Relaxation
FOR
DUMMIES®

by Shamash Alidina

Foreword by Cary L. Cooper

WILEY

A John Wiley and Sons, Ltd, Publication

Relaxation For Dummies®

Published by
John Wiley & Sons, Ltd
The Atrium
Southern Gate
Chichester
West Sussex
PO19 8SQ
England
www.wiley.com

MIX
Paper from
responsible sources
FSC® C013056
www.fsc.org

WILEY

About the Author

Shamash Alidina is a stress management expert, mainly using a scientifically researched approach called mindfulness. He is a renowned mindfulness trainer and consultant in the UK. A bestselling author of *Mindfulness For Dummies*, he regularly features on national television, radio, newspapers and magazines. Shamash has taught mindfulness in a secular way for over a decade. Previously he taught in schools where all the children practised meditation and mindfulness techniques on a daily basis.

Shamash holds two Masters degrees – in Engineering and Education. He trained in the clinically researched approach called Mindfulness-based Stress Reduction through the Center for Mindfulness in Massachusetts, USA and at the Centre For Mindfulness at Bangor University, which is part of its School of Psychology.

Shamash runs his own successful training organisation, LearnMindfulness.co.uk. He teaches mindfulness professionally to the general public, coaches, therapists, clinicians, trainers and corporate organisations, both in-person and through distance learning programmes accessible to all. He has trained in managing workplace stress and regularly coaches executives in mindfulness for optimising performance, creativity, decision-making and for reducing stress. He has taught mindfulness all over the world, including the Middle East, the Far East, the US and Europe.

Shamash currently lives in London and occasionally New York.

Dedication

I would like to dedicate this book to my wonderful grandma and grandpa who taught me so much about the value of culture, community and family. They both recently passed away. May they rest in peace.

Author's Acknowledgments

A tree doesn't grow from a seed alone – it needs soil, nutrients, warmth, water, sunshine and air. In the same way, I didn't write this book alone. Thousands of people helped to shape the content of this book, from the very close support of friends, family and colleagues, to the clients I have had the privilege to coach, the various lectures I've attended, the books and journals I've read, the online conversations on social networks and the authors and experts I've interviewed. This book has been a team effort.

I'd like to personally thank my immediate and extended family for their patience and support of this project: Fateh, Manju, Aneesh, Ashok, Parul, Vijay, Nirupa, Nikhil, Amisha, Amy and last but not least, Shona. I'd like to thank my friend Jo, who is so supportive of my work and always full of creative ideas and intelligent, positive suggestions; Margarita whose knowledge of psychology and spirituality helps me to put things into perspective; Garry, who's wisdom and sense of humour I always enjoy and deeply appreciate; Maneesh, who's wealth of knowledge in a wide variety of subjects is consistently enlightening and fascinating, and Rizwana, who's practical and perceptive suggestions aided me to speed up my writing. I'd also like to thank all the staff at my local Starbucks coffee shop – they were friendly, welcoming and encouraging for the hundreds of hours I spent typing away, drinking tea and eating porridge!

I've been thoroughly impressed by the support and professionalism of the *For Dummies* team at Wiley. I'd like to personally thank my project editor, Jo Jones, who has been incredibly patient and encouraging as I worked through writing the chapters for this book, from start to finish. I'd like to thank my commissioning editor, Kerry Laundon who was supportive of my passion to make this idea a reality, and always encouraging. I'd also like to thank my development editor, Colette Holden, my copy editor, Martin Key, my technical editor, Roger Henderson and proof-reader, Dawn Bates.

I'd like to thank some of the many supporters from my 'Relaxation For Dummies' and 'Learn Mindfulness' Facebook pages, and who have been closely following and encouraging me right from the ideas stage of this book. Those that come to mind, in no particular order, are: Caroline, Steven, Angel, Sarah, Andy, Mark, Anuk, Laura, Paul, Jenn, Mel, Amy, Stefka, Aseea, Meryl, Tracey, Lisa, Khurty, Mirja, Didi, Marie, Nancie, Gideon, Therese, Jacqueline,

Linda, Roisin, Nadia, Geoff, Maria, Aimee, Phil, Matthew, Claire, Carole, Alice, Ladio, Grethe, Carrie, Jen, Alastair, Hannah and Suki. I'm sure I've forgotten a few names and I'm so sorry for that – I certainly deeply value our online interactions and look forward to connecting with you online, if you like that sort of thing.

I'd like to thank one of the world's leading experts on stress management, Professor Cary Cooper, who took time out of his busy schedule to write the foreword to this book. And I'd finally like to thank Brian Tracy, personal development expert, for reading the script and offering his support for this book.

I'm deeply grateful for all your contributions.

Publisher's Acknowledgments

We're proud of this book; please send us your comments at http://dummies.custhelp.com. For other comments, please contact our Customer Care Department within the U.S. at 877-762-2974, outside the U.S. at 317-572-3993, or fax 317-572-4002.

Some of the people who helped bring this book to market include the following:

Acquisitions, Editorial, and Vertical Websites

Project Editor: Jo Jones

Commissioning Editor: Kerry Laundon

Assistant Editor: Ben Kemble

Development Editor: Colette Holden

Copy Editor: Martin Key

Technical Editor: Roger Henderson

Proofreader: Dawn Bates

Production Manager: Daniel Mersey

Publisher: David Palmer

Cover Photos: © iStock / Michał Krakowiak

Cartoons: Rich Tennant
(www.the5thwave.com)

Composition Services

Project Coordinator: Kristie Rees

Layout and Graphics: Carrie A. Cesavice, Joyce Haughey, Andrea Hornbegrer

Indexer: Claudia Bourbeau

Publishing and Editorial for Consumer Dummies

    Kathleen Nebenhaus, Vice President and Executive Publisher

    Kristin Ferguson-Wagstaffe, Product Development Director

    Ensley Eikenburg, Associate Publisher, Travel

    Kelly Regan, Editorial Director, Travel

Publishing for Technology Dummies

    Andy Cummings, Vice President and Publisher

Composition Services

    Debbie Stailey, Director of Composition Services

Contents at a Glance

Table of Contents

Foreword

The fast moving pace of life, the everyday stresses and strains of trying to balance work and life and the greater mobility of individuals, which means that the social support systems of the community and extended family are no longer there, have all led to a depletion of people's mental capital. We no longer have time to create or sustain important relationships, or to reflect on our lives and our lifetime objectives. As Henry David Thoreau once wrote in 1853; "How prompt we are to satisfy the hunger and thirst of our bodies; how slow to satisfy the hunger and thirst of our souls".

In the workplace, for example, the pace of work life has surpassed an individual's ability to cope, which means that people are suffering and need some respite to be able to develop a personal coping strategy. Studs Terkel, in his acclaimed book *Working*, summarised this as; "Work is, by its very nature, about violence – to the spirit as well as to the body. It is about ulcers as well as accidents, about shouting matches as well as fistfights, about nervous breakdowns as well as kicking the dog around. It is, above all (or beneath all) about daily humiliations. To survive the day is triumph for the walking wounded among the great many of us". It may be a bit over exaggerated, but it highlights some of the pressures in the modern day workplace.

This book outlines approaches to helping people to unwind, providing them with the space to reflect on what they are doing, and what they might consider doing in the future to make their life more meaningful. It provides a range of relaxation techniques that individuals can use to get themselves in a state to be able to tackle the problems and issues in their lives. It is the most comprehensive, and the most comprehensible, book ever written on the wide variety of relaxation techniques in the field, and the role they can play in enabling people to get the most out of their lives. As the US President Abraham Lincoln once said, "It is not the years in your life which are important, but the life in your years". This book will go some way to help you achieve some peace and serenity, so that you can go on your life's journey with better inner awareness.

Cary L. Cooper

Introduction

*F*or over a decade my work has given me the honour and privilege of
helping adults reduce their stress. I've been fortunate enough to help
thousands of people through personal consultations, workshops, books,
audios and online classes – a truly humbling thought. In that time, one thing
has stood out: most people don't know how to relax. Many of my clients use
simple techniques such as belly breathing and guided imagery for the first
time with pleasure and surprise. Others make exciting discoveries out of
techniques such as mindfulness meditation, t'ai chi and mindful eating.

Chronic stress not only feels unpleasant but also plays havoc with your
mind and body. Long-term stress increases your chances of having heart
disease, depression, obesity, digestive problems and sleep issues, among
other things. With chronic stress, your mind sees everything as a threat and
focuses on the negative. Relaxing deeply, which you can do rapidly with regular practice, reverses the harmful effects of stress on your body and mind.
Researchers have even shown that relaxation slows down your rate of ageing.

Relaxation is a skill. You may think you relax when you rest on your couch
watching TV or even when you sleep, but that's not the deep or nourishing relaxation that is explored in this book. To effectively relax you need to
switch on a part of your nervous system called the relaxation response, using
specific techniques. Rarely is this skill of relaxation taught in schools or the
workplace. I include a range of evidence-based techniques in this book to
turn on your relaxation response.

Relaxation not only prevents disease but also promotes wellbeing. If you're
under the right amount of pressure rather than overly stressed, the more
intelligent and creative parts of your brain function effectively. You can
process emotions well, thereby improving your relationships. You get fewer
mood swings, you see things in a more light-hearted way, and you understand situations from a bigger perspective. You make better decisions and
fewer mistakes.

In this book, I show you a whole range of different ways to relax. I include
many relaxation techniques, which form the foundation of a balanced and
relaxed life. Additionally, I encourage you to cultivate helpful attitudes so you
don't stress about things unnecessarily. I also explain lifestyle choices, high-
lighting proven ways of reducing stress through exercise and socialising.

Some techniques in this book take less than a minute to do. Others are subtle processes that you can continue to fine-tune your whole life. In this sense, you can refer to this book again and again. There isn't *one* perfect relaxation technique for everyone. I suggest you pick and choose what suits your lifestyle, temperament and needs. You can also experiment, mix different techniques together, and enjoy the variety of ways to experience relaxation – be creative!

Ultimately, a well-balanced life combines effective, regular relaxation techniques together with a wise attitude to daily living. This wisdom is already within you, and learning to trust your inner intuition allows you to access this wisdom regularly.

About This Book

Relaxation For Dummies provides you with practical techniques to develop the skill of relaxation. Each chapter is packed with insights about the art of relaxation, how to relax quickly and easily and ways to relax deeply. This book is for people who have chronic stress and want to discover ways to relax that are simple and scientifically proven to be effective. The book also comes with an audio CD of guided relaxation techniques for you to try. By listening to the CD regularly, you can be guided into a deep state of relaxation and wellbeing and learn the techniques so that you can make yourself feel more relaxed whenever you need to.

Conventions Used in This Book

To help you get the most from this book, I follow a few conventions:

- *Italic* emphasises and highlights new words or terms that I define.
- **Boldfaced** text indicates the action part of numbered steps.
- Monofont text displays web addresses.

What You're Not to Read

You don't have to read everything in this book. From time to time you'll see grey boxes – sidebars – that contain interesting bits of info and stories that may amuse or inform, but aren't crucial to your understanding of the funda-mentals. Read them, or not, whatever you want.

I hope you'll get something from the True Story paragraphs, which help you put the learning content of the book into an everyday life situation. However, these do not make essential reading so feel free to ignore them if you want.

Foolish Assumptions

In writing this book, I made a few assumptions about who you are:

- ✔ You want more relaxation in your life, but don't know where to start.
- ✔ You're willing to try the various relaxation techniques and strategies I have suggested a few times, before judging if they'll work for you.
- ✔ You're interested in understanding the potential dangers of chronic stress and adopting a range of strategies to experience relaxation.
- ✔ You're willing to set aside some time in your day to practise a relaxation technique.

Beyond those, I've not assumed too much, I hope.

How This Book Is Organised

I've organised *Relaxation For Dummies* into six parts. Each part covers a range of subjects to help you learn and practise relaxation and is further divided into chapters containing all the information you need.

Part I: Introducing Relaxation

Before you dive into the nitty-gritty of relaxation techniques and strate-gies, use this part to get a grip of the basics. In this part, I explain exactly what I mean by relaxation and how stress works to prevent you from feeling relaxed. I help you to discover effective ways to prepare yourself for relax-ation so that you're in the best possible place to begin training yourself in the skill of relaxation.

Part II: Exploring Relaxation Techniques Using Your Body

In this part, I show you many ways to relax your body, which naturally goes on to calm your mind and make you feel at ease. I offer a whole bunch of cool techniques to encourage you to discover the art of chilling out such as belly breathing, self-massage, t'ai chi and yoga.

Part III: Discovering Relaxation Techniques Using Your Mind and Heart

If you like the idea of calming your mind, or are attracted to exploring meditation, prayer or spirituality, this part is the one for you. Here, I offer a load of different techniques to try out. From guided imagery to problem-solving techniques, gratitude journals to self-compassion exercises, you're bound to find something that works for you.

Part IV: Everyday Relaxation

Relaxation is most effective if you can integrate the approach into your everyday life using the various techniques when you feel the stress levels rising. Stress often arises at home or in the workplace. In this part, I explore both of these situations and offer tips to ease the pressure. I help you relax in those situations and offer ways to prevent stress creeping up in the first place. I also include a chapter on sleep if you're having trouble nodding off.

Part V: Managing Problems Using Relaxation Techniques

Long-term stress has been shown to be the culprit for a range of different illnesses. Then the illness itself can compound your stress to higher levels. If you're suffering from a mental or physical health issue, reading through this part gives you some helpful tools for finding rest and relaxation. In this part, I explain how relaxation can help with anxiety, depression, anger, chronic illness, preventing burnout, and more.

Part VI: The Part of Tens

Every *For Dummies* book has one of these parts. The Part of Tens offers four fun-sized chapters covering top tips for the golden rules of relaxation, quick and deep ways to relax, and many exciting sources for further study that I personally love, including books, CDs, movies and websites. Yummy!

Icons Used in This Book

Sprinkled through the book you see various icons to guide you on your way. Icons are a *For Dummies* way of drawing your attention to important and interesting stuff and things you really need to know not to do.

Handy titbits to help you get the best from your relaxation studies. These little ideas summarise key relaxation concepts in bite-size chunks so you can access relaxation that little bit more easily.

This is stuff you need to know: whatever else you carry away from this book, note these bits with care.

Take careful note of the advice under this icon, and you'll avoid unnecessary problems.

These are examples of situations that I've encountered that I feel would help you to better understand how the techniques of relaxation can be used in everyday life.

This is a practical book. This icon offers you an opportunity to try certain relaxation techniques or strategies. By putting the theory into practice, you can begin to experience a greater sense of wellbeing.

Some of the concepts in this book can get a little tricky. If you'd like a little more explanation, look out for the tech stuff icon.

This icon indicates an audio track that guides you through the relaxation exercise.

Where to Go from Here

I've put this book together so you can dip in and out as you please. I invite you to make good use of the table of contents or the index and jump straight into the section you fancy. You're in charge and it's up to you of course. If you're a total beginner, or not sure where to start, begin with Part I and then you'll have a better idea how to proceed.

I wish you all the best in your quest for relaxation and hope that you find something of use within these pages. Above all, enjoy relaxing and, remember, you deserve it. Those close to you will also reap the rewards of your new-found sense of calm, so there's no need to feel guilty or selfish for giving yourself some 'me time'.

Part I
Introducing Relaxation

The 5th Wave   By Rich Tennant

In this part . . .

In this part you get to know what true relaxation is all about, discover what's stressing you out and begin your journey to a life of focused calm and peace of mind. Yipee!

Chapter 1

Discovering Relaxation

In This Chapter

▶ Uncovering the basics of relaxation

▶ Seeing how relaxation benefits all aspects of your life

▶ Making relaxation part of your daily routine

*T*he phrase 'just relax' sounds so simple. To relax you really just need to stop 'doing'. And yet 'stopping doing' is easier said than done. Your life has probably got more demanding over time. In those few moments that you have for yourself, relaxation may seem elusive. You may ask yourself questions like 'How do I relax?', 'What's the best way to relax?' or 'Why am I so stressed all the time?'

In this chapter, I help you begin your journey from anxiety and worry to discovering ways to find greater ease and peace in your life.

Understanding Relaxation

Relaxation is a state of mental calm and focus, free from unnecessary bodily tension. Relaxation is associated with a feeling of peace and tranquillity. You can achieve greater relaxation in two main ways:

✔ Using *relaxation techniques,* such as meditation, progressive relaxation or guided imagery.

✔ Doing *relaxation activities,* such as taking a bath, going for a walk, improving your time management skills or playing a sport.

Relaxation techniques reduce your stress and put you into a state of body and mind where you're deeply relaxed. This effect is called the *relaxation response* and is the opposite of feeling stressed. When your relaxation response is turned on, positive changes take place in your body and mind. You're better able to digest food and fight disease. You feel calm and at peace.

Relaxation activities help to reduce stress rather than put you into a state of relaxation. Most relaxation activities don't engage your relaxation response unless they encourage a calm focus of your attention, such as stroking a cat or doing a hobby that requires gentle attention.

You may not be good at relaxing at the moment, but you can definitely get better at relaxation. Relaxation is a skill and improves with practice. Learning relaxation techniques requires some time and effort, and you get the hang of them through trial and error, just like learning anything new.

Most people say activities like watching TV, having a cup of tea and chatting to a friend are relaxing. These activities do reduce stress and are certainly valuable, but they don't turn on your relaxation response so they're stress-reducing but not deeply relaxing.

The state of relaxation isn't sleeping. If you use a relaxation technique and you fall asleep, that's fine but after you fall asleep, you don't get any better at relaxing – you're just asleep. In true relaxation you feel calm and free of tension, but quite focused too.

Living a relaxed lifestyle requires relaxing activities, regular practice of relaxation techniques and a relaxed attitude, as I show in Figure 1-1.

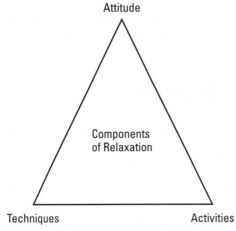

Figure 1-1:
Three components of a relaxed lifestyle.

Discovering the relaxation response

When you're stressed, your body turns on your stress response (see Chapter 2). Your blood pressure rises and your body prepares to run or fight. This is a process that's automatic and hard-wired in your body once triggered. No effective drug currently exists to counteract the harmful effects of chronic stress, so the best way to counteract stress with no known side effects is to regularly elicit your relaxation response.

The relaxation response is the opposite of the stress response. It is also automatic once triggered in the brain, releasing chemicals in your body that counteracts the stress response. When your relaxation response is activated, the following changes take place in your body and mind:

- Your muscles relax.
- Your blood pressure goes down.
- Your breathing slows down.
- You use less energy.

The part of your nervous system that controls stress and relaxation is called the *autonomic nervous system*. This system controls your heart rate, digestion, breathing rate, salivation, perspiration, pupil size, libido and urination. Some of these things are partly under your direct control, such as breathing, but some aren't, such as your pupil size and perspiration.

The autonomic nervous system has two sides: one side causes you to be stressed, and the other side causes you to relax: the *sympathetic nervous system* triggers your stress response – it's like your accelerator. The *parasympathetic nervous system* triggers your relaxation response – it's like your brake. The relaxation techniques in this book are designed to turn down the stress response, controlled by your sympathetic nervous system, and turn up your relaxation response, controlled by your parasympathetic nervous system.

You can think of these two systems as sides of a seesaw, as I show in Figure 1-2. The purpose of relaxation is to bring your seesaw back into balance. If you're too stressed at the moment, by putting in some relaxation techniques or doing your everyday activities with a more relaxed attitude, these will help to bring greater ease in your life.

Nobody is perfectly balanced all of the time. That's unnatural and an unhelpful aim to have. However, you can become better at noticing when you're leaning too far towards stress, and discover ways to shift the balance back, quickly and effectively. Using unhelpful coping strategies to manage your stress, such as isolating yourself, ignoring your problems or drinking excessive alcohol can end up leaning you further towards stress.

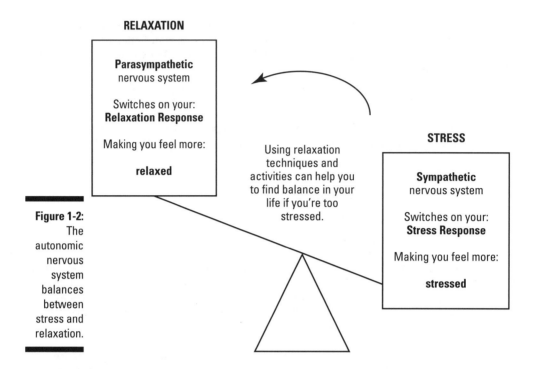

RELAXATION

Parasympathetic nervous system

Switches on your: **Relaxation Response**

Making you feel more:

relaxed

Using relaxation techniques and activities can help you to find balance in your life if you're too stressed.

STRESS

Sympathetic nervous system

Switches on your: **Stress Response**

Making you feel more:

stressed

Figure 1-2: The autonomic nervous system balances between stress and relaxation.

Benson, father of the relaxation response

Herbert Benson MD, pioneer in mind–body medicine, coined the term 'relaxation response' in the 1970s. Interestingly, he discovered the relaxation response in the exact same room in which Walter Cannon discovered the fight-or-flight (stress) response 50 years earlier!

The stress response takes place when a part of the brain called the hypothalamus is stimulated. Benson found that when a different part of the brain was activated, the opposite of the stress response occurred. He described the relaxation response as 'a physical state of deep rest that changes the physical and emotional response to stress, such as lowered heart rate, blood pressure, muscle tension, and rate of breathing.'

Benson discovered the relaxation response because he was repeatedly approached by meditators using a technique called transcendental meditation (TM). When he finally agreed to test them, which he was nervous about because he was a respected Harvard scientist and didn't want to get a reputation of being associated with esoteric ideas, he discovered that the meditators did relax well. They managed to reduce their blood pressure. But the meditation used a secret word, called a mantra. He tried the technique with a different word but the effect was the same. He eventually found that any word, phrase or object that you focus on with a passive attitude could trigger the relaxation response.

Figure 1-3 shows the different functions that the autonomic nervous system controls, and what happens when the stress response or the relaxation response are triggered.

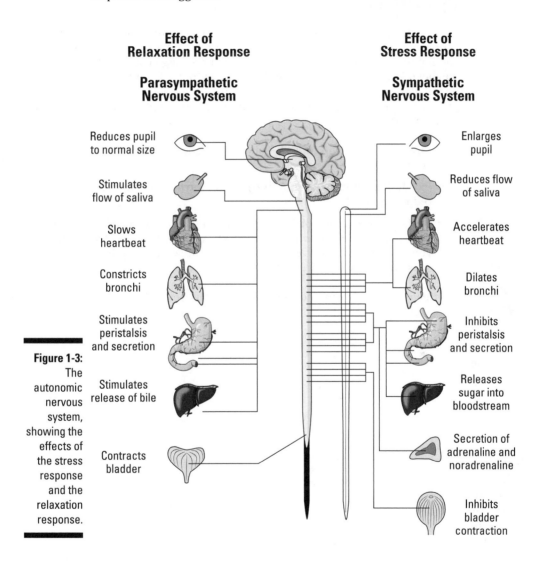

**Effect of
Relaxation Response**

**Parasympathetic
Nervous System**

**Effect of
Stress Response**

**Sympathetic
Nervous System**

Reduces pupil to normal size

Stimulates flow of saliva

Slows heartbeat

Constricts bronchi

Stimulates peristalsis and secretion

Stimulates release of bile

Contracts bladder

Enlarges pupil

Reduces flow of saliva

Accelerates heartbeat

Dilates bronchi

Inhibits peristalsis and secretion

Releases sugar into bloodstream

Secretion of adrenaline and noradrenaline

Inhibits bladder contraction

Figure 1-3:
The autonomic nervous system, showing the effects of the stress response and the relaxation response.

Considering different dimensions of relaxation

You can think of relaxation in three dimensions – body, mind and spirit, as I show in Figure 1-4. Effective relaxation operates on all three dimensions. Each of the dimensions is like the legs of a three-legged stool. The stool is balanced in the way that your life feels. If you took a leg out, the stool would be unbalanced. In the same way, if you didn't give each dimension your proper attention, your life would feel out of balance and stress would creep in more easily.

- ✔ **Physical relaxation (body):** Using techniques to ease the tension from your body.

- ✔ **Psychological relaxation (mind):** Using ways of calming your mind, reducing anxiety.

- ✔ **Holistic relaxation (spirit):** Reflecting on your own meaning and purpose in life, living your life according to your own values, feeling as if you're making a positive contribution in the world, and developing a sense of 'wholeness' in your life.

Spirituality certainly does not require a religious belief.

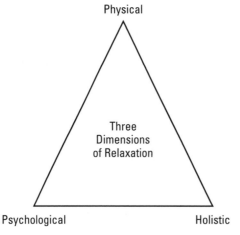

Figure 1-4: The three dimensions of relaxation.

Physical

Three Dimensions of Relaxation

Psychological   Holistic

Looking at the main ways to relax

In this section, I give a brief overview of the main techniques you can use to relax your body, mind and spirit. Although I separate these techniques into three different groups, the groups all overlap. For example, you can't relax your body using a breathing technique (body) if you don't also give your full attention to the process (mind) and have a sense of looking after your health (spirit).

Body techniques

Body techniques are based on releasing muscular tension in your body. (See Part 2 of this book for chapters about body-centred relaxation techniques.) The main body techniques are:

- Progressive relaxation
- Breathing exercises
- Physical exercise
- Yoga, t'ai chi and qi gong
- Biofeedback
- Massage and self-massage

Mind techniques

Mind techniques are based on being aware of your thoughts, and then stepping back from your thoughts, stopping your thoughts, changing your thoughts to be more realistic and positive, or seeing your thoughts in a different way. Mind techniques help to soothe your mind and include the following:

- Meditation, including mindfulness
- Guided imagery
- Self-hypnosis
- Cognitive behavioural techniques
- Music
- Problem-solving techniques
- Humour

Spirit techniques

Spirit techniques focus on holistic methods to create greater meaning and purpose in your life, and opportunities to explore old barriers you've created between yourself and others. Ultimately they're not techniques, but ways of living. Spirit techniques include the following:

- Gratitude and self-compassion
- Connecting with others through socialising or a shared interest perhaps
- Prayer, meditation, chanting and singing

✔ Volunteering, showing kindness to others and being generous

✔ Reflecting on your own inner thoughts and feelings and writing them in a journal

✔ Forgiveness

Appreciating relaxation as mind–body medicine

The natural healing force within each one of us is the greatest force in getting well.

Hippocrates

In the East, mind and body have always been seen as totally related and interconnected. Ayurveda (traditional Indian medicine) and traditional Chinese medicine seek to treat body and mind. In the West, however, for many years medicine focused on fixing the body and ignoring a person's thoughts, emotions and lifestyle as a possible contributor to the disease.

Now we know that mind and body are closely interconnected. The field of medicine called mind–body medicine uses the power of thought and emotion to aid the healing process. Most prestigious medical institutions around the world now have mind–body programmes. Mind-body medicine is no longer considered an alternative treatment to traditional medicine and has become an accepted part of mainstream medicine in some institutions.

When you're stressed, you release stress hormones into your bloodstream, affecting all your bodily organs. Negative, aggressive attitudes increase the chance of heart disease, obesity, diabetes and cholesterol. Your attitude can affect how long you live with a chronic disease or whether you contract a life-threatening ailment.

For example, research into people living with HIV found that those who had a faith in God, a sense of compassion towards others, a feeling of inner peace, or who were religious, lived longer than those who didn't have these values. In another study looking at women with late-stage breast cancer, the women in a weekly support group lived twice as long as those who weren't in the support group.

Not all pressure is bad for you. A sense of pressure releases norepinephrine, which helps create new memories and improves mood. Problems feel like challenges and the creative thinking stimulates new connections in your brain. The problem is when pressure becomes too high for you – what I define as stress. You need to reduce your stress, not eliminate all pressure.

Placebo effect – mind affects body all the time

Every high-quality experiment carried out using medication requires the experiment to be repeated using a placebo (dummy pill). This is because whenever people take a pill that they think will make them feel better, it often makes them feel better whether or not it is medicinal. In many cases placebos have been shown to reduce symptoms of pain, anxiety, depression, Parkinson's disease and inflammatory disorders. Scientists are not sure why placebos work so well – they suspect it is because hormones are released into your bloodstream due to expectations in your mind – with no actual medicine at all.

Having fun with relaxation

Relaxation is likely to be more elusive if you have a tendency to take life too seriously. If you are under a lot of stress or have depression, you probably don't think anything is much fun.

Try to work through the exercises and techniques in this book in a light-hearted way. After you find a technique that you enjoy, try to stick to the approach and reap greater benefit from it.

Children are good at having fun. Some researchers claim that children laugh on average 300 times a day, compared with 20 times for an average adult. Children have fewer responsibilities than adults, but we can still learn from them. You probably laughed a lot as a child and still have that capacity within you to have fun and relax. Slowly and surely, as you begin to put more 'me time' into your life, and enjoy a taste of relaxation from time to time, you'll find a smile appear on your face when you see the blue sky or the eyes of a child or hear the gentle sound of rain on your roof.

See Chapter 13 for more on cultivating humour and playfulness.

Discovering the Benefits of Relaxation

The more I research relaxation, the more I am astonished by its benefits. This helps to motivate me to ensure that I put relaxing activities and techniques at the top of my list of priorities. Health is important for everyone, and keeping stress at a reasonable level is a vital part of healthy living. I encourage you to enjoy relaxing through socialising and staying fit, as well as practising daily relaxation techniques to elicit the healing power of the relaxation response.

Effects of relaxation on your body

When you're stressed, your body is in a state of alarm or shock; your body is acting as if it's about to be eaten by a sabre-toothed tiger. You discover that you've no energy to start fighting that flu you have, or digesting breakfast. You're going to be sabre tooth's breakfast if you don't act fast! All your energy goes away from digestion, immune function, reproduction and growth.

When you relax, your body starts working on long-term projects to look after your health and wellbeing. Your immune system and digestion are energised. In a more relaxed state, you're less likely to get ill, you digest your food effectively and efficiently, and you feel generally more comfortable. Your muscles don't need to be tense when you relax, because you're not about to start running or fighting, so you save energy physically.

Research shows that relaxation has a positive effect all the way down to your genes, promoting long-term physical health. Relaxation slows down the rate of ageing by reducing the rate at which bits of your DNA wear out. Relaxation helps you live a longer, healthier, happier life.

Effects of relaxation on your mind and emotions

Relaxation turns on the more advanced, emotionally intelligent part of your brain. When you relax, you can think clearly and don't focus too much on your worries and concerns. Stress creates a tunnel vision type of thinking, whereas relaxation helps you see things from the stand of 'the bigger picture'.

Relaxation helps you with creativity. You're more positive and willing to take risks in your relaxed state of mind. You don't see everything as a threat but more as an opportunity. A relaxed mind is generally better able to focus. You can do your tasks more efficiently, without wasting energy. You are more hopeful about the future. You feel calmer and happier.

Effects of relaxation on your behaviour

Stress makes you react automatically to most things as if they are a threat, whereas relaxation gives you space to reflect. When you relax, you're more likely to respond wisely rather than react automatically to a new situation or what someone says. As you're more focused, you can pay attention to the tasks you need to do and get them done quickly. You complete your work with greater precision and less likelihood of mistakes.

Relaxation improves your relationships. Your emotional intelligence is heightened and you respond to your partner's requests with more understanding instead of starting arguments.

Being more relaxed means you don't move from one emergency to another. Instead of living life on survival mode, you step back and think about what you want from your life.

Lower levels of stress mean you don't snap at your children and other people so often. Your mood is more balanced. Children copy what their parents do, so by being in a relaxed state of mind, you're better able to offer a positive role model.

Uplifting your spirit with relaxation

If you're religious, you may pray, chant or attend worship. Your religion can give you social support, offers an opportunity to rest and reflect, and adds meaning and purpose to your life. Through this process, you're better able to handle difficulties in your life as you see them as part of a bigger picture.

If you're not religious, spiritual relaxation may mean seeking meaning through art, nature, a hobby, voluntary work, or living in a philosophical or ethically meaningful way. You may practise secular forms of meditation, such as the relaxation response meditation or mindfulness meditation. These techniques are among the most powerful ways to both relax, with all its benefits, and train your brain to be more emotionally positive and resilient in the face of future life demands and challenges.

Letting Relaxation into Your Life

Moving from a stressed, frantic lifestyle to one of relaxation and calm focus isn't an instant process. It has taken years to build up the various habits and tendencies that compound the stress in your life, so it will take some time to undo the stress – perhaps not years but at least a few months.

A life of greater relaxation is built on having the right attitude to relaxation in the first place (I talk more about attitudes in Chapter 3). From there, you may like to take stock of how stressed you are and the causes of your stress. Doing relaxation techniques without knowing the source of your stress may help you a little, but the underlying causes will still be there. A balanced combination of relaxation together with sorting out the specific causes of your stress is best, whether the cause is your inner thought processes or external demands.

Clarifying where you're starting from

Many of my clients first realise they have an issue with stress when they become ill, either with a physical illness such as a heart problem or with a psychological illness such as depression, clinical anxiety or panic attacks.

Humans are creatures of habit. To begin living a more relaxed lifestyle takes some determination and time. If you're a motivated and disciplined person, you can probably follow my suggestions in this book easily. But if you're like many people, finding the time and inner resolve to carry out the relaxation techniques, or reorganise your life balance to begin living in a more relaxed and calm way, is a big challenge.

The first step is to take stock of how your life is going at the moment, how much tension you carry around with you, how agitated and irritable you are on a daily basis, and what your health's like. In Chapter 2, I include some exercises to help you identify how stressed you are and how urgently you need to begin your journey from too much stress to a relaxed, calm, focused way of living.

Overcoming resistance to relax

There may be a range of reasons why you don't actively pursue relaxation in your life. Here are some possible reasons and what to do if they apply to you:

- **You don't know how to relax.** You know you need to relax, but whenever you have the time, you simply read a paper or call up a friend. But you still feel a constant underlying tension in your body and worries in your mind. You don't know how to let that tension go. Trying out the relaxation audio tracks and creating a relaxation plan will help you.

- **You don't think you have time to relax.** You wake up as late as possible and rush from one task to another. Any spare time is filled with errands to do, or you have a very low energy level. Time management skills can help you to find time to relax. If the President of the United States can find time to relax, you can too.

- **You feel guilty or ashamed spending time on relaxation.** This is a common reason. We live in a society where anything we do for ourselves feels selfish. But remember, when you're on a plane, you're always instructed to put your own oxygen mask on before you help another, even your child. Why? Because if you don't look after yourself, you can't look after others. It's the same with relaxation. If you don't take time to rest, you get ill and inefficient. How can you then help others? If anything, it's selfish *not* to take out time to relax.

✔ **You don't think you need to relax, despite your lack of health or wellbeing.** You may think stress is just 'normal'. You may ignore health warnings and put them down to everyday modern living. Looking more carefully at any symptoms of stress you're experiencing may help you to see how high your stress levels are, and how urgently you need to act. If you have a stress-related illness, a visit to your doctor may motivate you to take action.

✔ **You don't have the willpower to relax.** You know what you need to do to relax, but can't find the inner resolve to actually carry it out. Crashing out in front of the TV or staying in bed for an extra 20 minutes instead of doing your daily relaxation is just too tempting. Your stress makes you feel fatigued and you get into a negative cycle, unable to find the energy to relax. Reading a book such as this, joining a relaxation or exercise class, or relaxing with a friend can give you a little nudge in the right direction.

If you keep putting off your relaxation time, practise a relaxation technique for a minute. Tell yourself 'I'll do just one minute now, and do more if I feel like it'. Most of the time, people start to enjoy the relaxation technique and extend the time they spend on it.

Starting to use relaxation techniques and activities

If you're like most of my stressed-out clients, you make little time for relaxation. You may lead a very busy and intense lifestyle with a lot of responsibilities or work in an environment that's very challenging for you. You may like the idea of relaxing more but just don't know where to go or what to do. But you do know that something needs to change.

I suggest you read the first three chapters of this book. Then look at the range of relaxation techniques and activities throughout the book and choose one technique that appeals to you. Apply your chosen technique on a daily basis for a few weeks and notice what effect it has on you. If the technique works for you, continue to use it. If you find the technique has no effect at all, drop it for now and move on to try a different approach. This process of trial and error will lead you to the perfect technique or combination of techniques for you.

Everyone is different. Every person has a completely unique upbringing, set of genes, attitudes and life experiences. Each person achieves a balance of relaxation techniques and activities that's right for them. No one perfect technique works universally for everyone. The techniques I include in this book have been tested on thousands of people and found to work for the majority of people, but you need to find your particular preference.

Building relaxation into your daily life

To live a more relaxed and healthy life, more able to cope with the pressures that life throws at you, I recommend you practise a relaxation technique daily that you enjoy and that's suitable for your temperament and personality.

Try to look for opportunities to ease off from time to time. You don't have to wait till your stress levels are sky high and you have a stomach ulcer before you reach for this book. As mindfulness meditation expert Jon Kabat-Zinn says, 'Weave your parachute every day rather than leave it to the time you have to jump from the plane.'

Practise relaxation when you feel relatively calm as well as when you feel stressed, to buffer you against future stressors. For example, if you're waiting in traffic, do some deep breathing. When you've finished writing your report, go for a gentle stroll around the block. After putting the children to bed, soak in the bath for a while. Do some mindful yoga stretches at home before you head to your aerobics class. Be creative and think of clever ways to integrate relaxation in your life. In this way, relaxation becomes a way of life that you look forward to instead of yet another thing to add to your 'to do' list.

Here are a few suggestions to build relaxation into the daily grind:

- ✓ **Use 'waiting time' as time to do some simple relaxation techniques.** You could do some guided imagery as you wait in the queue at the post office.

- ✓ **Each time you finish one activity, and before you start another, take a few moments to relax.** For example, once you arrive home in your car, just sit for a few moments and connect with one of your senses to help you to let go of the stresses of driving before entering your home.

- ✓ **Make a list of things you do on a typical day.** See if there are any activities you find draining that you can stop, and any activities you find relaxing that you can start or do more of. For example, cut out surfing online everyday and join a local meditation class instead.

Everyone has days when they don't feel like doing their relaxation technique or find relaxation boring. That doesn't mean you need to give up. Just like going to the gym, you reap the rewards from relaxation in the long term. Try to keep practising, whether you like it or not, and then enjoy the benefits. With experience and practice, you'll come to enjoy using relaxation techniques and be able to enter a state of relaxed focus and inner calm within a very short time – that's something to look forward to! Just be as patient with yourself as you can, and you'll get there in time.

Chapter 2

Understanding Stress

Modern-day living is immersed in stress. The pace of life seems to accelerate, leading to higher levels of anxiety and constant rushing. Some pressure is good for you, but when that pressure is too high and continues for too long, you may have chronic stress, which has a negative impact on your body and mind.

Stress is the key underlying reason for up to 90 per cent of doctors' visits according to Centers for Disease Control and Prevention in the US. I began to take relaxation more seriously when I realised chronic high levels of stress cause a range of serious health issues. In other words, *stress kills*. Discovering ways to relax is probably one of the most important skills you can learn for your health.

In this chapter, I explain the biological basis of stress, help you work out your own personal stress level, and show you which parts of your life may be stressful for you.

Explaining the Science of Stress

Stress is the feeling of being under too much pressure. Pressure turns to stress when you think you can't cope with the demands on you. For instance, some people are able to cope with, and enjoy, raising children whilst others find the same responsibility incredibly stressful.

Almost anything can cause stress, but common causes include difficult relationships, demanding workloads and money issues. Stress can impact on all aspects of your life, but stress particularly affects four areas: your thoughts, your feelings, your body functions and your behaviour. Common symptoms of stress include problems with sleep, problems with eating and digestion, difficulty concentrating and back problems.

One person's challenge is another person's stress

My work is probably too challenging for some people, and too easy for others. Right now, I have publishers asking me to meet book deadlines, clients that wish to have stress management coaching, friends to meet, business clients looking for coaching, a new DVD to produce, papers to write, planning for a workshop to run tomorrow, a series of meetings next week, a call to make to my website designer, and a course on mindful eating to write up. Plenty to do. For me, this is an enjoyable challenge – I need the pressure to keep me engaged and enjoying life, making a positive difference in

the world. Sometimes the demands become a little too high and I need to make extra time for mindfulness meditation, exercise and socialising – my favourite ways to relax. This is difficult when deadlines are looming and the stress begins to creep in. I then know that if I don't relax soon, not only will I take even longer to meet my demands, but the quality of my work will deteriorate.

Think about all the demands on your time. Do you find it an enjoyable challenge, or too much to cope with?

Some pressure is good for you. A challenging job, a blind date, or the desire to bring up your children well all help you get out of bed in the morning. Without any pressure, you may feel bored and isolated. Some people with no pressure take drugs or commit crimes to find some stimulation.

In Figure 2-1, I show how too little or too much pressure causes stress. When the balance is right between your demands and what you believe you can cope with, you're at your optimal level of health, wellbeing and performance.

Stress arises if you think you can't handle a threat. If you're confident you can handle a situation, you see the situation as an enjoyable challenge rather than a threat and you feel under pressure rather than stressed. Your perception of your own ability makes all the difference.

Fathoming the fight-or-flight response

The stress response is sometimes called the *fight-or-flight response*. This is a primitive automatic response, hard wired into your body and brain, designed to prepare your body to either fight or run away from a threat to survival.

The fight-or-flight response has evolved in humans over many thousands of years to protect us from the dangerous creatures that lurked around. The humans that survived were the people with the most effective fight-or-flight response. We now have their genes, which is why we get stressed so easily.

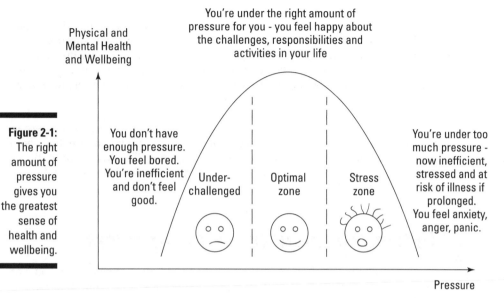

Figure 2-1:
The right amount of pressure gives you the greatest sense of health and wellbeing.

High levels of pressure activate our fight-or-flight mechanism stimulating certain nerves and releasing chemicals like adrenaline and cortisol into the bloodstream. Together these cause significant changes in your body and brain: your digestive system, which includes saliva production, is turned off, so your mouth goes dry; your stomach tingles; you begin to sweat, and your muscles tense, ready to fight or flee. For more on the physical changes that take place in the fight-or-flight response, check out Figure 1-3 in Chapter 1.

Stress facts

Here are a few facts about stress from a recent survey by the American Psychological Association:

✔ Money, work, and family responsibilities are the key causes of stress, and the most common reason for not doing something about the stress was being 'too busy'.

✔ Two out of five adults reported overeating or under eating in the past month due to stress.

✔ Almost half of all adults have been awake all night over the last month due to stress.

✔ Lack of willpower was seen as the main reason for not making lifestyle changes that would reduce stress.

So, if you find yourself lacking willpower to deal with your stress, have problems eating the right amount of food, find it difficult to sleep or your finances are causing you stress, you're certainly not alone. Following the tips in this book and getting extra support will help you to start undoing some of the stress. Remember, you can learn to relax and every small step counts.

The fight-or-flight response changes the way you perceive things around you too. You see anything as a potential threat to your survival – just like when you've got a huge list of things to do and you snap at anyone who tries to get in your way. You may even attack your computer or photocopy machine if it doesn't behave. Fear becomes your dominant emotion, not kindness or joy. You can't make good-quality decisions as you focus only on short-term survival, not the long-term consequences of your actions.

If you have chronic stress, your life becomes a series of short-term emergencies. Going from one urgent need to another crisis, you constantly fight your way through life. Relaxation doesn't seem to be possible. In this state, burnout (which I describe in detail in Chapter 19) may be waiting for you if you don't seek help soon.

Getting to know the signs of stress

Some people don't feel any emotional stress but have physical symptoms of stress, such as teeth grinding. Other people have a strong emotional reaction to stress. In this section I list the main signs and symptoms of stress.

Read through this list and see which apply to you. The more signs and symptoms you have, the more likely it is you are stressed. But remember that everyone reacts to stress differently – you may have other symptoms too.

Physical signs of stress include the following:

- ✔ Rapid heartbeat
- ✔ Nausea or dizziness
- ✔ Often or easily ill with colds or flu
- ✔ Digestion problems
- ✔ Lack of libido
- ✔ Aches or pains

Psychological signs of stress include the following:

- ✔ Difficulty in remembering things
- ✔ Inability to focus
- ✔ Only seeing the negative
- ✔ Being anxious, worrying, overthinking

Emotional signs of stress include the following:

- ✔ Feeling frequently sad or depressed
- ✔ Short temper, irritability, frustration
- ✔ Feeling lonely and isolated
- ✔ Agitation

Behavioural signs of stress include the following:

- ✔ Eating too much or too little
- ✔ Habits like nail biting and teeth grinding
- ✔ Sleeping too much or too little
- ✔ Little interest in socialising
- ✔ Dependency on drugs, alcohol or nicotine
- ✔ Procrastination

Discovering the Sources of Your Stress

In order to relax effectively, in addition to using relaxation techniques, you need to find and reduce the sources of stress. Otherwise it's a bit like massaging away a headache, while you keep knocking your head against the wall. The relaxation eases the pain of the headache, but you really need to stop banging your head against the wall too.

Living in the 21st century

The stress response evolved for life-threatening situations. However, a long set of e-mails to respond to, looming deadlines and bumper-to-bumper traffic don't imminently endanger your life, and yet your body responds as if your life is in danger. You may be releasing toxic stress hormones into your blood-stream on a daily basis.

If you were running or fighting each time you were stressed, you would make use of the increased energy, muscle tension and focus, and effectively burn up the hormones. But with our sedentary lifestyles, the hormones are left to swim around the body. The stress response makes you hyper-vigilant, aggressive and reactive, leading to behaviour that threatens your health, such as arguments leading to violence. On a much bigger scale, the aggressive nature of stress can even lead to war.

Technology plays a big part in many people's lives these days. The constant connection with e-mails, texts and social networks may fill every moment in your life. This constant stimulation leads to a constant high level of agitation, leaving your body in a constant semi-stressed state.

When I was young, I worked in my dad's shop part time. On one occasion I heard an argument between two drivers. I stepped out to see what the commotion was about. It appeared to be a case of 'road rage'. After a couple of minutes of arguing, one of the men got out of his car, opened his boot and took out a baseball bat. He walked over to the other driver and was about to hit him. Fortunately his wife started screaming and protected the other man from being hit. Road rage is an example of the fight-or-flight response going wrong. Violence arises from stress going out of control. People become frustrated and angry in traffic, switching on their stress response. They then see all other drivers as a threat and can literally fight (hit another car or driver) or flee (drive very fast). That's why learning relaxation is so important.

Identifying common triggers

In this section, I list the most common causes of stress. Read through the list and see how many of them apply to you. The more you can identify with, the more likely you are to have stress levels that are too high and the sooner you need to take action to reduce your stress.

- ✔ **Conflicts at work or home:** Difficult relationships can cause a huge amount of stress. Learning ways to deal with disagreements, working out a compromise and focusing on solutions make things less stressful. Easier said than done though. See Chapters 15 and 16 for more tips.

- ✔ **Major life changes:** Life is always changing. A different job, a new baby, moving abroad, divorce. Each change causes stress. If you see these changes as positive challenges rather than yet another problem to deal with, you'll be better able to cope with them.

- ✔ **Not enough time:** If you feel overwhelmed by the number of tasks that you're facing, you probably feel stressed. You only have a limited amount of time, so you need to think about what's most important for you and prioritise. Trying to do everything is a recipe for a stress-filled existence that is unsustainable in the long term.

- ✔ **Not relaxing:** Relaxation is a skill. If you don't know how to relax, or just avoid taking time out to chill, you can end up in a constantly stressed state. The techniques in this book provide you with a number of coping strategies.

✔ **Taking things too seriously, and refusing to accept the inevitable:** If you only see the negative sides of life, and don't laugh at the mistakes and difficulties you face, you make things more stressful for yourself. Seeing things in a more light-hearted way, and accepting what you can't change helps to lower your stress levels.

✔ **Trying to please everyone:** If you're always taking on too much because you want to keep everyone else happy, you're going to end up having too much to do. Learning to disappoint people by refusing to accept their demands from time-to-time helps in the long run.

✔ **Unhealthy living:** Do you live on fast food, cigarettes and alcohol? Do you think exercise is going for a drive around the block? Think lunch is for wimps? Find sleep a waste of time? If so, you're more likely to feel stressed. A healthy, balanced diet, a daily brisk walk or other physical activity, and ensuring you sleep on time makes a big difference.

Dealing with your daily routine

Daily routines or habits offer you some control over your life and give you a sense of security and stability. A feeling of losing control is directly linked to stress, and as life is full of changes, stress is inevitable. Finding some aspects of your life to ground yourself, such as a healthy daily routine, is an effective way of coping with life's challenges.

If you begin your day by hitting the snooze button as many times as possible, then rushing breakfast, getting the kids ready and making a mad dash to work, you have already over-activated your system, switching on your stress response. If you go to bed late watching some boring movie and are struggling to stay awake in the office, constantly drinking coffee or smoking, your habits are just getting your heart to beat faster giving you a feeling of anxiety. No exercise in your daily routine means you lack energy and by the time you get home and do your chores, you have little energy left and end up on the sofa staring at the box, calling it relaxation.

1. **Set your alarm an hour earlier than usual.**

   Take your time to stretch and do some exercise to wake yourself up. Have a glass of water or fresh fruit juice. Do a relaxation technique for about 20 minutes to help you feel calm and refreshed. Treat yourself to a nutritious breakfast, and eat it whilst giving the meal your full attention, enjoying each mouthful.

2. **Throughout the day, take a few moments to check how you're feeling.**

   If you notice your stress levels getting too high, take action to reduce your stress as far as possible. Make sure that you don't react in ways that compound your stress.

3. **Leave your work behind when you're home.**

   Perhaps do some exercise before you get home. Do some activities that you enjoy in the evening, meet with friends or family if you can, or do something creative after doing any household chores.

4. **Have a calming bedtime ritual, doing some light reading rather than checking e-mails just before bed.**

   Go to bed on time most nights so that you wake up with enough time to ground and relax yourself before the day starts.

Discovering the effect of perception

Everything can be taken from a man or a woman but one thing: the last of human freedoms to choose one's attitude in any given set of circumstances, to choose one's own way.

Viktor E. Frankl

Understanding the effect of your perception on stress is one of the key ways to a less stressful and more relaxed lifestyle, living with a feeling of greater control.

Most people think that stress is totally caused by external events. If this were true everyone would react in the same way to a long queue at the bank or a demanding job. Just discovering the cause of your stress as an external event and removing it isn't the only way to reduce stress. How you see a stress situation (stressor) has a massive effect on whether your fight-or-flight response is switched on. If you see the confused look on your boss's face in a negative way (he doesn't like me) you're more likely to trigger your stress response.

The way in which you perceive everyday challenges has a significant effect on your stress levels. For example, if you get a parking ticket you can react in two ways. A negative way is to think about how stupid you were to make a mistake, or why annoying people choose a job giving tickets to cars. You may kick your wheel or start looking for the person who gave you the fine so that you can chase them. Another person may think: 'Oh well, I made a mistake. Luckily I have enough money to pay the fine this month. The ticket guy is just doing his job at the end of the day.'

Same situation, but two different ways of seeing it. Getting annoyed doesn't take a penny off the cost of your parking fine.

Perception is affected by your level of optimism (see Chapter 12), your locus of control or your stress hardiness (which I describe in the section 'Considering your personality', below).

When something is seen as stressful, two decisions need to be made. Your perception determines what decision you take and how stressed you feel. The two questions are:

1. **Is this a threatening situation for me?**

   If you get easily stressed, then you may see situations in your life as more of a problem than they actually are. For example, if your child is making a noise in a restaurant, is that actually a threatening situation?

2. **Can I cope with this threat?**

   You probably are better able to cope than you think. You can talk to your child, explain the consequences of bad behaviour and use this restaurant visit as a learning opportunity.

You can change your perception and therefore your level of stress. See Chapter 12 on changing your thinking patterns for ways of reducing your stress.

Considering your personality

Your personality is a combination of your characteristics or qualities that make you unique. Certain personality types have been found to be more susceptible to excessive stress. By discovering if you have the kind of personality that compounds stress, you can begin taking action that helps to reduce your tendency to stress out too much.

In this section you'll find out about a range of personalities and tendencies that affect your stress levels. You'll find out about type A personality, which was discovered to increase the chance of heart disease. And you'll learn about stress hardy personalities, which have an increased resilience to stress. Having a sense of being in control affects your stress levels – you will read more about this in the subsection called 'Looking at your locus of control', later in this chapter.

Type A and Type B personality

Two cardiologists, Meyer Friedman and Ray Rosenman, working together in the late 1950s, noticed that their heart patients had certain characteristics making them possibly more susceptible to heart problems. For instance, they always sat on the edge of the seat in the waiting room, impatient for their turn, rapidly wearing out the upholstery on the front edge and armrests. Only the seats that the coronary patients were sitting on had this wear, the other seats rarely got worn out. They suspected this impatient behaviour of their heart patients may be the reason they had heart problems in the first place.

It seemed to be the personality type of the patients, which was aggressive, competitive and impatient, increased their levels of stress and caused the heart disease. The scientists called this highly-strung set of characteristics 'Type A' personality. And people with a more easy-going approach to life were classified as 'Type B'. Type A personalities experience higher levels of stress and therefore disease. Find out if you're a Type A by looking at the characteristics below.

Type A personalities are:

- ✔ **Impatient with a sense of time urgency:** Always aware of how little time is available. Quickly agitated waiting in queues. Walk fast and talk rapidly, often interrupting others when they speak.

- ✔ **Aggressive or hostile:** Quick to get angry, irritated or frustrated. Small things become big issues. Appear rude.

- ✔ **Competitive:** Always keen to be the best. Winning is more important than anything else, whether at work or in sport. Focus is on achievement rather than enjoying the process.

By becoming aware of your tendency to behave with Type A characteristics, you can begin to make some changes in your attitude and lifestyle to reduce your chance of getting excessively stressed on a day-to-day basis.

As you can probably guess, Type B personalities are the opposite: more patient, relaxed, easy-going and can lack a sense of time urgency. Type B have lower levels of stress. There is also a Type AB personality, which is a combination of the two.

People with Type A personality often develop certain physical characteristics, such as tension in the face, grinding teeth and sweating. They are likely to have several other problems including high blood pressure, heart disease and social isolation. A range of health issues associated with stress is likely.

Although Type A is a personality type that is associated with high stress levels, you can change it by using many of the strategies outlined in this book. Actions you can take include changing your thinking to be more positive, recording in your stress diary (see 'Using a stress diary' later in this chapter for details), deep breathing, meditation, a relaxing hobby, changing your work, and learning to be assertive rather than aggressive.

Stress Hardiness personality

A personality type that is said to successfully cope with stressful events is called stress hardiness. By developing a stress hardy personality, you will be protected from the challenges in life that others may find too stressful to cope with. If you have a stress hardy personality style, you enjoy:

- **Challenge:** Perception of life as a series of challenges to test yourself, rather than as problems or difficulties to worry about.

- **Commitment:** Being responsible for your work and home obligations. The commitments give a sense of purpose to your life. I sometimes call this part of the 'holistic dimension' of your life, as it's about connection and finding meaning through helping others.

- **Control:** A sense of being able to cope with life's demands and being in the driving seat. The more you see yourself in control of life's demands, the less pressure you experience.

This stress hardy personality type was discovered by analysing the stress levels of executives in a high-pressured job undergoing restructuring. Those with the above-average stress hardy personality coped more effectively with the changes, reducing the risk of stress-related illness by 50 per cent compared to the others.

- Consider the problems you're currently facing. Can you see them as challenges to be overcome?

- Think about your current commitments. Can you see how they help you to find connection and give some meaning to your life?

- Reflect on the parts of your life that you can control that helps you to relax. Your attitude to life, how you use your free time and the friends you choose to spend time with.

Looking at your locus of control

Your locus of control is a measure of the level of control that you believe you have over your life. As having a sense of control is linked to lower levels of stress, considering and reflecting on your own locus of control can help to reduce your stress.

You can either have an internal or external locus of control or be somewhere in-between. Internal and external locus of control are explained below:

- **Internal locus of control:** This means that you feel that you are able to influence external situations and you control how you react to life's challenges. For example, if you think you may lose your job, you take steps to ensure that you keep your position. If you do lose your job, you apply for new jobs believing that you'll get a better position, seeing it as a chance to step up and make a fresh start. You feel that you're in some control of what happens to you.

  Here are a few way you can help to develop an internal locus of control and therefore reduce your stress:

- When you feel like you're trapped in a situation, take a step back. Consider what options you have. Talk to a friend or relative about your situation to get a different perspective on things

- Remember, no matter what the situation, you do have choices available. And if you don't appear to have any choice, you always have control of your own attitude – no one can take that away from you.

- Notice the kind of thoughts that pop into your head. If you have thoughts like 'I've got no choice', 'I should', 'I must', or 'I can't', think again. You almost certainly do have a choice, even if it's a tiny one. And change 'should' and 'must' thoughts to 'I choose to...'. That helps you to feel a little more in control. Sometimes just saying to yourself 'Why should I?' or 'Why must I?' is helpful.

✔ **External locus of control:** This means you feel external situations control you, and there's nothing you can do about it. Whatever happens is your fate or destiny and you can't influence it. So, if you lost your job, you would think it was inevitable and had no control over it. You also would feel you had no influence over what your next job will be.

It's impossible to remove all the causes of stress in your life. But you can change how you see your influence over your stressors. Having more of an internal locus of control makes you feel in charge of your life, reducing your likelihood of getting too stressed when you're faced with your next challenge.

Measuring Your Stress

Before you decide what sort of relaxation techniques and activities to integrate into your life, you need to know how stressed you are, and some of the key reasons for your stress. If your stress levels are low, you may not need to take urgent action. If moderate, you need to take action on reducing your stressors or seeing them in a different way. If your stress levels are high, you need to take urgent action to prevent burnout, if you haven't already reached that point (burnout is described in Chapter 19).

Rating your stress level

Try this quiz to have a go at measuring your stress level. Answer each of the following questions, and then count the number of 'yes' answers.

1. Do you often feel tired?

2. Do you often feel as if you're out of control of the important things in your life?

3. Do you find your work or daily chores a burden?

4. Do you use food to cope with stress?

5. Do you smoke, drink alcohol or use other unhelpful ways to cope with your stress?

6. Has your weight gone up or down recently?

7. Are you having difficulties falling asleep due to tension in your body or because your mind won't stop chattering?

8. Has your libido decreased recently?

9. Do you have high blood pressure?

10. Do you have any other health condition that you suspect is stress-related?

11. Do you often feel things aren't going your way?

12. Do you feel so down or sad that you struggle to cope with your daily activities?

> 0–3 yes answers = low stress level
>
> 4–8 yes answers = moderate stress level
>
> 9–12 yes answers = high stress level

You may have a medical condition that's causing your stress. Visit your doctor for a full assessment if you feel unwell and think your illness may be stress-related.

Using a stress diary

If you want to identify the sources of your stress and how you currently react to them, keeping a stress diary may be helpful. You may think you know why you're stressed, but the act of taking time to jot down notes usually leads to helpful insights. Most of the time stress arises and passes fairly quickly, and if you don't take time to observe and record you easily miss the reasons why your stress levels are higher than you may like.

Follow the steps below to write a stress diary that helps you to identify your sources of stress, identify patterns in your behaviour that compounds stress, and aids you to consider ways of removing the cause of your stress.

1. **Create a table with the following columns in your stress diary or on a computer spreadsheet:**

   • Date and time

   • Stressful event

   • Level of stress (0–10)

- What was the cause of the stress?

- What thoughts, feelings and body sensations did you have?

- How did you manage the stress? What did you do?

2. **After each stressful event that you thought was significant, record your answers in your stress diary.**

3. **After a few weeks, look at all your entries. Consider the following questions:**

  - What situations caused you the most stress?

  - What was the underlying cause of the most stress?

  - What is the most and the least effective ways you managed your stress?

  - Looking at the way you managed your stress, what could you do to improve the way you manage your stress?

  - Look at the thoughts you had during the stressful event. Were your thoughts balanced, or focusing just on the negative? See Chapter 12 for more on mind management and ways to be optimistic in a realistic and believable way to help lower your stress levels.

Measuring stress using your body

To find out how stressed you are, look at the physical signs you're experiencing. Take action to lower stress if things are hotting up too much. Consider these five signs to look out for:

- ✔ **Check your pulse.** Measure your pulse rate, either on your wrist or the side of your neck. Count the number of beats over 60 seconds. That number is your pulse rate. A pulse rate over 75 indicates that you may be under stress, but it may be your normal resting rate. The average pulse rate for an adult is actually 60–100 beats per minute (bpm). Generally, the lower the resting pulse rate, the fitter you are. If your resting pulse rate is higher that 120 bpm or below 40 bpm, visit your doctor.

- ✔ **Consider your breathing rate and depth.** Notice how you're breathing. Place one hand on your belly and one on your chest. If your belly is slowly expanding and contracting as you breathe in and out, you're probably relaxed. If your belly area is tense and you're only breathing using your chest, in a shallow and rapid rhythm, you're probably stressed. Learn more about breathing in Chapter 5.

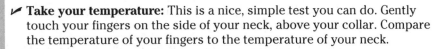

✔ **Notice whether you're sweating.** If you're perspiring even though you're not doing anything physically demanding, you're probably stressed. The sweat is caused by some stress hormones.

✔ **Scan for muscle tension.** Moving your attention gradually through your body is called scanning – it's a way of checking the tension in your body. You start at the top of your head and move your attention gradually down your body, checking for physical muscle tension. Check your forehead, jaw, neck, shoulders, arms and hands, chest, stomach, buttocks, legs and feet. You'll notice there is tension if you feel a sense of tightness, holding, discomfort or perhaps pain in a part of your body.

A much slower and more thorough version of this scanning is the mindful body scan meditation (see Chapter 10), which also helps to naturally release your tension with regular practice.

✔ **Take your temperature:** This is a nice, simple test you can do. Gently touch your fingers on the side of your neck, above your collar. Compare the temperature of your fingers to the temperature of your neck.

If your fingers feel cold compared to your neck, you're probably stressed. If your fingers feel about the same temperature or warmer than your neck, you're probably comfortably relaxed.

You can only reduce your stress if you notice when you're stressed. You can then begin reflecting on the cause of your stress, and plan a strategy to reduce that stressor. You want to be able to notice stress before it gets so high that it causes ill health or damages your work or relationships.

Trying a relaxation SWOT analysis

SWOT stands for Strengths, Weaknesses, Opportunities and Threats. This kind of analysis is traditionally used in business but works quite well for analysing your own stress levels. By doing a relaxation SWOT analysis you can discover your own strengths and weaknesses when it comes to managing stress. You also discover opportunities for greater relaxation in your life, and areas of your life that prevent you from relaxing effectively. Follow the steps below to do your own Relaxation SWOT analysis:

1. **Reflect and write down the following about you:**

   • **Strengths:** In what ways do you manage stress well? For example, you may go for walks regularly, drink herbal tea, call your friend or refrain from bursting out with anger. List them.

   • **Weaknesses:** In what ways do you cope with stress badly? Perhaps you start drinking alcohol, avoid people, internalise your negativity towards yourself or lose your temper completely.

- **Opportunities:** What simple things could you do to help lower your stress levels? Maybe you could start doing some short relaxation techniques every day, avoid spending time with negative people, walk part the way to work instead of driving all the way, or consider thinking about your stressors more as challenges to learn from rather than problems to avoid.

- **Threats:** What would prevent you from effectively managing your stress? Maybe you lack willpower to do daily relaxation techniques. Maybe you don't feel you have the time to exercise regularly, or you don't believe that you can make the necessary changes as you lack confidence and knowledge.

2. **Think about how you could use your strengths to overcome your weaknesses.**

3. **Think about how you can begin implementing some of the opportunities you have to manage stress.**

   Look back at the threats that prevent you from relaxing and consider what you can do to overcome them.

When I do this exercise with my clients, they often uncover more strengths and opportunities than they realised they have, and they tend to overestimate their weaknesses and threats. You may like to do this exercise again after reading more of this book to see what new ideas you have for integrating relaxation into your life.

Chapter 3

Planning Your Journey into Relaxation

In This Chapter

▶ Preparing to discover relaxation

▶ Finding ways to motivate yourself

▶ Creating a 30-day relaxation plan

Failing to plan is planning to fail.

Alan Lakein

*I*f you create a plan to relax, you're more likely to be successful. In this chapter I offer a range of ways to incorporate regular relaxation into your life. If you feel impatient and want to get on with the relaxation, feel free to jump ahead. However, this tendency to rush may be why you're feeling stressed in the first place. Consider putting on the brakes, slowing down and taking your time to prepare a plan to relax.

Getting Ready for Relaxation

Begin your journey into relaxation by nurturing helpful attitudes. In this section I show you how to prepare yourself for practising relaxation techniques on a regular basis, and how to nurture useful attitudes to make relaxation effective for you.

Cultivating useful attitudes for relaxation

To grow a plant from a seed, you need fertile soil with the right nutrients, and you need to provide air, water and warmth. With the right conditions, the seed happily germinates. In the same way, you need to cultivate the right attitudes for relaxation to grow and flourish in your life.

When I use the word 'relaxation', I mean triggering the relaxation response (which I explain in Chapter 1) rather than just fall asleep. This is a skill that takes practice and regular commitment.

In this section I describe the most helpful attitudes for you to cultivate in order to aid your relaxation. You may feel that you can't do them all, and that's okay. Just reading and considering these attitudes has some effect. Then, as you begin to practise relaxation, you naturally begin to find these attitudes easier to adopt. Re-read through this section from time-to-time to remind you about these attitudes on your journey to greater rest and relaxation.

Acceptance

Acceptance of what has happened is the first step to overcoming the consequences of any misfortune.

William James

As you practise your relaxation technique, bringing a quality of acceptance to the procedure is tremendously helpful. You can begin by accepting your physical sensations. So if you feel tense, and after trying a technique, you feel just as tense, or even more tense, see if you can just accept it. Denying that you're tense, or trying to fight with tension just generates more tension. It's like putting petrol onto a flame – it grows bigger.

You can also practise accepting your emotions as they arise whilst you relax. Let your emotions be there and allow them space to breathe. By acknowledging them, and even exploring them with curiosity, you are going from a sense of conflict with your inner experiences to being at peace with them. See Chapter 10 for more on mindfulness, which develops the ability to accept.

Open-mindedness and curiosity

You're bound to have some expectations about what you hope to get or experience from practising relaxation regularly.

But everyone's journey to greater relaxation is different. For some people the physical tension melts quickly, whereas for others they first begin to feel emotional or tense. Some find that their body begins to move involuntarily or they experience wild visions.

In a way, anything can happen as you begin to release your physical tension and calm your mind. Keep an open mind and see what happens with a sense of curiosity – let go of trying to feel relaxed.

Passiveness

The passive attitude is perhaps the most important element in eliciting the Relaxation Response. . .other thoughts do not mean you are performing the technique incorrectly. They are to be expected.

Dr Herbert Benson

When you practise a relaxation technique, you don't need to put in too much effort or try to do it perfectly. You may find your mind drifting off into other thoughts. That's normal. Try not to criticise yourself for this lack of concentration. When you have trouble concentrating, see it as an opportunity to be understanding and kind to yourself rather than beating yourself up.

By having a passive approach, you're not taking the process too seriously or trying too hard. Relaxation is ultimately a process of letting go and being with things as they are rather than trying to force a change.

Having said this, relaxation techniques do require some attention and focus too. It's about adopting a balanced effort. Just as a violin string works best when neither too taut or too loose, so relaxation techniques are most effective when your effort is neither too intense nor too docile. You'll learn this as you begin to try different relaxation techniques.

Patience

With time and patience the mulberry leaf becomes a silk gown.

Chinese proverb

If you don't have any patience, you'll easily get stressed. Not everything is instant and so you often feel the frustration of impatience. To be able to relax, you need to cultivate some patience.

Strengthening your muscles by going to the gym can be painful. Trying to be patient may also be painful to begin with. One minute after playing a relaxation audio you may be itching to stop. After five minutes you feel like running round the room. But as you persevere with practising daily relaxation techniques, your feelings of impatience will subside.

Cultivate patience by allowing feeling of impatience to arise from time-to-time, but continuing to wait.

Self-kindness

Kindness is a language which the deaf can hear and the blind can see.

Mark Twain

Be nice to yourself. Doing relaxation techniques can be challenging. You may have been suffering from stress for a long time. To begin a journey to relaxation can be challenging; your mind may come up with all sorts of reasons why you're useless or pathetic or doing it wrong.

Look out for your inner critic trying to put you down. Try dealing with your inner critic in the following ways:

✔ Smile and say to yourself, 'Ah, that's the old inner critic trying to put me down. Nice try!'

✔ Say to yourself, 'Stop!' and imagine a stop sign. Then get on with whatever you need to do next.

✔ Reply to your inner critic with some positive thoughts that you believe in, such as 'I'm not useless. I'm making an effort to relax. That's something many people don't even try.'

Self-mastery

You need to practise relaxation techniques regularly in order to gain any benefit from them. Regular practice takes a significant amount of discipline or self-control. You may be tempted to do 1,001 different things other than just relax. You may feel guilty or selfish even though all you're doing is looking after yourself, which would help you to look after others. You may think you're wasting your time.

Having an attitude of determination to practise even when you don't feel like relaxing will be worth it in the long run. That is self-mastery.

Trust

Follow your heart, but be quiet for a while first. Ask questions, then feel the answer. Learn to trust your heart.

Anonymous

You need to trust in your own inner capacity to relax. You weren't born tense or stressed – you've picked up certain beliefs and ways of seeing things along the way that cause you to feel stressed. Difficult life circumstances may have contributed to your stress. Believe that you can once again feel relaxed – everyone can.

If you find yourself overwhelmed with negativity about the process, just remember that even the tiniest belief that you can live a calm and relaxed life is valuable and will take you towards relaxation. It's like seeing a tiny light at the end of a tunnel. By following that light, you are led towards freedom.

You also need to have some trust in the relaxation technique you use. If you aren't convinced that it'll work you're less likely to reap the benefits of the technique. The techniques will still work, but are enhanced by your inner belief in the process.

Finding a suitable time to relax

I find the morning is the best time for me to practise a relaxation technique. My mornings are quiet and I have the time to myself. Other people choose to practise relaxation techniques just after coming home from work, as the practice creates a clear boundary between work and home.

Some people like to relax in bed as it helps them to sleep. If you do relax last thing before going to sleep, remember to also try to find another time during the day to relax. This is because you only trigger the healing effect of the relaxation response in your body when you're awake.

Try to relax at the same time every day if you can. Having a regular time helps to create a habit so you're more likely to do it every day. Your relaxation time becomes a special time for you alone.

Keeping a relaxation journal

In Chapter 2 I suggested that you keep a stress diary for several weeks to help you find out the key causes of your stress, how often they occur, what effect they have and how you cope with them.

From a more long-term point of view, I recommend that you keep a relaxation journal. In this journal, which can be a simple notebook, a beautifully bound diary or an electronic document, you record your daily reflections on the relaxation techniques and activities that you try.

Try recording the following every day, just before and after doing your relaxation exercise:

1. **Note the date and time.**

2. **Before starting the relaxation exercise, write down your answers to the following questions:**

   - How relaxed are you currently feeling (where 0 is not relaxed at all, or the most stressed you can imagine yourself to be, and 10 is totally and completely relaxed)?

   - What is your mood, and how strong is it (e.g. quite angry or slightly sad)?

3. **After the relaxation exercise write down your answers to the following questions:**

   - What relaxation technique or activity did you do, for how long and where?

   - How relaxed do you feel now (on a scale of 0– 10 again)?

   - What is your mood now?

4. **Write a few sentences about how you found the process.**

- What thoughts went through your head?

- How did you feel?

- How do you think your relaxation is going?

- Do you need to make any changes?

If you keep your diary for a few weeks and find the process too analytical, try simply writing or drawing your reflections on how you think your relaxing is going and leave out the scoring bit.

Recording your own guided relaxation

I include lots of different relaxation techniques in this book. You may like to read the techniques, memorise some of them and then practise them with your eyes closed. However, many people like to be guided through a relaxation technique. I include some guided relaxation tracks with this book. You can also record your own so that you can relax in your own style:

1. **Choose your recording device, such as a handheld tape recorder or a microphone connected to a computer.**

   Work in a quiet room without too much background noise.

2. **If you want some background music on your recording, play some music on a separate music player.**

   If you prefer, just have silence.

3. **Take a few minutes to relax.**

   Taking time to relax before you start helps to relax your voice. Now record the instructions for the relaxation technique at the right pace for you. Take your time. Remember to leave pauses between instructions to allow you to deepen your experience when you listen back to it.

4. **After you finish, play the recording.**

   You may find it strange to hear your own voice, but you'll soon get used to it. After a while, you may love to record your own audios as you can design them with all the words and soothing music that you love.

Creating a Relaxation Plan

When you join a fitness club, the club trainer helps you to create an exercise plan. The trainer asks you what you hope to achieve over the next few months, such as losing weight, changing your body shape or boosting your general health. Based on your goals, the trainer helps you create a set of exercises to do, several times a week, to achieve your aim. The trainer probably advises you to measure your progress as you go along.

Achieving greater relaxation involves a similar process to achieving greater fitness at the gym. You need to know what you hope to get from relaxation, plan the relaxation exercises that you will be doing on a regular basis, commit yourself to practising the relaxation techniques almost every day and get some support from experts or friends, to improve your chances of success. In the following section I walk you through the process of building your own relaxation plan.

Beginning the journey to wellbeing

Let your mind start a journey thru a strange new world. Leave all thoughts of the world you knew before. Let your soul take you where you long to be . . . Close your eyes, let your spirit start to soar, and you'll live as you've never lived before.

Erich Fromm

You may feel excited or anxious about starting your journey to relaxation. You have found a book that resonates with you. You like its style and content. You want to learn ways to relax. You imagine a future life free from stress, anxiety and tension. After years of stress and 'dis-ease', you want to start a new chapter in your life, a life where you look after yourself and not just others, a life where you can access your inner resources to achieve a sense of wellbeing.

As the old saying goes, a journey of a thousand miles begins with a single step. If you have only 10 minutes spare every day to commit to relaxation, your first step may simply be to read through this book. Then take a notebook, and begin writing down the kind of techniques you want to try for 10 minutes every day. Use your notebook to reflect briefly on how the session went, and how relaxed you felt before and after practising each technique. Use spare moments in each day to assess if the muscles in your body feel tight, and let go of any tension that you can, and see whether you can gently accept any further underlying tension just as it is.

As you begin your journey to relaxation, take the opportunity to reflect on how life has been for you in the past year or so. What's gone well and what's not gone so well? Have a lot of changes taken place? Have you experienced the death of a loved one, a marriage or the arrival of a new baby, or taken on a new mortgage? All of these major changes contribute to stress.

The story of the two salespeople

A British shoemaker manager sent two salespeople to Africa to determine whether the continent had any sales potential. The manager asked them to report back when they returned to work.

The first salesperson went to the boss and said 'There's no potential for selling shoes in Africa. Nobody wears shoes.'

The second salesperson visited the boss with excitement, saying 'There's massive sales potential in Africa. Nobody wears shoes!'

If you're feeling highly stressed at the moment don't just think to yourself, 'I've always been stressed and always will be so there's no hope.' Change your thinking by saying to yourself, 'I'm highly stressed at the moment so there is massive potential to improve my health through relaxation.'

Completing a wheel of life

The wheel of life is a helpful tool to show you which areas of your life are low on stress and which areas need your attention. You may be so busy struggling with one area of your life that you just fail to see all your other needs and responsibilities. Although there are always times when you need to focus your attention on one area of your life, you can end up knocking yourself totally off balance and then not get anything done well. Completing a wheel of life forces you to take a step back and take stock of how things are going in all the areas that are important to you. This bird's-eye view can be revealing, helping you see the bigger picture.

Many of my executive clients complete a wheel of life and decide that they're giving too much attention to work, even though their families are more important to them. On the other hand, when I coach people who have left their careers aside to spend more time at home, they often feel underchallenged in the area of work or study. Try completing your own wheel of life using the example in Figure 3-1.

1. **Think about eight key areas in your life that are important to you.**

   They could be career, friends, family, partner, physical home, exercise, nutrition, personal development, sports, leisure time, a hobby, holidays. Takes a few minutes to think about what matters to you.

2. **Write down one key area in each sector of the circle.**

3. **For each area, mark how satisfied you are with the way things are going.**

   0 is totally unsatisfied and 10 is totally satisfied.

4. **Join up all the points and see what sort of shape is created.**

5. **Reflect on your scores.**

   Which areas have low scores and which areas have high scores? Choose one area that you want to improve and think about what you could do to improve your score.

6. **Set a goal.**

   Write down what you are going to do to improve that area of your life. For example, if you want to improve your relationship with your partner, you may organise a date, book a weekend away, or take some time out to talk about your relationship with your partner to think of ways to make things better.

7. **Think about any reasons why you may not achieve your goal and think of ways to overcome them.**

   For example, you may be short of cash this month and unable to afford a weekend away. How about just a day trip somewhere romantic instead? Get your creativity going, and call a friend up for help if you're struggling with ideas – that almost always helps.

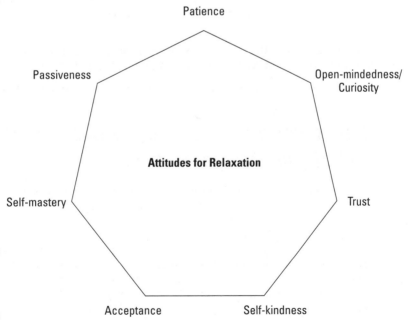

Figure 3-1:
Wheel
of life.

Prioritising the key causes of your stress

To relax effectively, you need to find out the key causes of your stress – your stressors. You then need to know which ones are causing you the most stress and prioritise to reduce these first. You only have a limited amount of time so use that time effectively by focusing on reducing the most significant stressors in your life.

Follow the steps below to help you discover which areas of your life are causing the most stress.

1. **Look at your journal entries for the past few weeks. (See Chapter 2 on using a diary to identify your stressors).**

   In this way you find the most frequent and significant stressors in your life.

2. **Jot down the areas in your life that are causing you the most stress.**

   These are your key external stressors.

3. **Consider the thoughts you have when you're stressed.**

   These are your key internal stressors. See Chapter 12 on mind management to identify the sort of negative thoughts that cause stress to be triggered.

4. **Make a list of the causes of your internal and external stressors, starting with the ones that are causing you the most stress.**

   You now have a list of stressors that cause you the most difficulty.

Discovering the most effective relaxation techniques for your stress

You may have all sorts of different factors causing you stress. For example, you may have more work than you can cope with in the office, causing you to arrive home late every day. But when you get home you need to ensure your son completes his homework instead of just playing on the computer, as well as cook dinner and clean. Every night your daughter is struggling to sleep, and she disturbs your own sleep. You are beginning to feel too stressed to cope – you don't have time to exercise or see friends, and your frustration is putting a strain on your relationship with your partner. How do you decide on the best way to relax? This section will point you in the right direction.

Use the following key to give you some ideas for ways of managing your stressors:

✔ **You have a constant feeling of stress but don't really know the cause:** Use the relaxation techniques from Part 2 if you prefer techniques to relax your body, or the exercises in Part 3 if you prefer an approach to focus on calming your mind. Parts 2 and 3 feed into each other: relaxing your body also calms your mind, and calming your mind also relaxes your body.

✔ **Your main source of stress is due to work:** Try the exercises in Chapter 16, which covers all sorts of workplace issues.

✔ **You think primarily in a negative way:** Have a go at the exercises in Chapters 12 and 13, on mind management for improving your attitude. You may also consider meditation, which I talk you through in Chapter 10.

✔ **You have stressful relationship issues:** Read through Chapter 15 for help with personal relationships and Chapter 16 for ideas on working through workplace relationships.

✔ **Your mind is too busy:** Consider using the exercises in Chapters 9 and 10 on guided imagery, self-hypnosis and meditation. You may also find Chapter 7 on yoga and t'ai chi helpful.

✔ **You have mental or physical health issues:** Choose the relevant chapters from Part 5.

✔ **The main cause of your stress is lack of sleep:** Start with Chapter 14 and add any relaxation techniques from Chapters 4-11 that you like.

✔ **You have poor nutrition and fitness:** If you're not exercising enough, consider starting with Chapter 6. If you think your nutritional intake is unbalanced, read Chapter 15.

Try to identify your key stressors and take steps to reduce them. If you can't identify what's causing you stress, simply practise one of the many relaxation techniques outlined in this book on a daily basis. This is likely to help, and may help you to identify the cause. Practising meditations such as mindfulness may be particularly helpful for you. As you raise your level of awareness you will find it easier to spot the reason why you're feeling stressed.

Developing long-term resilience to stress

Stress resilience is your ability to cope effectively with life's pressures. If you're resilient you can handle the problems and issues that come your way without feeling too stressed.

You may know someone who doesn't seem to be too bothered by the disasters they face. They seem to keep going, without significant difficulty, and even laugh about the stressful situation. That's resilience. Fortunately, resilience is not just something you're born with. You can develop resilience through taking some simple steps.

By developing your long-term resilience to stress, you won't need to use relaxation as a way to calm yourself down. You will lead a life in which you're grounded in a state of peace and wellbeing. To build such a satisfying and attractive foundation requires you to develop the following areas of your life:

- ✔ **Develop an internal locus of control.** Do you believe that you're in control of your life or that life is controlling you? In Chapter 2 I show you how to develop an internal locus of control. For example, your friend has asked you to do the school run one day next week and you agreed, but actually you're really busy that morning. You feel trapped. Get back in control by picking up the phone and discuss a possible solution with your friend, or ask your partner for some advice.

- ✔ **Encourage optimism.** Optimism is more than just thinking positively. Partly, it's about taking credit when you do things well, and not overly blaming yourself when things don't go your way. In Chapter 12 I suggest lots of ways to be more optimistic.

- ✔ **Foster a sense of purpose and spirituality.** To increase resilience, seek a sense of meaning to your life. You may achieve this through a religious belief, or a secular philosophy and doing things like volunteering, spending time in nature and cultivating deep, meaningful relationships based on trust and care. See Chapter 11. You can also create meaning by having a long-term vision of where you want to be, and taking small steps every day to achieve them.

- ✔ **Harness humour and playfulness.** Learn not to take things so seriously. Stand back and see the bigger picture and laugh at your predicament instead of just worrying about it. The movie *Life is Beautiful* shows the power of doing this in the most challenging of circumstances. See Chapter 13 on humour.

- ✔ **Look after yourself.** Take active steps to live a balanced lifestyle. See Chapter 16 for work/life balance tips. Exercise and eat well to protect yourself against stressors. Take time to do relaxation techniques of your choice on a regular basis. Using these techniques lowers your average level of stress on a day-to-day basis, so what would normally trigger a high level of stress in the past no longer has that effect.

- ✔ **Nurture a social support network.** Socialising is one of the most powerful ways of reducing stress and feeling more relaxed. When things go badly wrong, do you have someone to talk to? If not, begin developing a network of people you help, and who help you. See Chapter 15 for ideas.

- ✔ **Practise mindfulness.** Are you aware of the inner thoughts and feelings that are driving your actions? Do you give your full attention to the situation you're in and the demands on your life, so you can prepare for possible future stressful situations adequately? See Chapter 10 for more on mindfulness exercises, which build long-term resilience through reshaping your brain.

If you're physically fit, running up a flight of stairs may not be difficult. In the same way, if you increase your mental fitness by doing relaxation techniques regularly, coping with life's demands becomes less difficult.

Using the 6 As for relaxation

If you're looking for a simple, yet comprehensive way of staying in control when feeling stressed, you've come to the right section. I've identified six key ways to reduce most sources of stress, and they all conveniently start with the letter A to help you remember. Almost every source of stress can be managed or coped with in a more effective way by using one of the 6 As for relaxation:

- **Accept the stressors that you can't change.** If your child has misbe-haved, accept the situation. Then take steps to teach your child how to behave more appropriately next time. Accept your feelings too. If you're feeling down, acknowledge the fact. If you deny your feelings, they tend to grow and overwhelm you.

- **Accomplish a healthy lifestyle.** Eat a balanced diet and exercise regu-larly. Seek to balance your work and home life. Look after your mental health by having a goal to focus on, connect with positive people around you and take time out to just do nothing. Let your body rest. Make sure you sleep well too.

- **Adapt the way you see your stressor.** You can change your perspec-tive and your way of seeing whatever is stressing you out. In this way, you'll feel more in control of the situation, which is vital for effective stress reduction. See your problems as a challenge, a game or a chance to learn. Focus on what's positive about your stressor. Write down any negative thoughts you're having about the situation, and challenge them. Let go of perfectionism. Be more realistic about what's possible. Take a step back. Consider if it'll matter in three months. . .or three years. And be grateful. Notice how many things have gone well as you work through this stressor rather than just what's hard or difficult.

- **Allow time for relaxation and fun.** Make time to do things that you enjoy every day. Treating yourself is okay. Look after your wellbeing by doing a relaxation technique regularly that elicits the relaxation response within your body: a healing, restful state.

- **Alter your strategies.** If you can't avoid whatever is stressing you, think of ways you can handle the stress more effectively. If relationships are the cause of your stress, use assertiveness to express your feelings with-out being aggressive. Compromise rather than just fighting to be right 100 per cent of the time, or totally giving in to the other person's wishes.

Managing your time well, maintaining an organised workspace and breaking up large tasks into smaller, manageable chucks helps too.

✔ **Avoid the stressor.** Step away from whatever's causing you stress in the first place. Learn to say no rather than taking on more work. Wake up earlier so that you're well prepared for the day rather that frantically rushing. Take time to plan ahead so things that normally stress you don't arise in the first place. Stay away from people that frustrate you if you can.

Write down a short summary of the 6 As for relaxation on a small piece of card and keep it in your wallet or purse. When you're faced with a stressful situation and don't know how to deal with it, look at the card and choose the most appropriate action for you at that time. When you're stressed, it's hard to think straight – having a list of ideas to reduce your stress can be helpful.

Committing to a 30-day relaxation plan

Planning out 30 days of relaxation exercises is a good way to integrate more relaxation into your life. Many people claim that it takes about 30 days to create a new habit or stop an old habit, so a 30-day relaxation plan may be just enough to make relaxing a new habit for you.

If you've read this chapter and Chapters 1 and 2, you may have an idea about the kind of things that are causing you stress and the range of different techniques available in this book to help you to achieve greater relaxation.

For your 30-day plan, choose three things that you want to implement into your life and then commit to them for 30 days. Having the willpower to stick to your decision is what people most often struggle with. Counteract this with the following tips:

✔ **Be kind to yourself when you fail.** You're not perfect. If you slip up on one day, give yourself a break. Rather than totally giving up, think about what you've done, and start again.

✔ **Choose realistic aims.** If you've never managed to stick to doing 30 minutes of a relaxation technique daily, start with five minutes a day and build it up by five minutes every week.

✔ **Join a group.** If you're a member of a running club, you're probably more likely to go running. If you have a yoga class to attend, you'll look forward to seeing your friends there and you'll learn some new postures or breathing techniques.

✔ **Make sure you're prepared.** If you want to do guided imagery every day, ensure you have a CD to listen to, or have studied it so you know how to do the technique.

✔ **Tell your family or friends about your commitment.** Better still, see if they want to do your chosen activities with you. For example, go walking every evening with a neighbour. That will make it much harder to quit.

✔ **Write your commitments in your diary.** Use the diary that you use most often because then you'll hopefully see it there every day.

So now you should be ready to plan your 30 day relaxation plan. Use the steps below to help you plan how to use the next 30 days most effectively, and how to evaluate how helpful each technique is for you.

1. **Decide which three relaxation techniques and strategies you wish to implement over the next 30 days.**

   They could be meditation, yoga, jogging, guided imagery, walking, deep breathing, badminton or whatever you think is right for you. Be creative and think about what you enjoy as well as what you need. Try to include at least one relaxation technique because that triggers your relaxation response, which is a powerful way to a more relaxed life. Then add one or two relaxing activities that you enjoy, like walking or socialising with friends.

2. **Write down the techniques and strategies in your regular diary.**

   Think of it as an appointment with yourself.

3. **Each time you do one of the techniques, jot down how you feel before and after the practice.**

   You could rate how relaxed you felt before and after, giving yourself a score out of 10. Write down and explore your feelings too; even a couple of sentences are helpful.

4. **After 30 days, evaluate your progress.**

   What went well? What could you improve? What are you pleased about? Plan your relaxation for the next 30 days, in the light of your experience.

See www.relaxationfordummies.com for a 30-day e-course on relaxation.

Stressed-out city worker

An executive in his late thirties was referred to me with frequent headaches and stomach ulcers, caused by stress. After an initial consultation I found that he worked 14-hour days minimum and hardly ever had time for his own family. Working through some assessment activities revealed an imbalance between what he wanted out of life and what he was doing. At first, he could only relax in my consultation room. After a few sessions, he began to see relaxation and meditation as safe activities he could do on his own, and was willing to create a relaxation plan that he wanted to implement. He began to book appointments in his digital diary to remind him to stop, be mindful and do a relaxation technique. In those 30 days he eased off considerable tension, causing his headaches and ulcers to almost totally go away in the process. Over the longer term he managed to reduce the medication he was on too, with the permission of his doctor. He really enjoys mindfulness meditation now, and practises the techniques to this day. He looks fresher, calmer and more in control.

Part II
Exploring Relaxation Techniques Using Your Body

The 5th Wave   By Rich Tennant

"Here's a tip - if you hear yourself snoring, you're relaxing too deeply."

In this part . . .

In this part you begin using your beautiful body to help you to relax. From breathing techniques and yoga, to different forms of exercise you're bound to find way of relaxing that appeals to you.

Chapter 4

Trying Progressive Relaxation

. . . .

. . . .

*Y*ou can't have a relaxed body and a tense mind at the same time. One goes with the other. So, a way of calming your mind is by relaxing your muscles. That's the idea behind progressive relaxation. By regularly practising progressive relaxation, you calm and relax your mind at the same time.

In this chapter I introduce you to progressive relaxation and applied relaxation, two similar techniques for relaxing the muscles in your body that have been well tested over many years and found to be effective for lots of people.

Discovering Progressive Relaxation

Edmund Jacobson developed the progressive relaxation technique in the 1920s. Jacobson measured how tense people's muscles were and investigated ways to relax the muscles, eventually coming up with the technique he called *progressive relaxation*.

Jacobson found that muscles get tense due to stressful thoughts or situations. By relaxing muscle tension, the thoughts that create the anxiety subside. In time, the habitual tendency to immediately tense when in a challenging situation is reduced.

Jacobson also found that day-to-day stresses leave a certain amount of tension in people's muscles – he called this *residual tension*. Progressive relaxation was designed to release this residual tension completely, which results in the person having a calm mind, having greater energy and feeling better able to face life's challenges.

Notice where in your body you feel tense right now as you read this. Take some time to scan around your body and note any areas of tightness. Now relax those tight parts of your body. If you can't relax those parts, don't worry you're certainly not alone. Progressive relaxation gives you a way of relaxing those tense muscles through a step-by-step process.

If I'm tense, my shoulders are usually the area that feels tight and uncomfortable. By becoming aware of my shoulders, I can release some of the tension. But only through immersing myself in a relaxation technique can I totally relax the tension. By practising various relaxation techniques over the years I am now able to ensure that there isn't tension in the first place. If any tension does pop up, I can relax before the tension gets out of control. With experience and regular practice, you can do the same.

Understanding Muscle Tension and Relaxation

If all your muscles were completely relaxed all the time, you would be in a heap on the floor. You need to tense your muscles even whilst sitting on a chair or to hold up this book. When you want to move, your muscles contract, or tense up, to move your body.

Problems arise when your muscles are tense for no reason. For example, you don't need to tense your forehead to read this sentence. You don't need to hunch your shoulders to hold this book. Clenching your jaw doesn't aid your ability to read. If your muscles are excessively tense, you may be looking for ways to relax them.

Imagine holding a heavy bag all day. Eventually you'd want to put it down. Holding unnecessary tension is like carrying a heavy bag with you. By practising progressive relaxation and letting go of your muscle tension, you put the bag down, so you can rest, and don't feel so tired all the time. Then you have the energy to do other things.

Here are some benefits of relaxing your muscles from time-to-time:

✔ You have more energy, as you're not wasting effort tensing muscles.

✔ You're able to think more clearly and solve problems, especially emotional issues.

✔ You're less likely to suffer from ailments such as tension headaches and back pain.

✔ Your body feels pleasant and warm rather than feeling discomfort and pain caused by tense muscles.

✔ Your mind becomes calmer.

✔ You feel more positive and in control of yourself.

You may not feel all the benefits of progressive relaxation straight away, but after you practise the technique for a few weeks you'll probably notice some positive changes.

Progressive relaxation has been shown to be beneficial for managing many health conditions, including the following:

✔ Anxiety and panic

✔ Tension headaches and migraines

✔ High blood pressure

✔ Insomnia

✔ Asthma

✔ Chronic pain

✔ Chronic obstructive pulmonary disease

✔ Digestion problems

✔ Epilepsy

If you have a medical condition, check with your health professional before carrying out progressive relaxation or any other exercise in this book.

You can only hope to reap the rewards of progressive relaxation if you practise at least once, and ideally twice, a day.

Exploring Progressive Relaxation

Progressive relaxation is a very simple relaxation technique in principle. Edmund Jacobson's original technique can take months to learn, so in this chapter I show you a shorter, simple version.

You can choose between two different types of progressive relaxation – active and passive. Some researchers have shown that the active process in which the muscles are tensed first makes relaxing more difficult and the muscles take longer to relax. Edmund Jacobson emphasised the importance of passive progressive relaxation to remove residual tension in the muscles. However, he recommended that people practise the active process first to learn what tense and relaxed muscles actually feel like.

In *active progressive relaxation* you tense your muscles and then let them go. The idea is that you need to tense a muscle in order for you to feel what tension in that muscle feels like. Most people don't know which of their muscles are tense. By actively tensing your muscles you become more aware of the muscle and what it feels like to be tense. You do this by holding the tension for a few seconds and feeling that tension, and then you let it go and feel the relaxation in the muscle in comparison. When you let that tension go, your muscle does the opposite of the tension, which is of course, relaxation. If your muscle doesn't fully relax, you simply come back to the tense muscle later on and repeat the process. Just as when you swing a pendulum one way, it swings back again, so if you tense a muscle, it swings back towards relaxation.

Passive progressive relaxation is about learning to relax your muscles without actually physically tensing them. You simply go through each muscle in the body in turn and become aware of any tension there. Just the awareness of the tension itself together with a memory of how your muscles feel when they're relaxed helps to gradually dissolve the tension. You may prefer to use the passive relaxation technique if:

- ✔ You have injuries or a physical disability and cannot tense your muscles.

- ✔ You find it more relaxing to become aware of your muscles without the effort of tensing them.

- ✔ You are at work or in a public place where it would not be appropriate to start tensing and relaxing your muscles.

 Passive progressive relaxation is based on you knowing what your muscles feel like when they are tense and relaxed. For this reason, you may want to try active progressive relaxation first. Do active progressive relaxation a couple of times a day for a week and then move on to the passive technique.

Before you dive in to start practising progressive relaxation, it's useful to consider some of the key principles that make the experience most effective for you. The points below give you tips to best prepare you. By following them, you'll find it easier to concentrate, and are more likely to feel relaxed by the end of the progressive relaxation exercise, especially after a week or two of regular practice.

- ✔ **Avoid working too hard on any muscle or joint injuries.** Progressive relaxation isn't supposed to be painful. If you do have injuries in certain areas, either skip that muscle group or don't tense the muscle too much.

- ✔ **Choose a time to practise when you won't be disturbed.** You can practise at home or work. If neither of those places is suitable, consider where you can practise easily on a daily basis.

- ✔ **Consider your posture.** Progressive relaxation can be practised either lying down on your back on the floor or mat, sitting in a comfortable chair, or even on your bed. If lying down, allow your arms to be by your sides, with palms facing up if that feels okay. Ensure you're on a sufficiently padded surface so that you're relaxed. You'll find that your temperature drops quite rapidly when you're lying still so you may like to cover yourself with a blanket.

✔ **Find a place where you will feel warm, comfortable and safe.** These feelings are associated with relaxation and so will help you to be at ease.

✔ **Practise when you're alert and awake.** Avoid having a heavy meal just before you start your relaxation exercise.

✔ **Turn off your phone.** Switch off any other distractions that may disturb you too.

✔ **Wear loose, comfy clothing.** Take off your shoes and your spectacles or contact lenses if that makes you feel better.

Another helpful tip to help you relax in progressive relaxation is to use 'cues'. Cues are any word or phrase that you repeat in your mind to help encourage you to relax. If you use the same cue every time, you will associate relaxation with that particular word. You can then use that word whenever you feel stressed, to help encourage relaxation into your daily life.

Here are a few examples of cues you can use in your progressive relaxation to get you started:

✔ 'Letting go'

✔ 'Peace and calm'

✔ 'Let it be'

✔ 'Tension dissolving'

✔ 'Loosening and easing'

✔ 'Accepting my present moment experience'

You may prefer to use a phrase that you feel comfortable with, that embodies relaxation. Use these phrases when you're practising progressive relaxation, either formally as an exercise, or informally throughout the day when tension is popping its head up above the surface.

Trying an active progressive relaxation

In this section I guide you through an active progressive relaxation session. You can do this either by reading this script and then practising on your own, or by asking your partner or a friend to read the script to you slowly. Alternatively, you can record the script yourself (as I explain in Chapter 3) or listen to the guided progressive relaxation track that accompanies this book.

After you've practised the relaxation a few times, try practising from memory at your own pace.

Relaxation is not the same as going to sleep. Relaxation is a skill. You may prefer not to practise relaxation in bed or at the end of the day, unless you want to use the process to help you go to sleep. In this case you need to repeat the exercise when you are awake if you wish to learn the skill of relaxation. If you keep falling asleep during your relaxation practice, try doing it at different times of the day, practise in a chair or keep your eyes open. Don't become anxious or worried if you fall asleep. In time, and with practice, you'll learn to stay awake. Remember to give yourself credit for the time you do manage to stay awake.

Here are a few guidelines for practising this progressive relaxation.

- ✔ **Allow the tension phase to be for about 5 seconds and relaxation for about 20-30 seconds.** You don't need to be exact about these timings but remember to allow sufficient time to relax after each tensing phase.

- ✔ **Only tense the muscle group that you're working on.** For example, don't tense your face when you're tensing your fist. If you're squeezing other muscles at the same time inadvertently, let them go if you can. However, if you can't manage that, it's okay. You'll gradually get better with experience.

- ✔ **Avoid over-tensing your muscles.** You are far better off to err on the side of caution rather than squeezing your muscles to the point of pain.

- ✔ **Remember to feel the sensations of tension and relaxation.** This is part of the reason for carrying out the exercise, so you remember what relaxed muscles feel like.

Here are the steps for an active progressive relaxation:

1. **Begin by adopting a comfortable posture for you – perhaps sitting, or lying down on your back.** Ensure you are sufficiently warm, loosen any tight clothing and remove your glasses and shoes if you wish.

   Close your eyes if you prefer.

2. **Breathe in through your nose if you can, hold your breath for a few seconds and slowly breathe out.**

   You might like to say 'relax' or 'calm' to yourself as you breathe out. Repeat this breathing a couple of times and then allow your breathing to be smooth, and slow and calm.

3. **Clench your right hand. . .make a fist. . .feel the tension and strain in your hand. . .hold onto it for a few seconds. . .and relax.**

   Let your fist just relax. . .let go of the tension immediately and notice the sensations in your hand as your fingers uncurl. . .feel the sensations in your forearm too. . .focus on the sensation of relaxation now that you have unclenched your fist. . .compare how your muscles felt when they were tense to how they feel now. . .allow a sense of relaxation to flow into your muscles as you have let go of the tension. Breathing slowly and deeply. . .

4. **Straighten your right arm with your palm facing the floor.**

   Raise your fingers and palm to the ceiling and pull them backwards. Feel the tension in your arms. Hold the tension for a few seconds. . .and relax. Feel the relaxation flowing through your upper arm, lower arm and fingers. . .notice how the sensation of relaxation is different to the sensations of tension. . .

5. **Repeat Steps 3–4 with your left hand and arm.**

6. **Tense the muscles in your face.**

   Close your eyes tightly and wrinkle your nose. . .feel the tension. . .and let go. . .relaxing more and more deeply. . .feel relaxation spreading across your face. Feeling the sense of relaxation in your face. . .

7. **Clench your teeth and allow the corners of your mouth to go down, as if you are frowning.**

   Feel the tension in your jaw and mouth. . .and relax. . .feel the relaxation from your forehead all the way down to your jaw. . .breathing slowly and deeply. . .feeling calm and relaxed. . .letting your face be completely neutral and relaxed.

8. **Keeping your mouth closed, gently pull your chin down towards your chest.**

   Feel the tension in your neck. . .hold it for a few seconds. . .and relax. . . allow the muscles to let go and smooth out in your neck. . .continue to observe how the feeling of relaxation in your neck feels different to the tension and tightness.

9. **Focus on the feeling of relaxation as your body sinks down and relaxes more and more deeply.**

   Notice how your body feels more and more comfortable.

10. **Breathe in and then squeeze your shoulders back and together.**

    Feel the tension in your shoulders as you squeeze them together and back. . .hold it for a few seconds. . .and relax. . .let go of the tension in your shoulders and notice the sensation of relaxation in the muscles around your shoulders. . .feel the relaxation spread across your shoulders and down your back. . .breathing slowly using your belly if you can. . .

11. **Tighten your stomach muscles.**

    Notice the muscles that are tensing up in your belly. . .and relax. . .just feel the tension leaving this part of your body. . .let the relaxation replace any feeling of strain. . . now just feel the sensation of relaxation and the feeling of your breathing. . . let the breathing be slow and deep. . .allow the relaxation to ripple through your being. . .

12. **Move your attention to your right leg.**

   Lift your right leg very slightly and pull your toes towards your head. . .
   feel the sensation of tension in your leg and foot. . .keep the tension tight
   and hold it for a few seconds. . .and relax. . .let go of all that tension. . .feel
   the relaxation spread from your upper leg, to your lower leg and through
   your foot and into your toes. . .let your breathing be deep and slow. . .
   feel how the relaxation is so different to the tension. . .relaxing deeply
   and fully.

13. **Repeat with your left leg and foot.**

14. **Feel your whole body sink down and relax more and more deeply.**

   Noticing the heaviness of the body. . .breathing slowly and deeply. . .
   inhaling and exhaling. . .feel the sensation of relaxation flow through
   your whole body replacing any sense of tension. . .relaxing more and
   more completely. . .only noticing the feelings of relaxation. . .relaxing
   more and more deeply.

15. **Count from five to one, and as you do this, come back to an alert yet
    relaxed state.**

   Five. . .remembering the feeling of relaxation and comfort. . .four. . .
   becoming slightly more alert. . .three. . .keep the feeling of relaxation
   as you feel more alert. . .two. . .the feeling of relaxation is staying with
   you. . .one. . .gently open your eyes, only when you're ready, feeling
   relaxed and yet awake and alert.

If you found the sequence of muscles to be tensed confusing to remember, feel
free to relax in any order you prefer. You could start from your feet and move
upwards, or you could start from the top of your head and move downwards.
You need to feel comfortable with the process.

Trying a passive progressive relaxation

In this exercise you don't need to tense your muscles at all. You simply
become aware of the tension and let the tension go. Before you try this passive progressive relaxation, read the suggestions in the earlier section 'Trying
an active progressive relaxation'. Here are the steps you can try out:

1. **Begin by adopting a comfortable posture for you – perhaps sitting, or
   lying down on your back.** Ensure you are sufficiently warm, loosen any
   tight clothing and remove your glasses and shoes if you wish. Close your
   eyes if you prefer.

2. **Become aware of the feeling of your own breathing.**

   Take a deep, slow in breath, hold it for a few seconds. . .and slowly
   breathe out. . .with each out breath, feel a sense of letting go. . .let your

body sink deeper into the surface you are resting on. Let tensions in your body dissolve as you breathe out slowly and gently.

3. **Resume breathing at your natural, relaxed rhythm.**

Becoming slower, smoother and deeper as you start to relax.

4. **Begin by noticing the sensations in the top of your head.**

Feel a wave of relaxation begin to spread from your head into your fore-head. . .allowing your forehead to be smooth and relaxed. . .and then tuning into the sensations in your face. . .as you exhale you notice how the tension in your face begins to ease and release. . .leaving behind a feeling of relaxation. . .enjoy the feeling. . .notice any tension in your jaw and letting that tension go as you breathe out. . .feeling the sensations as you do so. . .letting go of any tension in the sides of your face and the back of your head. . .letting your head be heavy and warm and supported by whatever you're resting on. . .

5. **Allow the wave of relaxation to move down to your neck.**

Noticing any tension in the back, front and sides of your neck. . .allowing the tightness to melt away. . .taking your time and moving through your body with gentleness and warmth towards yourself. . .

6. **Move your relaxation into your shoulders.**

Ease any tension in your shoulders. Feeling the tension melt away each time you breathe out. . .and now allowing that relaxation to spread down your upper arms, elbows and lower arms and into your hands and each of your fingers. Feeling the wave of relaxation moving through your shoulders and into your arms and hands. . .Noticing how your shoulders and arms are feeling heavier and more and more relaxed with each out breath you take. . .easing the tension and tightness away and replacing it with a feeling of warm wellbeing. . .

7. **Notice the tension in the upper part of your torso.**

Let that tension go. . .as you breathe in feel your chest and rib cage rising. . .and as you breathe out, feel the tension melt away from your chest and the upper part of your back. . .let the relaxation spread down to the lower part of your torso now. . .Notice the sensations in your torso as you breathe in, and feel the tension easing as you breathe out. . .feeling as relaxed as you wish to be. . .

8. **Let the relaxation spread into your buttocks and hips and pelvis area.**

Feel a sense of relaxation in this part of your body. . .let the tension ease with each out-breath. . .let the relaxation deepen. . .

9. **Let the wave of relaxation spread to the upper part of your legs. . .and then the knees and lower part of your legs.**

Notice the range of different sensations in a passive way. . .allowing any tensions to ease. . .feel the legs getting heavier, warmer and more relaxed with each out-breath. . .enjoy the relaxed feeling in your legs as you let go of the tightness in the muscles and feel more relaxed. . .

10. **Turn your attention to your feet.**

   Notice the range of sensations down in your feet. . .feel any tensions in your feet dissolving as you breathe out. . .letting go of all the tension. . .

11. **Allow any last bits of tension in your body to flow out.**

   Scan your body for any bits of tension and let them gently go. . .let the tension move down through your whole body and out of your feet as you exhale slowly and smoothly. Allow the sense of relaxation to deepen throughout your body. . .allow yourself to feel heavier and warmer as you feel more and more relaxed. . .

12. **Allow yourself to be as relaxed as you wish to be.**

   Remember this feeling of relaxation. . . notice how your body feels now. . .so that you can recall and recreate this feeling of relaxation whenever you want. . .enjoy the feeling of relaxation for as long as you wish. . .

13. **When you're ready to bring this exercise to a close, gently open your eyes and slowly begin to move your muscles.**

   You don't need to rush at all. . .begin to notice your surroundings. . . have a stretch and reconnect with your day, refreshed, relaxed and re-energised. . .feeling calm and peaceful.

You can carry out this relaxation from the soles of your feet and move upwards towards your head if you prefer. You can also practise this exercise more rapidly and whilst standing up by scanning through the body and allowing relaxation to spread through.

Trying a short progressive relaxation

If you find the full progressive relaxation too threatening, too challenging or just too long, you could always begin with the short version I present in this section and gradually extend the time you spend on the exercise. You'll probably find progressive relaxation more effective if you practise a short version on a daily basis rather than a long session once a week. Daily practice is the key, as it is with all the different relaxation techniques I describe in this book.

Here is a short progressive relaxation exercise. Remember to be aware of the sensation of tension and the sensation of relaxation in each muscle group. Also, try repeating each step if you can to deepen the quality of your relaxation. Allow the tensing to occur for about 5 seconds and the letting go and observing the sensations for about 30 seconds. Also, try to just tense the muscle group you're working on, rather than any other part of your body.

1. **Begin by adopting a comfortable posture for you, where your back is supported – perhaps sitting, or lying down on your back.** Ensure you are sufficiently warm, loosen any tight clothing and remove your glasses and shoes if you wish.

2. **Take a few deep, slow breaths.**

   Allow your breath to go all the way down, pushing your belly out on an in-breath if you can. Breathe out slowly and say the word 'relax' to yourself, or any similar cue word that you prefer.

3. **Raise your eyebrows and feel the tension in the forehead.**

   Notice the sensation there. . .and relax. Now feel the sensations in your forehead.

4. **Raise your shoulders up towards your ears.**

   Hold the tension there and notice the feeling inside your shoulders. . .and let go. Notice how your shoulders feel now. Enjoy any sensations of relaxation there.

5. **Close your mouth and clench your jaw.**

   Notice the tension in and around the area of your jaw. . .and let go

6. **Scan through your body and notice any areas that are tight.**

   Tense them up but not to the point of pain. . .and then let go and notice any feeling of relaxation and letting go in the muscles. Be aware of how the sensations feel.

7. **Breathe.**

   Finish this relaxation with a few deep breaths as you did at the beginning of this exercise.

For a short passive progressive relaxation, use the script above, but instead of tensing the muscles just feel the sensation of tension and then let go of that tension.

Integrating Relaxation Throughout Your Day

The secret to living a more relaxed life is to practise a relaxation technique that appeals and works for you *every day*. You can deepen your relaxation by also practising relaxation throughout the day. As you practise progressive muscular relaxation on a daily basis, you begin to become aware of low levels of tension in your body before you get extremely tensed up. You are more aware and sensitive to tense muscles. This is great! It means that you can take action to alleviate the tension as soon as you notice tension creeping into your body. Awareness is the key. The sooner you realise the tension has arisen, the sooner you can 'nip it in the bud' so to speak.

Here are the stages, 'the 3 As', you go through to relax during the day:

1. **An activating event.**

   Something happens (a thought, feeling or situation) that causes unnecessary tension in your body.

2. **Awareness.**

   You become aware of the muscle tension. You notice which muscle or muscles are unnecessarily tense.

3. **Action.**

   You relax the muscles by either tensing that muscle up further; feeling the sensation, and then letting it go. Alternatively, you can use a passive progressive relaxation approach, and simply feel the tension in the muscle and say to yourself 'relax' each time you breathe out and feel the tense muscle relaxing.

Through this process, you begin to feel more relaxed as you go about your daily activities. If you find that the muscle doesn't relax, try not to worry about it. The fact that you are aware of the tension is a huge step. As you become more and more aware of the tension, you learn to relax the muscle. Regular practice of the standard progressive relaxation technique helps you to do this, as well as any other relaxation technique in this book that you like.

Use different prompts to remind you to scan your body for tension and to relax the muscles. For instance, use situations such as waiting in a queue or at a red traffic light, hearing the sound of the phone or doorbell, before eating a meal, or simply between the end of one task and the start of another. You could even use small colour labels or sticky notes around the house or office to remind you to relax.

Making time on a daily basis to relax is key to achieving greater relaxation in your life. Even a few minutes of relaxation makes a difference. Then you can use this skill to relax as you go about your daily activities.

Overcoming Problems in Progressive Relaxation

You may find all sorts of issues and problems that come up when you try the progressive relaxation exercise, such as falling asleep or constantly losing concentration. That's not unusual. The points below include some very common issues that people often face and some ways of overcoming them:

✔ **Being unsure of what to do with the tension and relaxation:** You need to be aware of the sensations of tension and relaxation when you're practising progressive relaxation. If you find yourself overly focused when tensing and forgetting to become aware of the sensation of relaxation, look again. Give attention to both feelings – the awareness of what tense and relaxed muscles feel like is an important part of the process.

✔ **Cramping muscles:** You may find that when you tense a muscle, it cramps. This usually happens in the legs. To prevent this, ensure you're in a warm room and that your muscles are not overtired. Also, remember not to over-tense your muscles. If your muscle does cramp, try to massage the muscle or stretch it to ease the pain.

✔ **Falling asleep:** If you are using progressive relaxation to help with your insomnia, then falling asleep is positively welcome, I'm sure! However, if you want to develop the skill of relaxation, ideally you need to be awake. Here are some ways to stay awake as you practise:

- Practise the progressive relaxation when you're more alert and awake, such as in the morning or afternoon.

- Try keeping your eyes open as you carry out the exercise.

Be patient with yourself. After a few weeks, you may no longer fall asleep as you do the exercise.

✔ **Feeling worse at the end of the progressive relaxation:** Progressive relaxation is not an instant fix. You need to give the technique a couple of weeks at least before you can judge whether or not it's right for you. Just because you feel a little worse the first few times you practise, doesn't mean the relaxation process won't work for you in the long run. That's a bit like saying that the gym isn't working for you because it makes your muscles ache. However, you can do things to help you feel better. Try these ideas if you're having issues with the technique:

- Reduce the amount of force and the time for which you tense your muscles.

- Try the passive progressive relaxation technique where you don't actually tense your muscles at all.

- Use a different posture, such as lying on your bed or sitting in a different chair.

- Give more time to the relaxation phase after each tensing of the muscles.

- Vary the length of time you practise the exercise. You could try shorter or longer periods.

- Try a different relaxation strategy if you don't find progressive relaxation helpful at all. Relaxation is about finding the right technique for you.

✔ **Feeling dizzy during or at the end of the relaxation:** If you feel dizzy during the exercise, you may have low blood pressure or some other condition. Visit your health professional to be tested and ask for suggestions for how to proceed with your relaxation exercises.

✔ **Finding the process painful:** Progressive relaxation is not supposed to be a painful experience as such. You may be over-tensing your muscles if you are finding the exercise painful. In this case, it's best if you reduce the amount of tension you exert into your muscles.

If you find the process emotionally challenging, then you need to decide what's the best way forward for you. You may decide to stay with the experience to see if the challenging emotions subside, or you may take a break and come back to the exercise a bit later when you feel stronger.

Remember to check with a health professional before you start engaging in progressive relaxation if you have a physical or mental health condition.

✔ **Losing concentration:** You're bound to lose focus at some point during the relaxation, if not many times. That's normal. Avoid criticising yourself for losing attention if you can. As soon as you notice that you have lost focus, gently guide your attention back to the progressive relaxation process. You may find that you're quite focused the first time you practise, but as the novelty wears off, you lose focus more easily. You don't need to worry. This is a normal part of the process.

✔ **Not knowing how long to tense and relax:** Remember the tension phase is only for about five seconds and the relaxation phase for about 30 seconds. You don't need to be precise about the timings, but you need to ensure that you're feeling your released and relaxed muscles for much longer than you're tensing your muscles. You may be getting so involved in the tension phase that you forget to give a generous time to the relaxation phase, where you let go of your muscles.

Chapter 5

Practising Breathing Techniques

1 first heard about breathing techniques as a teenager. When I was recommended to try an exercise, I wasn't convinced. 'I breathe all the time,' I thought. 'How can a bit of breathing make a difference? It's all probably some needless Eastern ritual.' I was a stereotypical, overly judgemental teenager. The classic image of an Eastern guru carrying out all sorts of weird breathing approaches didn't appeal at all. The first time I really understood the power of breathing exercises was when, as an adult, I listened to a guided breathing exercise CD. I measured my level of relaxation before and after the audio track, as instructed on the CD, and found I felt much more relaxed and refreshed after just a few minutes. I was really surprised. I went on to discover a range of different breathing techniques, and I now use those techniques interchangeably throughout the day to keep me feeling cool, calm, focused and . . . relaxed. I often show my clients suitable breathing techniques, with almost immediate positive results.

Discovering the Power of Your Breath

Using your breathing to reach a state of relaxation is a well-accepted and researched approach. Breathing techniques are one of the fastest ways to reach a state of relaxation and the techniques can be acquired in a relatively short time. Most relaxation techniques, such as progressive relaxation and guided imagery, indirectly induce the relaxation response (see Chapter 1 for more about the relaxation response). Changing your breathing can directly engage your state of relaxation, making your breathing a powerful tool.

Most relaxation exercises use breathing techniques. You can use breathing techniques at any time, which makes them ideal for use in stressful situations or when you're out and about and wish to re-centre and ground yourself in the present moment in an inconspicuous way.

Relaxing breathing exercises involve either becoming aware of your breath with a certain attitude (*meditation*), or changing your breath in a particular way for the duration of the exercise (*breathing technique*). Carrying out daily breathing techniques can make you feel calmer within one breath and improve any bad breathing habits you may have, resulting in greater energy and relaxation in your daily life.

Although the exercises in this chapter are simple, you may find the process initially quite challenging, and may even feel more anxious to begin with. Be patient with yourself, and rest assured that with time you'll get the hang of breathing techniques and go on to use your breath as a powerful ally in your journey to greater relaxation, peace and calm. If you just can't get the hang of breathing techniques after a couple of weeks, seek additional help or try one of the other relaxation techniques in this book – use what works for you rather than beating yourself up for not being able to use breathing techniques.

If you feel dizzy or uncomfortable when doing a breathing technique, stop doing the exercise and have a break. I suggest that you see your doctor or health professional if this discomfort continues. Avoid straining or forcing your breath – take your time and go at your own pace. No exercise in this book is a substitute for medical treatment if you have a health condition, unless recommended by your doctor.

Moving house stress

Yesterday I had a call from a woman with a high level of stress. She was about to move from her existing home, where she'd lived for over 30 years. On top of this, one of her neighbours was a continuous nuisance for her and another played loud music late into the night. She didn't want to move because of all the friends she had in the area, but at the same time she wanted to move near one of her sons and away from the neighbours. Her legs and arms were beginning to tremble with worry, and she felt like she had a 'brain fog'. Her doctor had put it down to stress. She'd scanned through my book *Mindfulness For Dummies* (Wiley) and used the CD every day to help manage her stress, but now the level of anxiety had become too much with the prospect of moving away. I asked her to assess how stressed she felt, and she rated herself as highly stressed. Then, I guided her in a breathing exercise for about ten minutes. In just ten minutes she re-rated herself as quite relaxed and felt back in control. That's a big change for just ten minutes on the phone. Then we could talk about the cause of her stress and different ways of managing it – but it all began with some breathing exercises. You too can feel more in control by practising the exercises in this chapter or use the accompanying tracks.

Understanding Your Breathing

Here's a breathtaking fact: in an average lifetime a human breathes about 500 million times. No more terrible breath jokes . . . so don't hold your breath.

Breathing is essential for your wellbeing. The main purpose of breathing is to nourish your body with oxygen and get rid of excess carbon dioxide. You breathe subconsciously. You don't need to think about breathing. If you had to remember each time you had to breathe, you'd probably have forgotten long ago and dropped dead. Fortunately your body is far too clever to leave the important job of breathing to you and so makes sure you breathe automatically – to be precise, your autonomic nervous system controls your breathing (see Chapter 1 for more on your nervous system). However, unlike most of the other systems in your body, you can also have some control over your breathing if you want. Breathing is almost like a relaxation switch – by managing your breathing you can switch off the automatic stress response and turn on your automatic relaxation response as and when necessary.

To carry out breathing techniques, you need to understand how breathing works and how you currently breathe. In this section, I help you understand the various aspects of your breath.

Looking at how your lungs work

You use your lungs to breathe. Breathing takes place in two simple stages:

- ✔ **Inhalation:** The first stage of breathing is *inhalation*. Inhalation fills your lungs with air. You inhale by using your *diaphragm*, a sheet of muscle located just underneath your lungs (see Figure 5-1). When you inhale the diaphragm muscle and the muscle between your rib cage contract and air is drawn into the lungs.

- ✔ **Exhalation:** The second stage of breathing is *exhalation* – or breathing out. The diaphragm and rib cage muscles relax, pushing the air out of your lungs. Then the cycle repeats again.

When you breathe in, oxygen goes into your bloodstream and supplies all your cells. Without oxygen, your cells would die. This is the reason why breathing is an automatic process and essential for your life. When you breathe out, you get rid of a waste gas called carbon dioxide made by your cells. Your body needs the right amount of carbon dioxide too, so breathing out is just as important as breathing in.

The rate and depth of your breathing are largely determined by the amount of carbon dioxide (the waste product gas) in your blood.

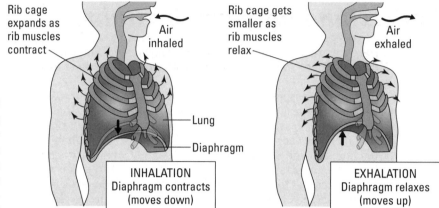

Rib cage expands as rib muscles contract

Air inhaled

Lung

Diaphragm

INHALATION
Diaphragm contracts
(moves down)

Rib cage gets smaller as rib muscles relax

Air exhaled

EXHALATION
Diaphragm relaxes
(moves up)

Figure 5-1:
Your diaphragm helps you breathe in and out.

If you breathe too rapidly or deeply – *overbreathing* or *hyperventilation* – you lose too much carbon dioxide. If you breathe too slowly or shallowly – *underbreathing* – you end up with a build-up of carbon dioxide.

The relaxation response is associated with a relatively slow rate of breathing. If you feel stressed or tense, simply by slowing your rate of breathing you immediately engage your relaxation response. This response results in a slower heart rate, reduced tension in your muscles and a calmer mind.

Finding out how you breathe

Before you begin exploring the wonderful range of different breathing exercises in this book, it's important to become more aware of how you currently breathe, and how your breathing is influenced by your state of mind. Discover how to do this in this section.

How your body responds to your breath

Begin understanding more about your breath by practising breath awareness. You can do this by becoming aware of the way your belly (abdomen) and chest move as you breathe in and out. This awareness is all about becoming curious about what's happening rather than trying to change anything.

1. **Begin by sitting on a chair. Ensure you are sufficiently warm, loosen any tight clothing and remove your glasses and shoes if you wish.**

   Place one hand on your belly (just around your navel) and the other hand on your chest. As you naturally breathe in and out, notice and explore how your hands move. Does your belly rise and fall? Does your chest rise and fall? Notice what's happening for the next few minutes.

2. **Now place your hands on your sides, just under your ribs.**

   As you naturally breathe, notice if and how your sides expand as you breathe in and move back as you breathe out. Remember, you don't need to force or change anything with this exercise. Simply observe what is happening for a few minutes.

3. **Lean forwards and place your hands on your lower back if you can.**

   See if you notice any movement there as you breathe. You may even be able to feel movement in your chest expanding backwards. Notice how that feels.

4. **Jot down your observations in your relaxation journal.**

   Find out more about keeping a relaxation journal in Chapter 3.

   Repeat this exercise after doing a few weeks of the various breathing exercises in this chapter and see if your breathing has changed. More expansion of your belly as you breathe naturally is a sign that you are getting more relaxed.

This exercise shows that breathing isn't just an expansion of the chest as many people think. Breathing involves an expansion in all directions. This is the reason why slouching when you're sitting or standing restricts your breathing and can add to your stress levels. Sitting or standing upright gives your chest the opportunity to open up and take in sufficient air.

How your thoughts and emotions affect your breath

A difference exists between intellectually knowing that your emotions affect your breath, and actually experiencing the effect for yourself. Here's an exercise to help you understand how your breathing is shaped by the kind of thoughts and feelings that you're going through.

1. **Begin by adopting a comfortable posture for you – perhaps sitting, or lying down on your back. Ensure you are sufficiently warm, loosen any tight clothing and remove your glasses and shoes if you wish.**

2. **Place one hand on your belly and one on your chest.**

   Feel your breathing for about a minute or so.

3. **Bring to mind a situation that is causing you some stress or anxiety at the moment.**

4. **Notice how your breathing changes for about a minute.**

5. **Now bring to mind a relaxing place that you've visited in the past.**

   Make one up in your mind if you can't remember one.

6. **Become aware of how your breathing changes, if at all, for about a minute.**

Breathing in ancient cultures

The Latin word *spiritus* means 'soul, courage, breath and vigour'. Ancient cultures often linked the breath to a sense of life force. *Qi*, a term from Chinese culture, literally translates as 'air' or 'breath'. Qi is also translated as 'energy flow'. The word *prana* comes from Sanskrit, the primary language of Buddhism and Hinduism, meaning 'breath' but also 'vital life force', like *qi*. In yoga, *pranayama* is the control of *prana*, which initially involves the control of your breath, leading to increased vitality. *Atman*, the word for 'soul' in Sanskrit, also means breath. The English word 'aura' comes from the Greek *aura*, meaning 'breath'. Even the word 'psychology' comes from the Greek *psykhe*, meaning 'mind, spirit, breath and life'.

The link between breath, spirituality and energy is close. Ancient wisdom cultures appreciated the importance of good breathing habits and techniques, not only for general wellbeing but also for energising yourself with spiritual freedoms.

What did you notice? You probably found your breathing was more rapid and shallow when thinking about something stressful, and a bit slower and perhaps deeper when thinking about a relaxing place. The point of this exercise is to help you see how stress affects your breathing rate. So, next time you notice your breathing rate is rapid and shallow, you may be overly focusing on some stressful thoughts. By doing a quick breathing exercise, you begin to feel more relaxed.

Appreciating the benefits of healthy breathing

Healthy breathing is breathing at a rate that is right for the situation that you're in. When you run, your breathing rate needs to be high. When you rest, your breathing rate needs to be lower. In this section, I show you some techniques to change your breathing, which I call *healthy breathing*.

Here are some of the benefits of healthy breathing:

- ✔ You feel more relaxed and in control.
- ✔ Your body gets sufficient oxygen and removes the right amount of carbon dioxide.
- ✔ You have more energy and are more alert and able to get more done in less time.
- ✔ You're less likely to fall ill as your immune system is strengthened by your more relaxed state.

✔ You feel a greater sense of wellbeing.

✔ You know how to relax yourself whenever you become excessively stressed.

Discovering the source of unhelpful breathing habits

Breathing is a very natural process, but as we grow up we pick up bad breathing habits for a number of reasons, such as:

✔ **Poor posture when sitting or walking:** This constricts your lungs, so you can't take a proper breath in or out.

✔ **Stress and anxiety over the long term:** The stress response results in a rapid breathing rate that can become a habitual pattern if you're chronically stressed.

✔ **Muscle tension in the body:** If your muscles are tense, especially around your shoulders or belly, you constrict the amount of air that your lungs can take in.

The great thing about improving your breathing or practising breathing techniques from time to time is that, just as feeling stress changes the rate of breathing, so changing the rate of breathing can make you feel more relaxed. As I show you in Chapter 10, mindfulness of your breathing – without actually changing your breathing – can naturally help to regulate your breathing and make you feel more relaxed and in control too.

Overcoming difficulties with breathing exercises

When you first practise the breathing exercises in this chapter, you may have a few difficulties. In this section I offer some simple ways to overcome these issues.

You feel anxious

Feeling anxious during breathing exercises is fairly common. Whenever you try something new, there's bound to be some anxiety. Your heart rate may go up and your breathing may become more rapid. Ask yourself what you're concerned about. Your body is far too clever to stop you from breathing altogether. You could have a little go and if you feel too anxious, stop, and try again a bit later. The more you practise, the lower your anxiety will become. Remember, you're in control so decide what's best for yourself rather than rigidly following whatever I suggest. You know yourself better than anyone else.

You feel worse by the end of the exercise

Feeling worse doesn't mean you've failed. You may be finding the breathing exercise tricky as it's something new. Try not to put too much effort into the exercise – go at your own natural pace. If you find yourself feeling worse, even after practising every day for a couple of weeks, seek professional guidance or try a different relaxation technique.

You feel a bit dizzy

This may be a sign that you're hyperventilating – breathing too deeply or too quickly. Try not to take too many deep breaths in succession. Make your breaths slower and shallower, or hold your breath for a few seconds. If you're in any doubt of the cause of your dizziness, see your doctor.

You fall asleep

If you fall asleep, you're very relaxed, which in one sense is a good sign. However, as relaxation is a skill, you need to practise staying awake when doing the breathing exercises. Try sitting up straight, keeping your eyes open or practising at a time of day when you're more alert.

You can't focus

Most people's minds are very busy and you may find that your thoughts take you away from the exercise. Simply bring your attention back to the breathing exercise as soon as you notice, without criticising yourself – this wandering of your attention is part of the process.

Exploring Relaxing Breathing Exercises

The breathing exercises in this section are designed to make you feel more relaxed. They are both simple and highly effective. If you take one thing away from this book, I recommend that you become aware of your breathing, and control it from time to time. You will then have a skill that you can use in minutes that is available to you for your whole life.

Relaxation is a skill. You may initially feel frustrated with the relaxation techniques as you try them out. Practise the techniques in this chapter for a week or so. If you see no effect at all, try something different.

Try practising the exercises in this chapter throughout the day, whenever you remember to do so. Then, when you feel stressed, you'll be better able to manage your tension as you'll be skilled at using your breathing technique. Little and often is the secret of relaxation and breathing techniques.

Beginning with diaphragmatic breathing

Diaphragmatic (pronounced dia-fram-a-tic) or belly breathing is when you breathe so that your lungs fill up with air causing your diaphragm to move downwards. The diagram in Figure 5-2 shows what happens in your lungs when you breathe diaphragmatically.

Figure 5-2:
Diaphrag-
matic or
belly
breathing –
a relaxing
way to
breathe.

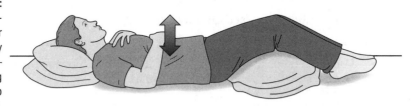

Try the following exercise to find out whether you belly breathe naturally:

1. **Sit on a chair or lie down on the floor.**

2. **Rest one hand gently on your chest, and the other on your belly, around your navel.**

3. **Notice whether one or both hands move as you breathe in naturally for a few minutes.**

If the hand on your chest rises when you breathe in, you probably don't do diaphragmatic breathing naturally at the moment. Don't panic – in a way, this is a good thing. You now have the potential to discover how to breathe dia-phragmatically and therefore feel more relaxed and calm whenever you wish. If you already breathe in a diaphragmatic way, great! However, if you want to deepen your belly breathing when you are in a stressful situation and need to relax you will still find this section useful.

Follow these steps to breathe diaphragmatically:

1. **Begin by lying down on your back. Ensure you are sufficiently warm, loosen any tight clothing and remove your glasses and shoes if you wish.**

2. **Place one hand gently on your belly (on or near your navel) and the other hand on your chest.**

3. **Allow your belly to rise gently each time you breathe in and fall each time you breathe out.**

4. You will begin to notice that your belly rises first, followed by your chest.

This is diaphragmatic or belly breathing.

5. Allow your breathing to be slow, deep and smooth.

Continue to notice the feeling of your breathing as your belly and chest rise and fall.

6. If your mind gets caught up in random thoughts, gently bring your attention back to the breathing.

Don't criticise yourself for thinking!

7. Try experimenting with breathing out with your mouth.

Use pursed lips as you breathe out, as if you're blowing through a straw, to help slow and extend your out breath.

Do this exercise for a few minutes to begin with, but as you become more experienced, extend this period to 20 minutes or so. Practise once a day, and ideally twice a day. Record your finding in your relaxation journal, noting how relaxed you felt before and after each exercise. See Chapter 3 on tips for writing a relaxation journal.

If your belly doesn't rise and fall during your in and out breath, or you just can't feel anything there, try the following:

- **Be patient!** Continue to focus your gentle, warm attention on your abdomen and see if your belly begins to gently rise and fall with time. The smallest of movements is a great start.

- **Don't force movement into your belly.** If you try too hard, your belly will just get more tense and tight. Bring a sense of gentleness to the exercise.

- **Exhale fully each time before you inhale.** By fully exhaling, your belly will naturally expand on your next in breath.

- **Massage your belly.** Warm your hands up by rubbing them together and then massage gently around your navel in particular. See whether this eases the tension a little.

- **Press your belly with your hands *very gently* as you exhale.** Reduce the pressure on your belly as you inhale. Do this for a few breaths. Then notice whether your belly begins to very gently rise on your in breath.

- **Rub your hands together until they're nice and warm.** Place one of your hands on your belly, one on top of the other. See whether you notice any movement of your belly.

- **Visualise a balloon inside your belly.** As you inhale the balloon inflates and as you exhale the balloon deflates. This image can prove helpful for some people.

Counting your breath

Focusing your attention on your breathing seems to naturally help the breath to calm and settle into a natural, smooth and slow rhythm for many people. One way of achieving this focus is called breath counting. This technique is simply counting your breaths. However, as you may find, it's not easy. The key is persistence. If you passively and persistently engage in the practice, you'll get better and better.

1. **Begin by adopting a comfortable posture for you – perhaps sitting, or lying down on your back. Ensure you are sufficiently warm, loosen any tight clothing and remove your glasses and shoes if you wish.**

2. **Notice the sensation of your own natural breathing.**

   Let each in breath happen in its own time rather than trying to draw the air in, and allow each out breath be a letting go

3. **The next time you exhale, say to yourself 'one'.**

4. **On your next exhalation, say to yourself 'two'.**

5. **Continue in this way, up to 'five'.**

6. **After you reach 'five', begin again from 'one'.**

7. **If you lose concentration, begin again from 'one'.**

8. **You may find your mind loses concentration easily, and you can't get beyond 'two' or 'three'.**

   Don't criticise yourself for losing concentration. Instead, gently smile to yourself and begin again from 'one'.

Whenever you realise that you've forgotten to count is a moment of awareness. You realise that you haven't been focusing. This awareness is an opportunity to congratulate rather than berate yourself for losing attention.

If you prefer, you may like to increase it to 'seven' or 'ten'. However, the most important thing is to cultivate persistence and patience with yourself as best you can. Try to accept that you'll lose concentration again and again – the idea is to keep starting again without getting overly frustrated.

The great thing about breath counting is that you can do it any time. And nobody would know. Well, unless you start doing it aloud! You can practise breath counting whenever you feel stressed. For example, you're in a queue at the supermarket and someone is taking five minutes just to find their credit card from the bottom of their handbag (or in the depths of their wallet), and you feel the heat rising in your body. Simply look away and start breath counting. You'll feel better in the long run and may avoid giving evil looks to disorganised customers.

Diving in with deep breathing

Deep breathing helps you feel more energised and calm. You may naturally breathe too shallowly. By carrying out some deep breathing for a period of time, your breathing will naturally deepen.

Most people don't know how to breathe deeply. Mistakenly, they expand the chest and tighten their belly. In the earlier section 'Beginning with diaphragmatic breathing', I explain the importance of the diaphragm in breathing. When you soften your belly, your diaphragm can move downwards, pushing your belly out slightly. This is the telltale sign that your breathing is deep.

1. **Begin by adopting a comfortable posture for you – perhaps sitting, or lying down on your back.** Ensure you are sufficiently warm, loosen any tight clothing and remove your glasses and shoes if you wish

   Try closing your eyes if that's comfortable for you.

2. **Place one hand on your belly and one on your chest.**

   Notice the feeling of your own breathing for a few moments.

3. **On your next exhalation, breathe out slowly and gently tense your abdominal muscles.**

   As your abdomen is pushed into your body, you push most of the air out of your lungs.

4. **As you inhale, imagine the air filling your lungs and making your belly rise.**

   Imagine you have a balloon in your belly and you're filling it up. Continue to breathe in until your chest expands too.

5. **Hold your breath for a few seconds.**

6. **Exhale fully and as slowly and smoothly as you can.**

   If possible take longer to breathe out than you did to breathe in. Allow your abdomen to sink in.

7. **Breathe into your belly.**

   Try filling an imaginary balloon as you count to four slowly. To help you count four seconds, say to yourself 'one thousand, two thousand, three thousand, four thousand'.

8. **Hold the breath for a slow count of two.**

   Say to yourself 'one thousand, two thousand' if that helps.

9. **Breathe out as you slowly count to six.**

   Have a sense of letting go as you breathe out. Savour any sense of relaxation in your body as you breathe out.

10. Let your breathing go back to normal and relax for a few moments.

After a few normal breaths, and when you feel ready, do some more deep breathing as you count again.

Give yourself a score out of 10 as to how relaxed you feel before and after the exercise. Scoring yourself helps to show you what effect the exercise has had and motivates you to try it again in the future. When you first try this exercise, you may feel more tense at the end. This sensation is fairly normal as deep breathing is a new experience for you. With time, you'll find the deep belly breathing a relaxing experience. With experience, you can do this in a seated posture or even when standing and waiting at the bus stop – you don't have to have your hands on your chest and belly.

Trying straw breathing

You may be in the habit of taking short, shallow, rapid breaths rather than slower, fuller breaths. Straw breathing encourages you to breathe out more slowly due to the use of the straw and results in deeper breathing too.

1. **Begin by adopting a comfortable posture for you – perhaps sitting, or lying down on your back. Ensure you are sufficiently warm, loosen any tight clothing and remove your glasses and shoes if you wish.**

2. **Exhale by blowing through a normal drinking straw until you have exhaled pretty much all the air in your lungs.**

   As you breathe out through the straw, try not to force your breath. Let your mouth and lips be relaxed, and allow the exhalation to be natural.

3. **Remove the straw and breathe normally for a few breaths.**

   Let your breath settle back into its natural rhythm.

4. **On your next exhalation, place the straw in your mouth and repeat the process.**

Try this exercise for a few minutes to begin with, but gradually increase the time you spend doing the exercise for 10–15 minutes if you find it relaxing or energising. If you don't have a straw, simply breathe out as if you have a straw in your mouth.

Combining Breathing Techniques

I describe several relaxation techniques in this chapter. However, you don't need to try each technique in isolation. In fact, many people find the relaxation techniques to be more effective when they combine them. Becoming aware of and controlling breathing is one of the fundamental relaxation techniques that people find powerful. However, breathing techniques combine well with other techniques.

In this section, I merge a few breathing techniques with some of the other relaxation strategies I describe in this book. To find out what's effective for you, try the techniques twice a day for at least a week. Note in your relaxation journal (see Chapter 3) what effect the technique has and then decide whether you want to stick with it for longer or whether you want to try some other techniques.

Breathing with relaxation affirmations

Affirmations are positive statements that condition your subconscious mind to develop a more optimistic outlook about yourself. My relaxation affirmations are statements that help you to feel calm and relaxed. Choose from one of the following relaxation affirmations or make some up yourself:

- ✔ I feel calmer.
- ✔ I am relaxed.
- ✔ My body is at ease.
- ✔ I feel more and more tranquil.
- ✔ I am at peace.

Try making up your own personalised affirmations to deal with whatever challenge you currently face. For example, if you feel tense and low on energy, you may say to yourself 'With each breath I take, I feel more energised and relaxed.' Choose statements that are positive rather than just avoiding a negative.

Ensure that you believe the affirmation. If you don't believe the affirmation, it has only a limited effect.

After you select an affirmation, try using it in the following exercise:

1. **Begin by adopting a comfortable posture for you – perhaps sitting, or lying down on your back. Ensure you are sufficiently warm, loosen any tight clothing and remove your glasses and shoes if you wish.**

   Notice how you feel at the start of this exercise.

2. **Become aware of the physical sensation of your breathing in your body.**

   Feel the breath around your nose, chest, belly or wherever you notice your breath.

3. **Each time you breathe out, say your affirmation to yourself.**

4. **Pay attention to both the feeling of yourself breathing out and your affirmation.**

5. **If your affirmation is quite a long sentence, say it to yourself during both your in breath and your out breath.**

6. **If your mind wanders off into other thoughts, worries and concerns, understand that's natural.**

   As soon as you notice you mind wandering, shift your attention back to your affirmation, with a sense of kindness rather than criticism towards yourself.

7. **Return to feeling the sensation of your breathing and notice how you feel now.**

Note down the effect of this exercise in your relaxation journal (See Chapter 3). Try rating how relaxed you feel at the start and end of the exercise.

Breathing with guided imagery

You can combine your favourite breathing exercise with imagery. Even if you aren't a visual sort of person, you can have a go at imagery to feel more relaxed. I talk a lot about guided imagery in Chapter 9.

1. **Begin by adopting a comfortable posture for you – perhaps sitting, or lying down on your back. Ensure you are sufficiently warm, loosen any tight clothing and remove your glasses and shoes if you wish.**

   Close your eyes gently if it's okay with you.

2. **Breathe out fully on your next out breath.**

   Place your hand on your belly as you breathe in. Try to make your belly expand. If you can't do this, see the tips in the section 'Beginning with diaphragmatic breathing' earlier in this chapter.

3. **Continue to do belly breathing for about a minute.**

   Allow your breathing to be smooth and natural. If you feel uncomfortable or are straining to breathe, you're probably overdoing it. Let it be a relaxed process. Let each in breath be a nourishing kind of breath and each out breath be accompanied with a sense of letting go.

4. **Bring to mind a place you've been to in the past that is relaxed and peaceful for you.**

   Think of a place where you feel safe and protected. A place of calm and relaxation. If you can't recall a place, make one up or combine images. If you can't decide between several places, just choose any one – try the others another time.

5. Let yourself relax into this peaceful place.

Notice the sights and sounds around you. Don't worry about how vivid or clear the images are. Just accept in whatever way the image is presented to you. What's the aroma in the air? How does your body feel in this peaceful, calm, relaxing place of yours. Become gently aware of as much detail as feels right for you.

6. Become aware of your breathing.

Imagine yourself breathing in a calm and relaxed way in your peaceful place. Notice and focus on any feelings of peace and relaxation. Allow the awareness of your breath to be warm and friendly. Invite a calm and relaxed rate of breathing. Continue to breathe in to your belly.

7. After 20 minutes, or however long you wish to practise for, bring the exercise to a close.

Become aware of the sensations of your body, and open your eyes. Become aware of your surroundings, but as you do so, bring any sense of calmness and relaxation with you to whatever you need to do next.

You can practise this exercise for just a few minutes if you like – such as when you're waiting in a queue. Visualise your peaceful place and allow your breathing to be deep and smooth and as relaxed as you can. Your brain will be tricked into thinking you're actually at that peaceful place, and your relaxation response will be engaged, rather than your stress response. You do need to practise and be patient with yourself, but in time you're bound to get better at it. However, if you try it twice a day for a couple of weeks and notice no benefit or sense of relaxation, try a different exercise and perhaps come back to this one at a later stage.

Smiling as you breathe

If someone tells you to smile when you're feeling down, you may not think very highly of them to say the least. But before you begin planning your revenge, take a moment to consider the benefits of smiling, which include a greater sense of wellbeing and positivity (see Chapter 13).

In this short breathing exercise, you use the fact that smiling, even when you don't feel like it, can have an effect of lifting your mood and making you feel more relaxed. As smiling uses fewer facial muscles than frowning, you'll begin to feel more relaxed straight away. Combined with a few deep, slow breaths, smiling results in a powerful way to relaxation and wellbeing in a relatively easy way.

1. Begin by adopting a comfortable posture for you – perhaps sitting, or lying down on your back. Ensure you are sufficiently warm, loosen any tight clothing and remove your glasses and shoes if you wish.

2. Close your eyes if that's okay with you.

If you feel sleepy or don't want to close your eyes, leave your eyes open and look softly downwards.

3. Take three slow, deep, smooth breaths.

Let your breath expand your belly and chest. Place one hand gently on your belly to help you to notice your breath. Inhale deeply and let your exhalation be longer than your inhale. Make the breath smooth and slow.

4. Smile gently, even if you don't feel particularly smiley.

Your smile can be a gentle subtle smile, or one of those big smiles that you reserve for looking gorgeous in photos. Just hold your smile and relax the muscles in the rest of your body.

5. As you smile, continue to feel your natural, smooth in breath and out breath.

You no longer need to control your breath. Just feel your breathing as it is. Continue for about 10 minutes or so, smiling and breathing.

6. Each time you find your smile has turned into a frown, lift the corners of your mouth and smile.

If your smile hurts, you may be overdoing it! Just keep the smile a subtle, gentle one in that case.

7. If you get lost in thought, bring your attention back to the feeling of the breath.

Re-engage your smile muscles if they have turned into a frown. Praise yourself for noticing that you were lost in thought rather than criticising yourself for not focusing.

Record your findings in your stress diary (see Chapter 3).

Chapter 6

Using Physical Activity to Relax

It is exercise alone that supports the spirits, and keeps the mind in vigour.

Cicero

*P*hysical activity is one of the most effective ways to relieve stress and feel more relaxed in the long term. Hundreds of research papers concluded that regular moderate physical activity improves mental wellbeing – which simply means that you feel less stressed and more relaxed after exercising. Although physical activity may not actually reduce the cause of your stress, exercise may help you find a solution, or at least take your mind off the problem for a while.

In this chapter, I give you many well-proven reasons to get moving. I offer some tips, tricks and techniques to overcome those unhelpful excuses that stop you from exercising. If you spend too much time in front of the TV, this chapter is just what you need.

Visit www.relaxationfordummies.com/exercise for web links and resources to help you get exercising and deal with stress more effectively.

Seeing How Exercise Leads to Relaxation

When you deal with the pressures and demands of everyday living, you begin to build up a certain level of muscle tension around your body. The reason your muscles are tense is because your body thinks it has been in a dangerous or life-threatening situation and needs to either run or fight the danger (see Chapter 2 for more on the fight-or-flight response). For example, if you have to give a speech at work and are scared of public speaking, you may sweat, your hands may tremble, and you may be tense physically – as if you're facing the barrel of a gun or a hungry tiger.

An effective way of relieving that tension at the end of the day is to use your muscles. Your body is designed to move, but nowadays a sedentary life due to technical advancements is the norm. Your body is designed to move about and releases all sorts of beneficial chemicals into your bloodstream when you do so.

Meeting the benefits of exercise

The amazing benefits of exercise are well researched. If a medicine existed with the same benefits as exercise, the drug would probably be one of the greatest discoveries of all time. Exercise is a powerful technique that rapidly reduces your feelings of tension and stress.

Here are some ways that exercise helps you to relax in the long run:

- **Exercise lifts your mood:** Physical activity releases chemicals produced by the brain called endorphins. These neurotransmitters help you to feel good about yourself, making you feel happier.

- **Exercise breaks the stress cycle:** A 30-minute power walk or a ten-minute run boosts your self-confidence and reduces symptoms of mild anxiety and depression. You're also more likely to sleep better – stress usually disturbs your sleep and feeds back to create more stress.

- **Exercise helps you live in the now and let go of worries:** When you exercise, your attention concentrates on the activity instead of your worries or regrets. You focus and live in the moment and so your stress levels are less likely to increase.

- **Exercise detoxes your brain:** Stress creates a lot of toxic waste products in your brain. When you exercise, the increase in blood flow clears out the toxins from your brain and helps you think more clearly and rationally.

- **Exercise improves your resilience to stress:** Research shows that people who exercise regularly have lower levels of the stress hormone cortisol, a lower heart rate and lower levels of anxiety. Exercise acts as a stress buffer, making you more resilient to the stresses of everyday life.

Knowing when NOT to exercise

Before you drop this book and go for a run, hold on a minute! Prior to beginning any exercise programme, I recommend that you see your doctor or health professional for a check-up. Consulting your doctor is particularly important if any of the following applies to you:

✔ You've ever had a heart condition and your doctor has told you to check before starting a new exercise regime

✔ You take medication for high blood pressure or have ever had chest pains

✔ You lose balance due to dizziness or sometimes lose consciousness

✔ You have a problem with your bones or joints that may be affected by a new exercise programme

✔ You have doubts, for whatever reason, that exercise may have an adverse effect on you

Finding the Right Exercise Routine for You

Exercises broadly fall into three categories – aerobic (cardiovascular), stretching (range of motion, flexibility) and strengthening (resistance) exercises. Ideally you need to do all three types of exercise to be physically healthy and therefore live a life with less stress. Here's the low-down on the different types of exercise:

✔ **Aerobic (cardiovascular) exercise:** Aerobic exercise is characterised by the large muscles in your legs and arms moving at a moderate pace. Examples of aerobic activities include walking, jogging, cycling, swimming and dancing. The idea is to get your heart pumping so that it strengthens, and to allow your lungs and muscles to work efficiently. You thereby lower blood pressure and improve your circulation.

✔ **Strengthening (resistance) exercises:** These exercises involve short bursts of effort using your muscles, such as weight-lifting, press-ups, resistance bands, sit-ups and squats. You end up building muscle so that everyday tasks become easier for you to do – you also improve your balance, posture, stability, bone density and joints. In other words, your daily activities don't stress your body as much. Additionally, you burn more calories even when you're resting.

✔ **Stretching (range of motion, flexibility) exercises:** Stretching exercises are especially helpful for relaxation by loosening your tense muscles. They also act as a protection for your joints, improve balance and posture, and reduce the risk of future injury. Yoga and t'ai chi (which I talk about in Chapter 7), as well as Pilates, offer a highly effective range of flexibility exercises. You can do a flexibility exercise by stretching your muscle until you feel some resistance, and then hold that position for up to about 20 seconds, without stretching any further.

Working out how much to exercise

The amount of exercise you begin with depends on your age and current activity levels. However, research recommends that adults try to do 30 minutes of moderate physical activity a day, on five days each week. Your daily physical activity can be broken into three ten-minute chunks spread over the day.

Physical activity is any physical movement that makes you feel warm and slightly out of breath. You don't necessarily have to go to the gym or run until you drop. You can include activities like walking briskly, housework, DIY, walking up stairs, gardening, swimming and cycling.

You may not be able to achieve 30 minutes of daily physical activity straight away. Instead, build up gradually, doing a little more each week as you become fitter.

Integrating physical activities into your life

The secret to staying fit is to use every opportunity you get to move your body. Driving everywhere and always using the lift is easy – but taking small steps to use your body more often is just as easy. In this section, I offer some suggestions for incorporating exercise into different lifestyles.

You're a stay-at-home parent

If you find yourself mainly at home, here are some suggestions for fitting exercise into your routine:

- ✔ Walk the kids to and from school if this is possible.

- ✔ Cycle your child around locally.

- ✔ Participate in exercise with your children.

- ✔ Go for a walk with other parents.

- ✔ Remember that housework is exercise too – cooking, cleaning and doing the washing get your body moving and you feel good about yourself once you've done it.

- ✔ Children need about 60 minutes of exercise every day – get them to help you with housework, let them run around in the park and encourage them to cycle, rollerblade, swim and play team sports.

You work in an office

It's easy to forget about exercise if you're one of the millions of people who works in an office. Try some of the following suggestions to help you ultimately feel more relaxed in your workplace:

✔ Walk or cycle part or all the way to your workplace.

✔ Walk to your colleague's desk instead of phoning or e-mailing.

✔ Make use of your lunchtime to walk or pop to the local gym.

✔ Go up and down flights of stairs rather than using the lift.

✔ Stretch and stroll around every half-an-hour if you sit at a desk most of the day.

You work from home

Lots of people work from home nowadays. Although this cuts down time wasted in your journey, it's easy to get caught up in the work and put off exercise. Try these ideas:

✔ Plan your day or week and put some sort of exercise in five days a week at least.

✔ Arrange meetings in person, and try to cycle or walk to the meetings.

✔ Take time to do some vigorous housework rather than relying on a cleaner.

✔ When you're on the phone, walk around at the same time.

✔ Participate in a team sport such as football, rugby, basketball, tennis or badminton in your spare time.

You're retired

If you associate retirement with simply putting your feet up, you'll lose your fitness level quickly. Here are some suggestions for ways to keep active:

✔ Go for a five-minute walk if you're not used to exercise, and gradually build up to walking 30 minutes. Remember you can do three lots of ten minutes a day and still benefit – you don't have to do 30 minutes exercise all in one go.

✔ Do some gardening regularly. All the moving, lifting, pulling and pushing make a great workout, and it's relaxing and refreshing to be out in nature – a great way to relax.

✔ Join a community-based activity group – conservation work for example. This kind of activity combines exercise with socialising, which are both powerful ways to reduce stress and relax.

Staying motivated

Motivation is the key to success with exercise. It's easy to exercise when you feel like it, but what about the times when you really can't be bothered?

Here are some tips to keep you going:

- ✔ **Choose an exercise you enjoy.** If you love the activity, you have no excuse to stop.

- ✔ **Do ten-minute bursts of exercise three times a day.** You don't have to push yourself to the point of pain – that can be demotivating and lead to injury.

- ✔ **Sign up for a charity walk or run.** You'll have a target to aim for and love the atmosphere once you're there. Also, you're helping a charity, which is great for your self-esteem too.

- ✔ **Do five minutes of exercise and see how you feel.** I find this very helpful. Rather than doing nothing, by making a start, you may feel up to doing more exercise.

- ✔ **Reward yourself for doing a certain amount of exercise.** You could go and watch a movie, buy that little gadget you've had your eye on or prepare yourself a really delicious fruit salad. If all your rewards are junk food, you'll undo all your hard work.

- ✔ **Visualise yourself doing the exercise and feeling good about it.** Images are a powerful motivator, and positive images result in a feeling of wellbeing.

- ✔ **Listen to music.** Playing upbeat music can be a positive motivator for some people.

- ✔ **Wear your workout clothes.** Once you've done that, you'll probably think, 'Ahhh, I might as well go!'

- ✔ **Exercise with a friend.** You're more likely to turn up as you don't want to let your friend down, and the opportunity to talk and compete with each other in a friendly way acts as a motivator.

Ultimately, you need to make a decision to be more active and stick with it. Start with something small and manageable and build it up as you go along.

Challenging your excuses for not exercising

Consider all the excuses you make for not doing exercise. Do any of the following reasons resonate with you?

- Exercise is boring

- I'm too unfit to exercise

- I'm too shy

- I can't afford to pay the gym membership

- I'll start in the future

Now for each of these excuses, try challenging them. For example

- Exercise is only boring if I choose boring exercises. I could exercise with my friend and then it'd be fun and I'll feel more relaxed afterwards.

- If I'm too unfit, that means I do need to exercise. I'll visit my doctor and plan a programme around her recommendations.

- Exercise doesn't have to be done in front of others. I can exercise on my own to begin with, and maybe change that after some experience.

- I don't have to go to the gym. I can go running, cycling or even do some skipping at home. There are many low-cost ways to keep fit.

- Tomorrow never comes! I need to make a decision on this rather than keep putting it off.

Discovering Some Popular Exercises

Many people struggle to find the best exercise for them. In this section, I describe a handful of popular exercises and discuss their benefits and drawbacks to help you pick and choose the best workout for you.

Walking works wonders

Walking is an underrated exercise and is relatively easy to do. You need almost no equipment, you can do it with other people, and still socialise at the same time (which is also great for relaxation), and you gradually walk faster as you get fitter.

Walking regularly has been shown scientifically to have a range of health benefits too – reducing the risk of heart disease, stroke, asthma, diabetes and even some cancers.

You need a few things for your walk:

- ✔ A pair of shoes that you find comfortable and supportive.

- ✔ Loose-fitting clothing that isn't too heavy (you don't want to be weighed down).

  However, make sure you're warm or cool enough, depending on the weather.

- ✔ For longer walks, proper walking boots and a jacket suitable for all weathers.

- ✔ Water, snacks, and, if it's sunny, sunblock and a hat.

Aim to walk for 30 minutes a day, 5 days a week. You don't have to do those 30 minutes in one go – you can break it up into three lots of ten minutes a day. If you find walking difficult, you can start with literally just a few minutes walk a day and as you get used to it, gradually increase the time you walk. The fitter you get, the faster you can walk. Brisk walking is healthy, energising, and ultimately relaxing.

Here are some ways to stay motivated:

- ✔ **Join a walking club.** You're likely to make active friends, discover new places to walk and have a regular time to do your exercise.

- ✔ **Go for a walk at the same time every day so it becomes a habit.** After you have a daily walking habit, you'll love it and won't want to stop.

- ✔ **Use a pedometer to measure the number of steps you take every day.** Record your steps in a journal or on a chart and place it on the wall to encourage you to keep going. Aim to walk 10,000 steps a day. Most people walk about 3,000 steps a day anyway, so it's not as daunting as you first think.

- ✔ **Walk with a friend or relative.** You can encourage each other to walk regularly.

- ✔ **Walk along different routes.** Changing your route helps keep your attention engaged on the surroundings rather than getting bored of the same route.

Running for exercise

Running is a low-cost activity that can make you very fit and reduce your stress quickly. You'll feel more relaxed and rejuvenated and have more energy after a run. Running reduces the risk of chronic diseases, such as heart disease, diabetes and stroke. Running also helps you manage your weight and boosts your mood.

Treat yourself to a good pair of running shoes from a specialist shop if you can. The shop can help you decide what shoes suit you best. Good shoes help to support and protect you from injury. Money invested in quality shoes now will pay back in the future – it's worth the investment in my opinion.

If you're a beginner, it's important to start gently. Begin by walking briskly and interspersing the walking with running. As your fitness inevitably improves, you'll be able to run for longer.

Begin with some warm-ups such as going up and down stairs, jumping up and down, raising and lowering your knees, and side stepping.

Here's a simple programme to get you moving. Use this plan to go from just simple walking to running 5,000 metres. The idea is to continue doing each stage of the programme until you're comfortable enough to move on to the next stage. Just check with your doctor if you're in any doubt about your health.

> **Stage 1:** Walk for any distance that feels comfortable for you – 10, 20 or 30 minutes perhaps.

> **Stage 2:** Build up until you can walk for 30 minutes fairly easily.

> **Stage 3:** Now intersperse your walking with running for a period of one or two minutes at a pace that feels comfortable for you. When running, you don't need to over-tense your muscles. Keep your shoulders and arms relaxed and your elbows bent. Run upright rather than in a slouch-ing posture, and run as smoothly as you can. Let your heel make contact with the ground first as you run.

> **Stage 4:** Gradually increase the amount of time you're running, until you're running for the full 30 minutes! Remember to do at least five min-utes of brisk walking as a warm-up before each run.

> **Stage 5:** Aim to run about twice a week on a regular basis.

> **Stage 6:** Congratulations – you're now a runner! Consider reading books or magazines to develop your running ability further.

Remember to spend at least 5 minutes cooling down at the end of your run. You can finish with walking and gentle stretching of your muscles.

Here are some ways to maintain your motivation:

> ✔ **Join a running club.** Contact your local running clubs and ask whether they are appropriate for your current level of fitness. Most running clubs cater for beginners. A club offers the support of fellow runners and helps you discover new routes in your area. You may be in a fun run before you know it, if you like that sort of thing! The social aspect of a club also takes your mind off your worries and helps you feel more relaxed.

✔ **Run with a friend.** Running with somebody else is a great way to catch up and get fit at the same time. You can encourage each other on the days you don't feel like going, which makes all the difference.

✔ **Have a target.** If you have a target or goal in mind that you want to achieve, you're much more likely to keep going when you don't feel like it or are demotivated. You could aim to participate in a race or build up to running 5km or 10km by a certain date. Just remember to make your goals realistic and set a date to achieve it.

✔ **Use a journal.** You could record your running in your journal, a diary or on a chart. Write down how long you ran for, where you ran, and how you felt. When you're feeling down, a quick glance will show you just how much you've improved in just a few weeks.

Going swimming

Swimming is a great exercise at any age. If you can't swim, it's never too late to learn. Swimming helps reduce the chance of several chronic illnesses, lifts your mood and exercises all the muscles in your body. All you need is access to a swimming pool, swimming togs and perhaps some goggles if your eyes are sensitive to the chlorine.

Here are some ways to stay motivated:

✔ **Join a swimming class.** Find one that meets your needs whether beginner, average or advanced.

✔ **Go at the same time every week.** When exercise becomes a habit, you're more likely to stick at it.

✔ **Swim with a friend or take the kids.** When you plan to be with others, you're much more likely to go. And exercising with your children sets a great example for them, showing the importance of exercise for adults as well as kids.

Enjoying cycling

Cycling is relatively cheap, can be a great way to travel and is a fun way to keep fit and burn off your stress. If you're just starting out to cycle, you don't need to spend huge amounts of money on a bike. You can pick up a good second-hand cycle fairly cheaply. Ensure the seat is adjustable and suits your body.

Some cities now have cycles that can be picked up from one location and dropped off at another place. Here in London, UK, the scheme has been a huge success.

Running as Superman

My main physical activity for the past couple of years has been brisk walking, but after researching for this chapter I decided to give running a go. I was on holiday in Devon and decided to add a few minutes of running into my daily walk. In the days and weeks that followed, I gradually increased the time I ran and reduced the time I walked. I'm now at a stage where I can run for almost 30 minutes. I just need to be careful I don't try to push myself too quickly, as I have a tendency to do that. The other day I signed up for a 5km superhero charity run with a friend, in which I plan to dress up as Superman, together with thousands of other participants. This all started from running for 1 minute as part of my usual walk.

If you live reasonably close to your work use cycling as a regular way to commute; it's good for your health and great for the environment. If you live too far from work, perhaps you can cycle for part of the journey and take a train or bus for the rest of the distance.

Starting dancing

Dancing can be done for a low cost (or free if you know how), is a great full-body workout, gives you the chance to meet new people and, best of all, is great fun. Joining a dance class helps to reduce stress and makes you feel more relaxed for the following reasons:

✔ When fully engaged in the dancing, your mind is off your worries.

✔ Meeting other people is healthy for you and helps to put your concerns into perspective.

✔ The full body exercise helps to ease tension in your body.

Learning various dance moves actually trains your brain to be sharper and may reduce the onset of brain disorders later in life. A whole range of different dance styles exists to suit all temperaments. Here are a few examples:

✔ **Ballroom:** There are many types of ballroom dancing to suit different tastes. Usually they involve learning specific steps so it's a great workout for your brain and your body too.

✔ **Bollywood:** My favourite – I grew up listening to Bollywood music from the Indian film industry. Bollywood dancing is a mix of some traditional Indian dances moves with modern energy, often depicting emotions and passion.

✔ **Contemporary:** Fluid and natural and not limited to a particular style. The movement and form tends to be quite personal.

✔ **Salsa:** This fusion of Afro-Caribbean and Latin styles is a passionate and fun form of partner dancing that's easy to learn.

✔ **Tap:** Using special shoes with metal plates on the sole to create wonderful sounds as you dance. Still popular today and can be contemporary.

✔ **Zumba:** An aerobic fitness programme based on a Latin style that's fun and popular, using bubbly music to keep you moving.

Trying Mindful Exercise

One of my specialities is teaching mindfulness. You can find out more about mindfulness in Chapter 10. Mindful exercise is about staying in the present moment as you exercise. This approach has the added benefit of not only training your body as you exercise but also training your mind to become more focused and away from your worries. For more information check out *Mindfulness For Dummies* (Wiley).

Discovering a powerful mind-body relaxation

Mindfulness is about paying attention to whatever you're doing with an attitude of curiosity, kindness and acceptance. Here are some reasons why doing exercises mindfully works:

✔ **You become sensitive to your body's needs.** By paying more attention to your body whilst you exercise, you can notice if you're being overly aggressive with your body and possibly causing damage to joints. You'll notice if you need to drink more water, take a break or go easy on that injured knee.

✔ **You are more aware of the intensity of your exercise.** Therefore you can increase or decrease the intensity according to what you feel you need to do.

✔ **You can let go of negativity.** You notice if your mind is beginning to drift into negative, habitual thought patterns and can bring your attention back to the present moment.

✔ **Your mind becomes calmer and more focused.** If you're mindful as you exercise, you're more likely to finish the exercise feeling calmer and more focused. Being mindful encourages you to make better decisions such as doing some sensible stretching exercises to finish, and eat a healthy meal.

Looking at ways to practise mindful exercises

No matter what exercise you choose to do, you can exercise more mindfully and thereby make the activity more enjoyable. You just need to either focus on the sensations in your body, on your surroundings, your thoughts or your emotions. And whenever you find your mind drifting off, just congratulate yourself for noticing rather than criticising, and bring your attention back to the present moment. The concept isn't difficult but it just takes a bit of effort, especially at the beginning. Soon, with a bit of luck, you'll love being mindful and then you won't need any effort at all to practise mindful exercises.

Here are some suggestions for ways to be mindful as you exercise:

- **Cycling:** Be aware of your physical body as you cycle – the way in which the sensations in your legs change as you cycle. Notice the sights, sounds and smells around you as you cycle. How does your breathing rate change? How do you feel physically towards the end of your journey compared to the beginning? Are any other muscles in your body needlessly tensing?

- **Swimming:** Notice the temperature of the water as you swim. Feel the sensations in your arms and legs as you move through the water. Become aware of how the rate of your breathing changes. Listen to the sounds around you, including the water. Be mindful of being too competitive and comparing how you're doing with others – just focus on each moment in your experience.

- **Tennis:** Feel the weight of the ball in your hand as you hold it. Notice if any part of your body tenses up unnecessarily as you play, such as your shoulders, forehead or jaw. Become aware of the negative thoughts that pop into your head when you lose a point, and decide if you're being overly self-critical.

- **Walking:** Make a clear decision that you're going to pay attention to your walking instead of just focusing on where you want to get to. Begin by feeling the physical sensation of your feet on the floor. Notice how the sensation changes as your weight shifts from one foot to the other. Expand your attention to the physical sensation in your legs. Extend further the feelings that you're experiencing as you walk to the rest of your body. Make sure that you walk upright rather than looking down or slouching. Relax any tense muscles within your body and just accept any underlying tension just as it is. Each time you notice that your mind has wandered off into other thoughts, be grateful that you've become aware of this, and shift your attention back to your physical sensations.

As an alternative, you can practise mindful walking by noticing your surroundings as you walk, such as the cool air, the clouds in the sky, or the sounds of the cars and the birds.

Mall walking and green gyms

Mall walking, which involves brisk walking through indoor shopping centres, is popular in the US and is catching on elsewhere. The benefits of a warm, dry environment, and an opportunity to socialise with other participants, are the main attractions. Plus it's free! By combining the walking with going up and down the stairs, you end up doing a decent, stress-busting workout.

Another great idea is green gyms. This free voluntary activity is a chance to do some exercise and help look after your local environment. Run by experienced leaders, you are encouraged to dig, weed, plant trees or clear paths, working at a pace that's right for you. You end up exercising aerobically, as well as improving your strength and stamina. Additionally you'll feel more confident and make new friends. A great way to relieve stress and relax outside – beats running on a treadmill.

The best way to find your nearest mall walking group or green gym is to type it into an internet search engine such as Google or Yahoo, followed by the name of your area.

Chapter 7

Yoga, T'ai Chi and Qigong

. . . .

In This Chapter

▶ Seeing how mind/body exercises offer special ways to relax

▶ Practising yogic breathing techniques to wind down

▶ Discovering basic yoga and t'ai chi routines for beginners

. . . .

*Y*oga, t'ai chi and qigong have been practised by millions of people over thousands of years. They were developed not just for reducing stress, but to improve overall wellbeing. Their popularity in the West continues to grow at a rapid rate, as stress levels climb and as science finds more benefits of these Eastern disciplines.

Some relaxation techniques, such as massage, focus on relaxing the body. Other techniques, such as meditation, emphasise ways to calm the mind. The great thing about yoga, t'ai chi and qigong is that they relax both mind and body at the same time. If you get frustrated by relaxation techniques that involve sitting or lying still, or just keep falling asleep when doing them, you may benefit from practising regular yoga, t'ai chi or qigong. They have the added advantage of training your mind to be more focused and make you feel grounded in the present moment.

In this chapter I help you understand these age-old techniques and show you a series of exercises to calm your mind and relax your body at the same time. Most of the postures, movements and breathing exercises are suitable for beginners and will give you a taste of the kind of practices you would learn in a class.

Check with your doctor if you suspect for any reason that these exercises may have an unhelpful effect on your health, and to make sure that they are safe if you are pregnant.

Practising Yoga for Relaxation

People have practised yoga for over 5,000 years. Yoga is best known for its physical postures, but it's also a powerful approach to relaxing and energising yourself. A recent study estimates that 16 million Americans practise yoga. There are many schools of yoga combining postures, breathing, meditation and philosophy in different ways. Hatha yoga is the most popular approach in the West, where people usually use yoga either for relaxation or to improve their fitness and flexibility.

Understanding how yoga relaxes you

The word 'yoga' means 'union'. Originally that meant union with God or ultimate reality, but nowadays yoga is seen as a way to unify your body, mind and spirit.

The physical poses of yoga are called *asanas*. True yoga is much more than just physical postures. Yoga includes ethical ways of living, breathing exercises and meditation – how you see yoga is up to you. By practising all the various aspects of yoga, practitioners claim to experience a deeper sense of peace and tranquillity. To enjoy the full benefits of yoga, begin with the physical poses and then have a go at some of the breathing and meditation exercises to explore how yoga helps relax and energise you at deeper levels.

Yoga includes the following techniques, which are effective in themselves to create a sense of relaxation:

- ✔ **Physical stretching:** Relaxation is associated with muscles that are not tense. By gently stretching physically, you are directly relaxing the muscles, which can lead to a more relaxed mind.

- ✔ **Breathing exercises:** Breathing is closely connected to the stress and relaxation system in your body. By learning breathing exercises, you can create an easy and direct way to feel more relaxed in seconds.

- ✔ **Meditation:** Meditation is not directly designed for relaxation, but for focus and spiritual development. However, one of its wonderful side effects is often a deep relaxation as well as greater resilience to future stress.

- ✔ **Physical exercise:** The act of moving raises your heart rate and helps to dissipate any stress within your body. Stress is essentially the activation of your fight-or-flight response – by moving your body, you're doing what your body is asking you to do when stressed, which is to move.

- ✔ **Mindfulness:** A good yoga practice is to be aware of the movements you are making. By being mindful – being aware of your breathing, physical sensations, thoughts, and emotions – you develop your capacity to be aware with a sense of kindness towards yourself, which helps to engage your relaxation response. This is the secret of effective and life-changing yoga practice.

Each of these techniques helps create a greater sense of relaxation for most people. Done together, the techniques are a potent way to relax. Now you can see why yoga is such a powerful approach for a range of reasons, one of which is relaxation.

Preparing for yoga

Yoga is considered safe for most people, including people using a wheelchair and people who are severely overweight. Pregnant women can attend special pregnancy yoga classes.

However, you can do more harm than good if you practise yoga incorrectly and I offer the following tips:

✔ Talk to your doctor before trying yoga if you have an injury or medical condition.

✔ Practise yoga with a qualified instructor who has plenty of experience.

✔ Always warm up before yoga.

✔ Wear clothing that allows you to move freely.

✔ Learn proper techniques and the basics of yoga. If you're not sure how to do something, ask questions.

✔ Don't push yourself too hard, and stop if you have pain.

✔ Drink enough water during your yoga class.

Exploring yoga breathing exercises

Yoga breathing exercises, called *pranayama*, are a great way to feel more relaxed and energised. If you have a physical condition that prevents movement, or just don't like the physical postures of yoga, pranayama may be for you. Otherwise, you can combine yoga postures and breathing exercises.

If you're pregnant or are suffering from a health condition, check with your doctor before doing breathing exercises.

The primary way of relaxing through breathing is belly breathing (which I describe in detail in Chapter 5). Here are a few other ways of breathing to try out.

Try to practise yoga breathing exercises by giving your full attention to the feeling of your breath entering and leaving your body. When you find your attention wandering to other worries, concerns, plans or anything else, turn your attention gently back to your breathing. Training your mind to keep in the present moment enhances the relaxation effect.

Bee breath (bhramari pranayama)

The bee breath is a simple way to increase your awareness of your exhalation. The longer you exhale comfortably, the more you feel relaxed. You'll find the sound helps to lengthen your out breath and allows your attention to rest in the present moment rather than on your worries or that to-do list that keeps popping up in your mind. Just *bee* yourself (sorry!).

1. **Choose any posture you like.**

   Hold a yoga posture if you feel like it.

2. **Each time you breathe out, hum gently with your mouth closed.**

   Breathe out for as long as feels comfortable.

3. **Listen to the sound and feel the vibration through your body.**

   Allow the hum to have a softness about it rather than aggressively pushing the sound out. Notice whether the vibration allows you to become aware of different parts of your body.

4. **Continue for 10 minutes.**

   Or carry on for longer if you have time.

Exhalations that are longer than your inhalations switch all systems in your body to relaxation. Bee breath is one tool to aid you to achieve longer out breaths.

Victorious breath (ujjayi pranayama)

This exercise, also called hissing or ocean breath, is designed to be both relaxing and energising. The breaths are long and smooth and make a sound a bit like the waves rolling in and out of the ocean. You may sound a bit like Darth Vader, but in a nice way.

1. **Lie down on a mat or other comfortable surface.**

   Take a few deep breaths through your mouth.

2. **On your next exhalation, imagine you're trying to say 'ha' without the 'a'.**

   Alternatively, imagine you're trying to fog up a pair of spectacles before you clean them. So, you are slightly constricting your throat, which creates a sound as you breathe out.

3. **Continue to exhale in this way until it feels a little easier to do.**

   Listen and allow the sound you create to be as smooth as you can.

4. **Now inhale in the same way you've been exhaling.**

   Make the same type of noise as you inhale.

5. **After you feel that you're beginning to get the hang of this type of breathing, close your mouth but continue to breathe in the same way.**

   With further experience you can do this whilst sitting up and during your yoga practise.

Alternate nostril breathing (nadi shodhana)

In yoga's original language, Sanskrit, *nadi shodhana* means energy channel clearing. According to yoga philosophy this breathing technique has the following benefits:

- ✔ It reduces the sense of stress.
- ✔ It purifies the energy channels in your body so that the energy within you flows more easily.
- ✔ It harmonises the two hemispheres of your brain.

1. **Find a comfortable sitting posture.**

   In traditional yoga this is done in a cross-legged posture, but you can use any posture you find comfortable.

2. **Create a fist with your right hand.**

   Let your thumb, ring finger and little finger stick out.

3. **Gently close your right nostril with your right thumb.**

   Inhale through your left nostril, and then close your left nostril with your ring finger, remove your thumb from your right nostril and exhale slowly through your right nostril (see Figure 7-1).

4. **Continue to breathe in through your right nostril.**

   Now close your right nostril with your thumb and breathe out through your left nostril again. This completes one cycle of this breathing exercise.

5. **Repeat Steps 2 and 3 up to ten times.**

Then let your arm come down and go back to your normal breathing pattern

Figure 7-1:
Alternate
nostril
breathing.

Trying some relaxing yoga poses

If you're a beginner to yoga, you might like to try this sequence of yoga poses. You only need about 10–20 minutes to practise these poses.

Corpse pose

This is the ultimate relaxation posture (shown in Figure 7-2). Your body is fully supported and your pose relieves stress, anxiety, lowers blood pressure and helps with reducing fatigue and insomnia.

1. **Find a place where you are sufficiently warm and undisturbed.**

2. **Place a blanket over your body.**

   Your temperature may drop if you're in the posture for some time.

3. **Place a rolled-up towel under your knees for extra comfort, especially if you have pain in your lower back.**

   Let your arm be on your side, slightly away from your body and allow the palms to face upwards.

4. **Place your feet on the floor in front of your body with knees bent.**

   Raise your pelvis off your mat and with your hands gently push your pelvis towards your tailbone to ensure that your body is in a neutral posture.

5. **Lower your pelvis and lie down as I show in Figure 7-2, gently pushing through your heels.**

   Ensure both feet are evenly placed.

6. **Reduce any excess tension by shaking your shoulders and then slowly roll your head from side to side a couple of times.**

   Let go of any frowning in your face.

7. **Let the ground support your body.**

   Each time you breathe out you relax more. Imagine sinking a little deeper into the floor.

If your back hurts in this posture, bend your knees and place your feet on the floor, about hip distance apart. Then either let your knees fall apart and rest on pillows, or let your knees lean on each other, with thighs touching.

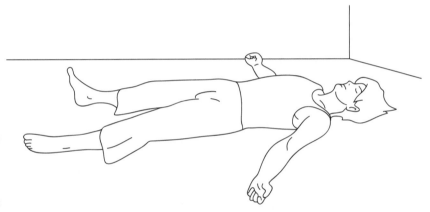

Figure 7-2:
Corpse
pose.

Sitting mountain pose

This posture (shown in Figure 7-3) helps you to embody the qualities of a mountain – giving you a sense of inner strength, stability, poise and a sense of uplift. You can use this posture together with other relaxation techniques such as meditation or breathing exercises if you like it.

1. **Kneel on the floor with your knees pointing forward and sitting on your feet.**

   If you can't kneel on the floor, simply sit on a chair. Use cushions wherever you feel you need to place them for extra comfort – under your knees or feet, and maybe on your calves too. Sit upright, balanced, yet not straining. Let your shoulders and face be relaxed, and your chest open. Sit with the qualities of a mountain – stable, balanced, and dignified.

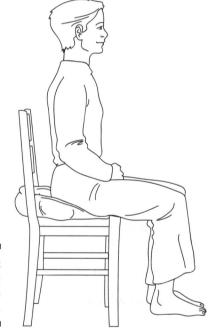

Figure 7-3:
Sitting
mountain
poses.

2. **Allow your breathing to be calm and smooth.**

3. **Feel the sensations in your body and the feeling of your own breathing.**

   With each out breath, have a sense of letting go and just 'being'. Don't try to relax, just notice the sensations and see if relaxation comes to you. In time, it will – you just need patience.

Pelvic tilts

This exercise (shown in Figure 7-4) helps to relax the muscles in your lower back, releasing the tension and any subtle pain in that area.

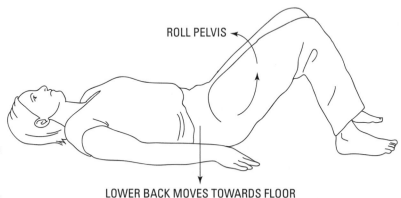

ROLL PELVIS

LOWER BACK MOVES TOWARDS FLOOR

Figure 7-4:
Pelvic tilts.

1. **Lie down on a yoga mat.**

   Become aware of your own breathing.

2. **When you feel ready, bring your feet up, as in Figure 7-4.**

   As you lie there naturally, you'll notice a slight curve in your lower back – this part of your body is not touching the floor.

3. **As you exhale, roll your hips towards your head.**

   Feel your lower back touching the floor.

4. **After a few seconds, inhale and go back to the neutral, relaxed position with the natural arch of your back.**

5. **Repeat the sequence 5–10 times.**

Cat and cow stretches

This stretch (shown in Figure 7-5) helps to release any tension in your shoulders and upper back.

1. **Kneel on all fours, with your knees underneath your hips and your hands underneath your shoulders.**

   Spread out your fingers. Try to make your head, neck and back flat like a table-top. See Figure 7-5 Step 1.

2. **As you inhale lift your head up to look straight ahead, together with your chest and sitting bones.**

   Let your belly sink towards the floor. See Figure 7-5 Step 2.

3. **As you exhale, curl your back upwards and let your head relax and go downwards.**

    See this posture in Figure 7-5 Step 3.

4. **Continue to flow in this sequence together with your breathing, 10–20 times.**

Step 1 - Neutral

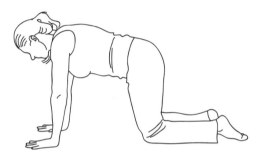

Step 2

Step 3

Figure 7-5:
Cat and cow
stretches.

Child's pose

This pose is particularly good for relaxation. It calms your mind, relieving any stress or fatigue. Additionally, your hips, thighs and ankles

1. **Begin in the sitting mountain pose, which I describe above.**

   As you exhale slowly lower your head to the floor and place your arms by your sides with your palms facing upwards. Let go of any effort to hold your head, neck or shoulders. (See Figure 7-6.)

Figure 7-6:
Child's pose.

2. **Each time you exhale, relax deeper into the pose.**

   If you feel you'd be more comfortable with pillows under your knees, feet or anywhere else, feel free to use them.

3. **This posture helps you to breathe into the back of your torso.**

   Notice each in breath going into your back and curving it towards the ceiling, allowing your spine to lengthen and widen.

4. **Stay in this posture for 5 minutes or any length of time you feel comfortable with.**

If you find your heels beginning to hurt in this pose, place a thin pillow or folded blanket between your calves and thighs.

Hugging-knees-to-chest pose

This is a great way to stretch your lower back and is particularly relaxing after doing exercise. (See Figure 7-7.)

1. **Lie on your back.**

2. **Bring your knees to your chest and hug them with your hands.**

   By keeping your chin slightly tucked in, you allow your neck to be aligned with the floor as shown in Figure 7-7.

3. **Hold the posture for a few minutes.**

4. **Continue to breathe smoothly and with awareness.**

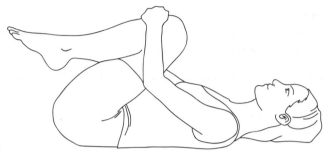

Figure 7-7:
Hugging-
knees-to-
chest pose.

Legs-up-the-wall pose

This is a great pose for rejuvenating tired legs and feet. It can also help to relieve a mild backache as well as feel relaxing for your whole body. (See Figure 7-8.)

Figure 7-8:
Legs-up-
the-wall
pose.

1. **Sit next to a wall.**

2. **Let your side slightly touch the wall and bring your knees towards your chest.**

3. **Using your hands to support you, lower your back to the floor, turn your hips towards the wall, and raise your legs up the wall.**

   If you can, straighten your legs, but if not, allow your legs to bend and move slightly away from the wall.

4. **Place your arms by your sides or rest them on your belly.**

   Feel your breathing in this posture for anything between a few minutes and 15 minutes – whatever feels right for you.

5. **When you're ready to come out of the pose, bend your knees towards your chest and swivel around.**

6. **Lie on your side for a few breaths before sitting up.**

Avoid inverted postures such as legs-up-the-wall if you're menstruating, if you have a serious eye problem such as glaucoma, or if you have back or neck problems.

Attending a yoga class

If you're new to yoga, it can be hard to decide which type of class to go to. For relaxation, I suggest you look out for a hatha yoga class, especially a class described as 'gentle' or 'restorative'. Although the term 'hatha yoga' includes many different forms of yoga, hatha yoga classes tend to be gentler and focus on relaxing awareness of breath together with the postures.

Some of the major styles of hatha yoga are Ananda, Anusara, Ashtanga, Bikram, Iyengar, Kripalu, Kundalini and Viniyoga. Different teachers use and combine these styles in different ways, so experiment and see which approach works for you.

Visit the British Wheel of Yoga's website on www.bwy.org.uk or Yoga Alliance's site on www.yogaalliance.co.uk for information on a yoga teacher in your area.

Some yoga tips:

✔ Aim to practise yoga at least twice a week, and daily if possible.

✔ Wear clothing that you feel comfortable in. Very loose clothing may get in the way, however.

✔ Let go of ideas about competition. Be aware of your bodily sensations as you stretch and show yourself kindness and acceptance rather than self-criticism and frustration.

✔ Be patient and remember that some days you'll be able to do more than others.

✔ Eat after your yoga class rather than just before. Allow at least 2 hours after eating before doing a class.

✔ Tell your teacher if you have any injuries so that they can tell you the best ways to look after yourself as you do the various poses. A good teacher makes sure that you don't harm yourself.

Practising yoga at home

If you haven't done any yoga before, I recommend that you begin with a yoga class with a qualified teacher so that he or she can correct any postures you're doing incorrectly. After you have some experience, you can start practising yoga at home.

Consider the following options to help you with your home yoga practice:

- ✔ Use a book to teach yourself and practise daily, such as *Yoga For Dummies* (Wiley).

- ✔ Use a yoga DVD to learn and practise yoga. You can choose from hundreds of different teachers, styles and levels to suit you. One suggestion is *Yoga For Stress Relief* by Barbara Benagh.

- ✔ Use a website to learn and practise different yoga postures. Try www.yogajournal.com or www.yoga.about.com.

- ✔ Look out for a class run by your local authority. There are many around and you can usually find a list of classes at your local library.

- ✔ Book a private one-to-one class with a yoga teacher – many are willing to travel to private addresses. This method is probably the most effective but most expensive option. You could lower the cost by getting a group of friends together for each class with the yoga teacher.

Trying T'ai Chi and Qigong to Relax

T'ai chi and qigong originate from China and involve co-ordinating gentle physical movements and deep breathing with awareness. Regular practice has a range of physical health benefits as well as relaxation.

The flowing movements with your breathing cause you to focus in the present moment and let go of concerns about the past and worries about the future. They help to bring your mind and body into a harmonious whole – one of the hallmarks of effective relaxation techniques.

T'ai chi and qigong are considered to be 'meditation in motion'. If you have difficulty sitting still for more traditional meditation, t'ai chi or qigong are an ideal alternative. You get most of the same health benefits as meditation as your mind is being trained in the same way (focused on the present moment with acceptance). For more on mindfulness, see Chapter 6 and 10.

The legend of Master Chang

Master Chang was a semi-mythical Taoist priest, who is credited with originating t'ai chi. He thought most martial arts were too energetic and dependent on physical strength. As the legend goes, one day he was carrying out his devotions in his hut when he heard a commotion. He stepped outside to see that a bird and snake were fighting. Each time the bird tried to attack the snake, the reptile simply curled itself differently and fought back. However, the bird also used its wings to circle and strike back at the snake. The Master reflected on his observation and that night had an inspiring dream where he was visited by an Emperor. The Emperor taught him the secret of the Tao, which the snake and bird had demonstrated. The next morning the Master jumped to his feet and began developing a martial art that depended on internal power, or chi. The basis of this art was that 'yielding overcomes aggression' and 'softness overpowers hardness'.

You can practise t'ai chi or qigong on your own or in groups. In countries with Chinese communities and other enthusiasts, you may see groups of people practising the beautiful, slow, flowing movements early in the morning, in front of the rising sun. Their bodies are continuously moving with gracefulness, and each movement is carefully co-ordinated and named to evoke aspects of nature.

What's the difference between t'ai chi and qigong? Well, t'ai chi is actually the part of qigong that encourages relaxation.

The word 'qigong' is made up of two Chinese characters, *qi* and *gong*. *Qi* is translated as life force or vital energy that flows throughout the universe, including your body. *Gong* means a skill or accomplishment through steady practice over time.

So, qigong means 'cultivating energy skilfully' and is a major part of Chinese healing medicine. T'ai chi is a soft internal style of qigong, whereas something like kung fu is a vigorous style. Actually t'ai chi was originally a martial art but has been adapted over time as a way of managing health.

T'ai chi and qigong have been found to have similar benefits so you can try whichever class you like.

Understanding the key principles of t'ai chi and qigong

At the core of t'ai chi and qigong is the philosophy of yin and yang and qi. The idea is that everything in the universe has the qualities of yin or yang. *Yin* has the qualities of water – softness, cool, light, going inwards and downwards. It is considered the feminine principle. *Yang* has the qualities of fire – heat, light, going upwards, and outwards. It's the masculine energy and has the qualities of hardness.

According to practitioners, you can balance the opposite qualities of yin and yang to enhance the flow of qi within you. Through this balance you feel both energised and relaxed. This balancing is achieved through the three key aspects:

- ✔ **Movement:** In t'ai chi the body is moved from one movement smoothly into another, all the time allowing the weight to sink into the ground and being aware of stability, poise and balance. Body weight is shifted from one foot to the other. Simple t'ai chi uses 13 movements but there can be many more.

- ✔ **Breath:** T'ai chi uses deep breathing. The idea is you exhale out stale air and any toxins and inhale fresh, nourishing air, releasing any stress and promoting relaxation.

- ✔ **Mindfulness:** Being aware of the movements of your body and keeping your mind in the present moment as much as you can.

These three aspects explain why qigong and t'ai chi are sometimes called a movement meditation.

T'ai chi and qigong are suitable for people of any age. In fact, as a low-impact exercise, it's particularly good if you're unable to challenge your body too much. Some forms involve high-speed movements, but most are calming and slow, encouraging relaxation.

Discovering the benefits of t'ai chi and qigong

Deep breathing and mindful movement have been shown to create a sense of relaxation. T'ai chi combines these together to create a powerful relaxation approach.

T'ai chi has been researched for its health benefits, both in the East and in the West. Here are some of the preliminary Western findings suggesting that T'ai chi:

- ✔ Boosts a sense of wellbeing.
- ✔ Reduces anxiety and depression.
- ✔ Increases energy.
- ✔ Eases chronic pain.

✔ Enhances cardiovascular fitness, particularly in older adults.

✔ Decreases the number of falls in older adults.

✔ Lowers blood pressure.

✔ Improves the quality of your sleep.

✔ Develops your balance and muscle strength.

Beginning learning t'ai chi and qigong

As a beginner, I recommend you find a t'ai chi teacher. If you have any injuries, an instructor may be able to adapt the movements to suit your needs. Books and DVDs can guide you in t'ai chi but can't tell you if you're practising incorrectly of course. Try finding a teacher by asking your local community centre, adult education college, or health club. Alternatively, look on the website of the Tai Chi Union for Great Britain on www.taichiunion.com.

T'ai chi instructors don't have to be licensed or accredited so check their training and experience, and use personal recommendations when you can.

T'ai chi is a safe practice. However, as with all exercise, avoid practising just after a big meal or if you have an active infection. Speak with your health provider for advice if you are pregnant, have a hernia, joint or back problems, fractures or osteoporosis – they may be able to tell you how to adapt the routines.

Trying some simple routines

Remember to do all these practices slowly and gently, with awareness. Breathe deeply throughout the practice. As you become more aware of your breathing, it will naturally begin to synchronise with your movement – you don't need to force it. Set aside any worries or concern and focus your attention on your bodily movements. If you experience pain at any time, stop the practice.

Swinging your arms

This is a nice, simple way to warm up and gently stretch your back.

1. **Stand in a neutral posture.**

2. **Rotate to the left and then the right.**

   Keep your body straight and let your arms swing naturally as shown in Figure 7-9.

3. **Gradually build up some speed if you wish. Or just continue to rotate slowly.**

1.   2.

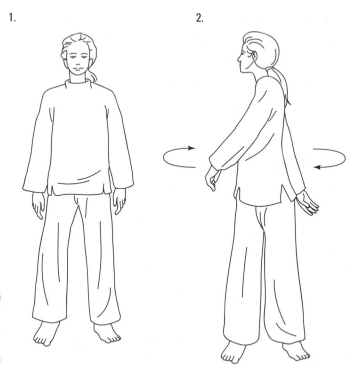

Figure 7-9:
Swinging
arms.

T'ai chic circle

This is a good exercise to encourage you to breathe deeply to help you to relax.

1. **Stand in a neutral posture.**

   Let your body be relaxed if you can.

2. **Turn your hands so they face upwards, as in Figure 7-10.**

3. **As you breathe in, raise both hands up in a circular way.**

   Keep your shoulders down.

4. **When your hands reach the top, begin to breathe out.**

   As you do so, bend your elbows and press your hands downwards softly.

5. **Repeat for a few minutes.**

   Or continue for longer if you find the exercise enjoyable.

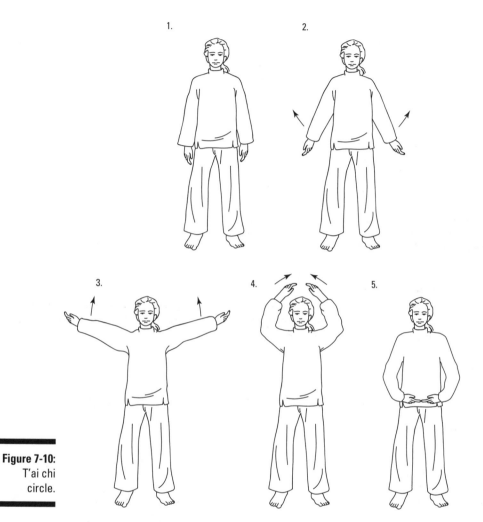

Figure 7-10:
T'ai chi circle.

Shoulders up and down

If you find you hold tension in your shoulders, this is an ideal exercise for you. It's an easy way to begin easing tense shoulders anytime during the day. (See Figure 7-11.)

1. **Stand in a neutral, relaxed posture.**

2. **As you breathe in, raise your shoulders up to their maximum height as shown in Figure 7-11.**

3. **As you breathe out, slowly lower your shoulders back down again.**

4. **Continue for a few cycles to help loosen tension in your shoulders.**

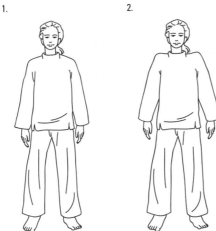

1.   2.

Figure 7-11:
Shoulders
up and
down.

Waist rotations

This exercise should be done slowly, ensuring you don't overstrain yourself. It's a great way of loosening tight muscles in your back and massaging your internal organs. (See Figure 7-12.)

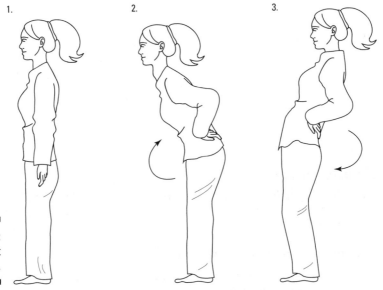

1.   2.   3.

Figure 7-12:
Waist
rotations.

1. **Stand in neutral, relaxed posture.**

2. **Place your hands on your lower back.**

3. **Fix your gaze on a stationary object in front of you.**

   This helps you balance through this exercise.

4. **Move your pelvis forwards.**

   Continue to gaze ahead.

5. **Begin to rotate by your waist in any direction you wish.**

   Follow an imaginary circle round with your mid-section. The sequence is shown in Figure 7-12

6. **Remember to breathe deeply as you do your rotations.**

7. **After several rotations, gently stop.**

   Come back to neutral and repeat the rotation in the opposite direction.

Chapter 8

Massage, Acupressure and Reflexology

· ·

In This Chapter

▶ Investigating different types of massage

▶ Discovering self-massage

▶ Using acupressure and reflexology on yourself

· ·

Human beings need four hugs a day for survival, eight hugs a day for maintenance and 12 hugs a day for growth.

Virginia Satir

*O*ne of the first things people crave when they feel stressed is a massage. Millions of people get massages every year, and for good reason. Massage is an enjoyable experience that relieves your muscular tension. This release of muscle tension may also calm your mind.

The essence of massage, reflexology and acupressure is touch. In many Western cultures, touch has become a rarity. But you don't need to be a scientist to know how good a hug or a supportive pat on the back feels. Touch is a natural expression of affection, and regular touch makes you happier. Children brought up in families that habitually touch each other are found to be healthier, sleep better, are more sociable and have a greater sense of well-being. Grown adults crave touch too. Massage, reflexology and acupressure offer a chance for you to experience touch in a safe and accepted way, leading to a range of health benefits, partly due to the relaxing effect of touch.

In this chapter I tell you all you need to know to find a massage therapist or enjoy a good old self-massage. I also explain what reflexology and acupressure are, and offer some ways for you to use these techniques on yourself to relax.

The power of human touch

Lots of scientific experiments have been carried out to try to discover the effect of even fleeting human touch on behaviour. Here are some of the findings:

✔ A gentle touch on the back or arm from a teacher made students twice as likely to volunteer to help out afterwards.

✔ A sympathetic touch from a doctor made a patient feel they were in the consultation room for twice as long as those that didn't – in other words, they felt more looked after.

✔ Research at the Touch Institute in Miami found a massage from a partner eased pain and depression, and strengthened the relationship.

✔ Scientists at Berkeley found that basketball teams that were 'touchier' than others were better at basketball. Players who hugged or 'high-fived' the most were found to be the better players within the team. The reason for this may be due to the relaxing effect of human touch, allowing the areas of the brain that's dealing with stress to re-focus on the game.

Discovering Massage

Massage is a treatment where a therapist manipulates your muscles and other soft tissues to help improve your wellbeing. Massage has been used in most cultures for centuries.

Massage has been used in China for over 4,000 years according to medical literature. Modern, Swedish massage was introduced to the West in the 1850s. In the 1970s massage gained public interest as a mind–body therapy and following positive research outcomes and greater interest, there are now millions of massage appointments every year, helping people to both relax and heal.

Massage works through the positive mood chemicals released from being touched, together with a stimulation of soft tissues sending electrical impulses throughout the body. In other words, being touched feels good.

According to the American Massage Therapy Association, massage is effective for a range of conditions including arthritis, lower back pain, insomnia, headaches, anxiety, circulatory problems and recovery from a sports injury. Massage has been found to boost immune function and increase a sense of wellbeing.

And as you may know, massage helps you to relax.

If you don't normally use massage, you may like to begin with a Swedish massage, one of the most popular types. Some massages, like sports massage and deep tissue massage, are more painful and you can sometimes feel sore for several days after – perhaps not the ideal way to relax!

Choosing a massage therapist

Choosing the right massage therapist for you is an important part of the process, especially if you plan to book a series of sessions. No matter what type of massage you choose, if your therapist is not adequately skilled, you probably won't feel relaxed. Consider the following points when making the decision:

- **Ask for a recommendation.** See whether any friends, family or colleagues can recommend a massage therapist. You could also ask a health professional, such as your doctor, osteopath, physiotherapist or counsellor.

- **How qualified and experienced is the therapist?** If you're going to get a massage, it's important to know your therapist's qualifications. Did she do just a weekend training course or a full year? Is she accredited with a particular organisation or national body? Find out if she has just started working as a therapist or has several years under her belt.

- **What type of massage does the therapist offer?** Some therapists like to combine different types of massage, whereas others just stick to one type. Find out what type the therapist offers and if that meets your needs.

- **How did you feel during and after the first massage session?** A good massage therapist will explain what she will do and make you feel comfortable and relaxed. If you found the experience painful and perhaps even stressful, seriously consider getting a different therapist. You ought to experience some benefits having had a massage. If you don't feel relaxed after the session, consider changing your therapist. Trust your intuition and if the massage didn't feel special at all, that may be a sign to move on to someone else.

- **Did the therapist communicate with you?** If you're having a session for the first time, you should be informed about what to expect, and asked about your medical history, injuries and your personal needs of the massage.

- **What additional features helped to make the massage relaxing?** Some therapists use acupuncture, scented oils, reflexology, chanting, music, joint manipulation or stretching. If you like the sound of any of those, ask if the therapist offers them.

This may sound like a lot to consider, but remember you're investing both time and money, so take your time to find the right person for you. You may like to find a qualified massage therapist through the General Council for Massage Therapies. Their website is www.gcmt.org.uk.

Tell your massage therapist what you want from the massage and communicate how you feel during the massage. Let the therapist know if the pressure is too hard or too soft, or if he or she is missing an important area. Make sure the lighting, heat, sounds and posture are right for you – this is *your* time.

Discovering popular types of massage for relaxation

Here is a list of the most popular types of massage for achieving relaxation.

- **Swedish massage:** This is probably one of the most common massages, developed by a Swedish physiologist called Henri Ling in 1812. It can be called Swedish massage therapy or simply massage therapy. If you're having massage for the first time, a Swedish massage is the best place to start. During a Swedish massage, the therapist uses massage oil on your body and smooth gliding strokes, kneading, stretching and perhaps some tapping. Swedish massage ranges from gentle to vigorous, so be sure to let the therapist know what you prefer to aid your relaxation.

- **Aromatherapy massage:** The therapist rubs essential oils from plants into your skin. Essential oils such as lavender stimulate areas deep in the brain that deal with emotions and memory to create a feeling of emotional relaxation.

- **Hot stone massage:** The therapist places gently heated smooth stones on key points on your body. Sometimes the therapist massages the stone in certain areas. The warmth of the stones helps to relax your muscles so the therapist can massage in a deeper way. The heat also helps to improve your circulation and calms you.

- **Shiatsu:** In this traditional Japanese therapy the therapist uses pressure to manipulate certain points in the body. Although Shiatsu means 'finger pressure', the therapist may also use other manipulative techniques. The points correspond to energy centres according to traditional Chinese medicine, allowing your body to heal and balance itself. In some ways Shiatsu is similar to acupressure (which I talk about in the section 'Trying Acupressure and Foot Reflexology' later in this chapter), but Shiatsu tends to be relatively quicker.

- **Thai massage:** This is also called Thai yoga massage and lasts from an hour to two hours. It is more energising that some of the others on this list, but still leads to a feeling of relaxation. The therapist uses her hands, feet, elbows and knees to move you in yoga-like postures without you doing any work as such. The massage is usually done on the floor, using a padded mat, and no oils are used so you can usually wear comfortable clothes.

Reflexology and acupressure are sometimes considered to be types of massage. For more info on these, see the section 'Trying Acupressure and Foot Reflexology' later in this chapter.

If you're on a budget, contact your nearest massage school. You often get a discount for experiencing massage with a student, but do so at your own risk. Make sure the massage is supervised by an experienced. I do know a friend who regularly receives massage from a massage school and finds the experience very relaxing.

Exploring Self-Massage to Relax Your Body

Self-massage is so natural you probably do it without even realising. If you rub your face when you feel tense, caress your temples when you have a headache, or rub your feet after standing up all day, you are practising self-massage. You can be your own massage therapist at any time. By discovering some simple techniques, you can enhance your feeling of relaxation with self-massage. Self-massage only takes a few minutes, but if you do it from time-to-time throughout the day, you'll ease excess muscle tightness and help remove toxins, leaving you relaxed.

Self-massage has two benefits over using a therapist: you can act immediately when you feel tension, and it's free. However, the effectiveness of a therapeutic massage is wonderful to experience from time-to-time too.

Understanding the principles of self-massage

To practise self-massage effectively, you need to follow a few key principles. By keeping them in mind, you are able to optimise your experience of self-massage, and probably use it more often too. The principles are:

✔ **Breathe deeply:** Deep breaths enhance your feeling of relaxation. Try to make your exhalations slightly longer than your inhalations. Have a sense of letting go and relaxation with each out breath. (For more on breathing techniques, have a look at Chapter 5.)

✔ **Be aware:** Feel the sensations of the tension, and notice what it feels like to massage that area of your body. Just being aware of the tension with a sense of warmth and kindness sends a message to your brain of safety and helps turn off your stress response.

✔ **Use the right amount of pressure:** Let times of self-massage be enjoyable. If you find the process painful, either use less pressure or stop. You could also try stretching the painful area first. For example, if your shoulders are too painful to massage, try raising and lowering your shoulders (which I describe in Chapter 7) and then try again.

✔ **Take your time:** The feeling that you don't have enough time is the reason for the tension in the first place. Even if you really don't have much time, set aside a few minutes and tell yourself 'This is time for me I do have time to relax.'

Practising different techniques for different parts of your body

Here you'll find specific self-massage techniques that tend to relax muscles in parts of your body that normally love to hold tension when you're stressed. Give them a try and see if the massage works for you.

Ask your friend, partner or family member to give you a massage. They could use the self-massage techniques in this section just as effectively.

Shoulders

The shoulder is one of the first areas to become tense for many people. Try the following exercise to ease the tension in your shoulders.

1. **Sit in a comfortable posture and loosen any tight clothing.** If you're wearing a coat or jacket, take it off if you can.

2. **Run your right hand over your left shoulder.** Start from the top of your neck near the base of your skull and stroke your way down to the end of your shoulder and down to your elbow using your fingers. Then slide your hand back up to your neck again. Do this about three times; do more repeats if you have time. Then repeat on the other side.

3. **Begin again in the same locations, but this time knead the muscles using your finger and the palms of your hands in a rhythmic way.** Repeat at least three times on each side again, remembering to go from your neck down to your elbows. Don't squeeze too hard or too softly – use a pressure that feels comfortable and eases the tension. Remember to breathe smoothly.

4. **Create a fist with your right hand and begin to lightly tap your left shoulder.** Try to keep your wrist quite loose and flexible. Use the right pressure for you. Then repeat on the other side.

5. **Using the fingers of your right hand, apply a pressure on the left side of where your neck meets your shoulder.** Hold that pressure for a few seconds and then move down into the left shoulder. Again, apply a constant pressure for a few seconds. Continue to apply pressure in this way as you make your way to the end of the shoulder. Repeat on the other side.

Abdomen

Abdominal massage can help with digestion and sometimes can cure digestive problems such as bloating or tightness in the stomach area.

1. **Stand up or sit in a comfortable chair.** Loosen tight clothing, especially around the waist.

2. **Place your right hand at the top of the right side of your pelvis and lightly rub your hand in a circular motion upwards until it reaches the base of your ribs.** Then work across your abdomen till you reach the ribs on your left side. Move your hand down, continuing to apply a light circular motion and pressure, until you reach the top of your pelvis on your left side. And then move across your lower abdomen back to the top of your pelvis on your right side. Continue in this way for about three minutes.

3. **Repeat the process in Step 2, but this time only use your fingertips, rubbing in a circular motion.** Spend a minute moving up the abdomen, a minute to go from the right to left side of your ribs, a minute to go down the left side of your abdomen and a minute going across the bottom of your abdomen. Remember to always move in this clockwise direction, which is the way your food moves in your gut. Continue for about ten minutes or however long feels comfortable for you.

Hands

You use your hands all the time – for lifting, typing, cleaning, writing. Tension is bound to build up so now may be a great time to ease that tension with a little massage.

1. **Place your left hand on a pillow on your lap.** Stroke the back of your left hand from your wrist to your fingertips and back again several times.

2. **Squeeze the whole of your left hand using the fingers and palm of your right hand, working your way from your wrist to your fingers and back down again.**

3. **Massage each of your fingers and your thumb in your left hand making a circular motion, ensuring that you include the finger joints.**

4. **Gently pull each finger from the base and slide towards the end of the fingertip and slide off.**

5. **Rub the palm of your left hand using your right thumb in a circular motion feeling into the soft tissues and easing out any tension. Include your left wrist too.**

6. **Give your left hand a gentle shake, and then repeat the process for your right hand.**

   You may want to end this massage by applying some hand cream or lotion, which can be like a massage in itself.

Face

A face massage can help you to ease a headache or make you feel less stressed and more relaxed. A face massage can also improve your skin and enhance your complexion. Use massage oil if you prefer.

1. **Begin by rubbing both of your hands together to generate some heat and then place both your hands on your face.** Place your fingertips on your forehead and the heels of your hands over your chin. As you breathe out smoothly move your hands out towards your ears. Imagine you are wiping tension out of your face. Continue to breathe slowly and smoothly through the self-massage.

2. **Using the fingers of both hands, apply a light pressure in the centre of your forehead, with the fingers almost touching.** Smoothly move your fingers out to the side of your forehead, past your temples, down the sides of your face, along your jawline and allow the fingers to meet at your chin. Repeat three times.

3. **Massage around your eyes very gently, making a light, circular motion with your fingers.**

4. **Tap both sides of your upper jaw with your fingers, and then gently apply pressure on your upper jaw using your fingers for a few seconds.**

5. **Beginning with the chin, apply a gentle pressure and work your fingers along your jawline to the upper part of your jaw.**

6. **Using a finger from each hand, apply a gentle pressure between your eyebrows. Move along your eyebrows to your ears.**

7. **Massage behind your ears using your fingertips, making gentle, circular motions.**

8. **Place two fingers just outside your nostrils and apply a gentle pressure. Breathe in and out deeply and slowly for a few breaths.** Now make a circular motion with your finger in this area for a few seconds.

9. **Stroke your finger from the bridge of your nose across your cheeks. Make your way down all the way to your chin.**

10. **Spread your fingers over the top of your head and your thumbs behind your ears.** Move your scalp slowly forwards and then backwards. Then make circular motions with your fingers on your scalp for about 20 seconds.

11. **Relax your eyes by placing your palms gently over your eye sockets and enjoy the complete darkness for ten seconds or so.** Then smoothly slide your palms outwards and take a few deep, refreshing breaths to finish.

Feet

If you're on your feet all day, you'll really appreciate this massage. Your feet have to carry the weight of your body and if you walk or run, even more pressure is placed. Use these techniques to help you relax and your feet will be smiling!

1. **Hold one foot between your hands.** Place one hand under your sole and the other on your ankle. Stroke up and down your feet. Remember to breathe smoothly and deeply and avoid over-straining your shoulders and neck in these movements.

2. **Holding the foot with one hand, work your way through each of your toes with your other hand – rub each toe in a circular motion and gently pull each one too.**

3. **Rub along the centre line of your sole and then using both your thumbs create lines of massage going outwards from the centre.** Now make circular motions with your thumb over the sole of your foot, including the ball, arch and heel.

4. **Make a fist with your hand and tap all over the sole of your foot, pushing in wherever you feel it needs massaging.**

5. **Now carry out a chopping action on the sole of your foot. Tap away your tensions as you breathe out slowly and smoothly.**

6. **Rub the top of your foot from your ankle to your toes using your palm and fingers and then repeat this process, squeezing from around the ankle and moving down your foot.**

7. **Finish by stroking both sides of your foot using both your hands.** Move up and down your foot, from the ankle and heel, up to your toes and back down again, at least three times and in a soothing and relaxing way.

Repeat the massage for your other foot that has been waiting patiently!

Integrating self-massage into your daily routine

Self-massage is a great way to keep yourself relaxed as you go about your daily activities. Here are some suggestions, but feel free to use other ideas you can think of too:

- ✔ **Tap out tension every morning and evening.** Begin and end each day by lightly tapping your body with a fist. Start with your shoulders and move down your arms. Using both fists, tap your lower back, the sides of your hips and make your way down your legs all the way to your feet. Repeat three times if you can.

- ✔ **Ease headaches by pulling your hair.** Spread your fingers through your hair and gently create a fist, holding on to your hair. Pull your hair for a few seconds and release. Then continue to repeat this process until you've done your whole head.

- ✔ **Hug away tension in your shoulders.** If you've been working on your desk for a while, give yourself a hug. Reach each hand out to the other shoulder, squeeze, and as you breathe out, let your arms stretch slightly farther. When you're done, slowly slide your hand along your arms right through to your hands.

- ✔ **Give your tired feet some love.** Wash and soak your feet in warm water. Then massage your feet by squeezing, tapping and using circular rubbing motions. Don't forget to massage your toes too. You could finish by massaging in your favourite scented massage oil.

- ✔ **Massage your neck to ease computer stress.** You could do this every half an hour or so, especially if working on a computer. Clasp your fingers together and place your palms around the back of your neck. Use the heels of your palms to gently squeeze both sides of your spine. Move up and down your neck.

- ✔ **Massage your hands as you apply hand cream.** As you rub lotion into your hands, use the time to massage your hands too. Use circular motions in your palms and your fingers, and enjoy the sensation as you do so.

- ✔ **Rub your belly after eating.** Use a very gentle pressure and rotate your hand on your belly in a clockwise direction. This is a relaxing feeling and aids digestion too.

Try to use times when you're waiting for a train or in a queue to do some simple self-massage.

Trying Acupressure and Foot Reflexology

Acupressure involves applying pressure in specific points on your body to enhance the flow of energy (qi) according to ancient oriental medicine. Acupressure is considered to be the mother of acupuncture, a similar treatment that uses needles instead of pressure. As acupressure can be done by applying pressure with your own fingers rather than requiring any special equipment, it makes an ideal self-help treatment.

Reflexology is a form of complementary medicine using massage and pressure, mainly on feet, to relieve mild medical symptoms and create relaxation. Thought to have originated in China thousands of years ago, reflexology was first brought to the West by Dr William Fitzgerald in 1913.

Applying acupressure for relaxation

Please don't use acupressure:

- ✔ As the only treatment for a medical condition. Acupressure can often be used to supplement, but not instead of, professional medical treatment.

- ✔ If you are pregnant.

- ✔ If you have a heart condition.

- ✔ If the acupoint you are using has any form of break in the skin or has a bruise, mole, wart or varicose vein.

- ✔ If you've just had a meal or exercised. Wait at least 30 minutes after that.

To carry out acupressure on yourself, you need to apply pressure on the acupoint using your fingertip, a knuckle or the rubber end of a pencil (not the sharp end!).

Here's how to carry out acupressure:

1. **Sit or lie in a comfortable posture and loosen any tight clothing.**

2. **Turn off any loud music and your phones so that you won't be distracted.**

3. **Use the diagrams in Figure 8-1 to choose an acupoint to start on.**

4. **Explore the area using a fairly deep pressure, using your finger, knuckle or the end of a pencil (as in Figure 8-2) until you feel a slight twinge. This is your acupoint.**

5. **Apply pressure for 10–30 seconds on that acupoint. The experience is supposed to be relaxing.** If you don't enjoy the sensation, stop.

6. **Now apply pressure on the same point on the other side of your body.**

7. **Continue to try the different points on the chart in Figure 8-1 and see which points work best for you to help you relax.**

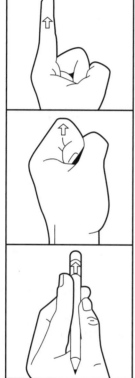

Figure 8-1:
Acupoints
for creating
relaxation.
Try them
out to see if
they work
for you.

You may be interested in getting some acupuncture from a professional therapist too. If so, it's important to check they're properly qualified. You could begin by looking at The Acupuncture Society, which is a professional body of acupuncture practitioners at www.acupuncturesociety.org.uk.

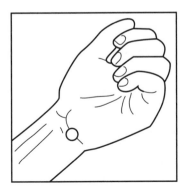

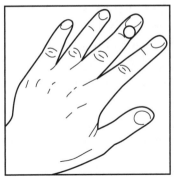

Directly under your little
finger, on the big crease.

Just above the nail on the middle
finger, on the side which is closest
to the thumb.

Figure 8-2:
Different
ways of
applying
pressure
on the
acupoints.

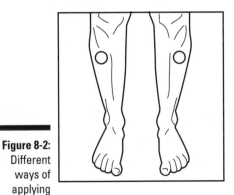

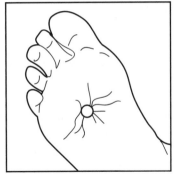

Measure about a palm's width
below the knee cap and find the
dip between the outside of
your shin and your leg muscle.

In the middle of the sole of your
foot, just next to the ball of your
foot.

Using foot reflexology to de-stress

✔ Don't use reflexology as the only treatment for a medical condition.

✔ If you are pregnant, check with a health professional that it's okay to
have reflexology.

✔ If you have a heart condition, check with your health professional before using reflexology.

✔ If your foot has any form of break in the skin or has a bruise, mole or wart, don't use foot reflexology.

✔ If you've just had a meal or exercised, wait at least 30 minutes before getting some reflexology.

Like acupressure, reflexology works by applying pressure on certain points of your body. According to practitioners, different parts of the foot are related to parts of your body and by applying pressure there, energy begins to flow more freely, restoring a sense of balance. Find time for reflexology and discover podiatric paradise.

Usually you need to go to a qualified reflexologist, but here's how to give yourself some reflexology:

1. **Remove your shoes and socks, turn off your phones and find a quiet place.**

2. **Sit on a comfortable and firm chair and place your left ankle on your right knee, so that you can reach the sole of your foot.**

3. **Support your left foot using your left hand so it doesn't slip off your knee.**

4. **Using the edge of your thumb or the knuckle of your right hand, apply pressure on the various points. Press quite hard for about 30 seconds on each point, but ease off if the experience is uncomfortably painful.**

5. **When you've finished with the left foot, swap over and work through your right foot.**

Fill a shoebox with golf balls and leave it under your desk at work or computer at home. Whenever you feel the need for some foot reflexology, pop open the box and roll your feet. The golf balls will contact all your acupoints simultaneously.

If you enjoyed the experience, you may like to take a course in reflexology or get some treatment from a professional reflexologist. Remember to check that they have completed a recognised course and have some experience.

Part III

Discovering Relaxation Techniques Using Your Mind and Heart

The 5th Wave   By Rich Tennant

"I think you'd be less tense if we did some relaxing visualization. Okay, close your eyes and imagine you're on a deserted island..."

In this part . . .

In this part you'll find relaxation techniques like guided imagery, meditation, self-hypnosis and problem-solving systems to help to de-stress. If you like to get a grip on your mind and emotions, this part may be just the one for you.

Chapter 9

Guided Imagery, Self-Hypnosis, Autogenics and Music

What's wrong with right now, if you don't think about it?

Bob Adamson

*Y*our mind has an extremely powerful effect on how you feel. The stories you tell yourself about your life, the memories of past hurts or joys, the images of how your next meeting or date will go all affect how relaxed you are at a particular time.

In this chapter, I show you several techniques to help you feel more relaxed. By practising the techniques in this chapter regularly, you'll get better at achieving a state of relaxation. You'll find that you can use these methods any time you have a few spare minutes and no matter where you are.

Using Guided Imagery or Visualisation

Imagination is more important than knowledge.

Albert Einstein

All the things you see around you that are man-made were first conceived in someone's imagination. Humans would have probably become extinct long ago without imagination. All discoveries, from creating a fire to sharpening a weapon, were born through imagery. Imagination gives you the possibility to project into the future and create something unique.

In this section, you discover how to use guided imagery to help you relax. Guided imagery is a way of directing your thoughts and imagination to create a relaxed and yet focused state of mind, and to help you find solutions to your current challenges in life. Visualisation is very similar to guided imagery, so I use the terms interchangeably.

A large part of this chapter involves using scripts to help guide you in the relaxation techniques. Here are a few tips on the use of scripts:

1. **Begin by sitting in a comfortable posture.** If sitting is uncomfortable for you, then any posture you prefer is fine. Loosen any tight clothing and remove your shoes if you wish. Ensure you won't be disturbed.

2. **Take a few moments to settle down and compose yourself.** You could take a few deep breaths to help you calm down if you like.

3. **Read the script slowly in your mind.** After each sentence, give yourself a few moments to really allow the meaning to be fully understood. Close your eyes when the script invites you to imagine a particular scenario or scene. Take your time as you work through the script.

    If at any time you feel uncomfortable with the imagery exercise, remember you can come out by simply opening your eyes, feeling the sensation of your body on the chair, looking around and having a stretch perhaps.

If you don't like reading scripts as you relax, you can either record the script and play it back, or use the CD that comes with this book.

As with all relaxation techniques in this book:

- ✔ Ensure you're fully awake and alert before using any kind of machinery after doing a relaxation exercise.

- ✔ Do not use the techniques to replace medical treatment. (However, relaxation techniques can often be used in conjunction with medical treatment and in some cases can help speed up the recovery process.)

Relaxation is worth waiting for

New research reveals that over their lifetime an average person in the West spends about six months waiting in queues, including waiting in shops, banks, post offices, on train platforms and on the phone. Use that time to carry out a short relaxation exercise and you'll feel better, rather than worse, when it comes to your turn in the queue.

Discovering the power of imagery

Imagery doesn't just mean visual images. Imagery includes thoughts that you can see, hear, smell, taste, touch or feel. When you daydream you see images but also hear and feel as if you're there. Daydreaming is your inner world.

You can find out the power of imagery by reading the script below slowly.

This exercise demonstrates the power of imagery:

> *Sit down and turn off any distractions for a few minutes. Imagine you are at home. You step into your kitchen and see a lemon. You decide to cut the lemon in half and do so. You pick up half the lemon and look at it, You notice the colour. Take your time to imagine the lemon in your hand. Then you bring the lemon towards your nose and smell it. Imagine what it may smell like. You decide to squeeze the lemon juice into a glass. Notice what happens as you squeeze the lemon, and the lemon juice begins to come out and into the glass. No pips fall into the glass – just fresh lemon juice. You pick up the glass and begin to drink the juice and notice the sour but perhaps refreshing taste.*

What did you notice in the exercise? Did you salivate? Most people do salivate when imagining this example. This illustrates that just imagining a particular situation in your mind has an effect on your physical body – an example of your mind/body connection. Although you're not aware of it, perhaps some acid and digestive chemicals were secreted in your stomach too, preparing to digest for you. All from your imagination.

If you can bring about all these reactions in your body through just imagination, you can use this same technique to help you to both relax and to better manage situations you find stressful.

Here's another one for you to try:

> *Begin by noticing how you're feeling emotionally. . . Now find a quiet place where you can do this imagery for a few minutes. Sit down and turn off any distractions. Think back to a time when you were proud of your achievements. Maybe it was receiving a certificate, having a baby, passing an exam or getting a job. Imagine you're back there right now. Notice what you're seeing. What are you hearing? How does your body feel in that situation? Is there a particular smell or taste there? What sort of thoughts are going through your mind? What sort of emotions do you feel there? Continue to stay there until you're ready to come out of this imagery exercise.*

Notice how you feel now. Have your feelings changed in the past few minutes? You may feel better, worse or just the same. If you don't feel better, that doesn't mean imagery doesn't work for you. You just need a bit more practice, and perhaps need to try some of the other exercises in this chapter. With practice you can get better at imagery and making your emotions a little more positive, without forcing them at all.

Cultivating the right attitude

The attitude you bring to a guided imagery exercise does shape the quality of the experience itself. This is because guided imagery is a mental exercise and so is easily influenced by your mental state and approach. Consider cultivating the following attitudes to help you maximise the benefits of guided imagery:

Try to think about the following when you use guided imagery:

- ✔ **I can do it!** If you think you're not a visual person, that doesn't mean you can't do imagery. About 50 per cent of people are not visual, so you're not alone. You can imagine the sounds or smells, the tastes or feeling, or just use words. Use what works for you.

- ✔ **I may feel better or worse at the end.** When you first try guided imagery you may feel slightly worse instead of better. Try to be okay with that. You can't really control your emotions 100 per cent and so if you feel worse, just be patient with yourself. As with any new skill, you need to practise.

- ✔ **My images don't have to be perfect.** You don't have to imagine the situation you're visualising in a perfect and detailed way. Just do the best you can. A vague or unfinished picture in your mind is fine.

- ✔ **I can use imagery anytime it's safe to do so.** You don't have to have 30 minutes in a room alone to use imagery, although practising for extended periods from time to time is helpful. With a bit of experience, you can use imagery when waiting in a queue, travelling on public transport, or at your desk at work. You can even keep your eyes open so that no one else knows that you're on a tropical beach or in a magical forest.

Using guided imagery exercises to relax

Essentially, guided imagery for relaxation has five steps:

1. **Get into a comfortable posture.**

2. **Begin with belly (diaphragmatic) breathing (which I describe fully in Chapter 5).**

    Imagine that you're breathing in relaxation and breathing out stress.

3. **Think of a relaxing place for you.**

4. **Imagine being in this place with all your senses.**

   Make the place as real as you can manage, and feel what it's like to be there.

5. **Stay in your chosen relaxing place for as long as you wish.**

   When you're ready to come back, count up from 1 to 10

Below is a script for a guided imagery to help you to relax. This first one is generic so you can imagine whatever you want. Use the book the first time you try it, and in future ask a friend or partner to read the script to you, or record your own voice, going at the pace that's right for you. Pause between sentences to help deepen the experience.

Find a place and time that's right for you. You may like to lie down or sit in a comfortable chair. Switch off any potential distractions. Imagine a scale that you can use to measure your level of relaxation. 0 is totally stressed and 10 is completely relaxed. Where would you rate your level of relaxation right now? Remember your number or write it down somewhere.

Begin by using your breath to relax with some belly breathing. As you breathe in, allow your belly to expand and as you breathe out, allow the belly to contract (see Chapter 5 for more on belly breathing). If you like you can imagine there's a balloon in your belly that inflates as you breathe in and deflates as you breathe out. On your next in breath, breathe in to a count of four, hold your breath to a count of two and breathe out to a count of four, six or eight, whatever you can manage. Now let your breath become natural and normal again.

Now imagine somewhere beautiful, peaceful and safe for you. You can imagine a place you've been to before, or some place you've created in your mind. That doesn't matter. Notice what you see. The colours and shapes. Notice if there are any sounds. Are there some sounds or is it silent? Notice if there is a scent in the air – there doesn't have to be – just be aware of how it is for you. Be aware of the time of day. Is it day or night? What time of year? And notice how you're feeling in this special place you're in. Enjoy this beautiful place without having to do anything or go anywhere. Allow yourself to absorb the peace and calm of this wonderful place, as if you're a sponge. There's nowhere else you need to go at this moment. Just give yourself time to be. Rest in this serene, tranquil, soothing space knowing that you can return here any time you wish. And when you're ready, prepare yourself to come back to your surroundings again. Remember you can continue to stay in this peaceful place for longer if you wish. That's absolutely fine. When you're ready and choose to do so, begin slowly counting from 1 to 10. With each number, feel more refreshed and relaxed. Stay with any feeling of relaxation and bring that feeling into your wakeful state. When you're ready, gently allow your eyes to open and notice the colours around you. You can take a deep breath and stretch in any way you please, and come back to the outer world, refreshed and awake.

Before you fully engage with your next activity take a few moments to reflect on your level of relaxation on a scale of 0 to 10, 0 being not relaxed at all, and 10 being totally calm and relaxed. How does your score compare to your level of relaxation at the beginning of this exercise? If you found yourself less relaxed at the end, that doesn't mean anything is wrong. Remember, you're only just beginning to learn to use imagery. With more practice you'll find that you do feel more relaxed through doing this exercise.

Try this exercise twice a day for about three weeks or at anytime you feel stressed or tired. You could also try using it before eating a meal, or afterwards.

Write about your experience in your relaxation journal (see Chapter 3) or notebook. You could even do a drawing to express your experience.

Natan Sharansky, a human rights activist, was imprisoned in the USSR for nine years, accused of spying on behalf of the US. In his book *Fear No Evil*, he mentions how he had seen some chess problems in magazines and began to visualise playing and working out the solutions whilst in solitary confinement. In other games he'd lost, he analysed variations for up to 40 different moves to find solutions. He was visualising to preserve his sanity rather than to improve his chess. However, after he was released he played against and beat world champion chess player Garry Kasparov. Sharansky said 'I had many years of playing chess in my head while in prison in the Soviet Union, so I was very well prepared!'

Accessing an inner advisor

If you have a problem or challenge that prevents you from accessing relaxation, try adding the following script to your guided relaxation imagery. This script is about talking to your own inner advisor, who represents your subconscious or innate inner wisdom as I see it. If you're religious, you may think of your inner advisor as your soul or some form of spiritual guidance. How you see it is up to you. Try it and see what happens.

Consider a problem or issue that you'd like some guidance or help with to make you feel more relaxed. Bring an image to mind that is wise and kind. The image may be a spiritual person, an animal or something else such as some form of energy. The image can be real or imaginary but make sure that it feels wise and kind or loving and if it doesn't, send it away and invite one that does.

Thank the inner advisor. Explain your situation to the inner wise figure and then ask for help. Pay careful attention to the response you receive. Notice both what is communicated to you and the way in which the advice is received. The guidance may be through words, pictures, sounds or a feeling. Just be open to receive the guidance. Take time to reflect on what the inner wisdom you have received is telling you, as if you've heard words from someone you really respect. Imagine what may happen to you if you act out on the advice offered and how you would cope with the challenges that arise. Can you see how the solution offered may improve or solve your problem? If not, what would help?

If you don't receive guidance from the inner advisor, then ask your advisor to reflect further on the issue, and plan to meet again in the future.

If you receive guidance, imagine acting out the solution and imagine a successful outcome. Imagine how you feel to have a successful solution and notice your reactions. Become aware of the feeling of being successful and amplify the feeling as much as feels good for you.

Reflect on what you've discovered with this wise counsel today. Be clear what you want to bring back with you when you return to wakefulness in the outside world.

After the guided imagery, if you receive guidance that helps you to reach your solution, write it down. If you think this guidance is helpful, write down the steps you need to take to move towards the solution. Write your plan down. Feel and amplify the feelings of positivity on achieving your solution. Be clear about the steps you need to take to achieve the solution and begin to take those steps as soon as you can, if appropriate.

Overcoming resistance

You may have some sort of resistance to guided imagery. This is not unusual so don't immediately give up. Instead, I would invite you to look through this section to see if you can find out and overcome the cause of the resistance.

Here are some ways you may experience this resistance:

- ✔ Not wanting to practise imagery
- ✔ Finding the process very difficult or uncomfortable
- ✔ Unable to create any form of imagery
- ✔ Wanting to do anything else but the imagery exercises
- ✔ Experiencing strong, difficult emotions each time you practise
- ✔ Constantly questioning how helpful the imagery is
- ✔ Always falling asleep during imagery

Resistance is a form of defence mechanism, which is a healthy response in some life situations. When someone says something unkind to you, you may defend yourself by either reacting back or moving away from them. In the same way, if the imagery is bringing up sensitive and emotional feelings, your body may not be ready to deal with these feelings so rapidly and cope by creating a defence mechanism in the form of resistance.

One way to deal with an inner resistance is to explore that resistance through imagery. Allow yourself to get into a relatively relaxed state through deep belly breathing as explained in Chapter 5, or any other approach you like. Now try to visualise what form the resistance takes. You may see a rock or a wall, a person, or something else. Explore the resistance and communicate with the resistance. Ask yourself what purpose the resistance serves, what it does for you, how it got there and if there's a way you could meet its needs. How can you work together to deepen your imagery experience?

Alternatively, you could connect with your inner advisor – imagine someone or something wise and kind. Ask the inner advisor about the resistance you're experiencing and work together to find a suitable way forward.

If you still have difficulty and want more support, you may like to get in touch with a professional in your area who has trained in guided imagery. Go to www.relaxationfordummies.com/guidedimagery to access a list, and to find links to audio downloads of guided imagery exercises.

Discovering Autogenics

Autogenics, or autogenic training, is a technique to raise your level of bodily awareness and create a state of relaxation. Autogenics is said to promote self-empowerment and peace of mind. You learn to switch off the 'fight-or-flight' stress response and switch on the 'rest and recuperate' relaxation response.

A key aspect of autogenics is learning to develop a passive concentration, which helps to reduce chronic stress.

The main benefits of autogenics are:

- Greater ability to relax at any time
- An increased ability to focus on a task
- Improvement in sleep quality
- Reduction in panic attacks and anxiety
- Increased confidence and feeling of control
- Reduction in stress-related illnesses and disorders, such as high blood pressure

Preparing to practise autogenics

Autogenic training is about teaching your mind and body to relax. This requires the following five principles:

- ✔ **Quiet environment with low-level lighting:** This kind of environment helps to reduce external stimulation so that you can focus effectively.

- ✔ **Passive concentration:** This is a state of alertness, but also a 'detached' awareness, which means that your attention is relaxed and non-striving – you're not trying to achieve anything. This technique is more of an 'allowing' rather than a 'doing' to achieve relaxation or anything else. This passive concentration is the same as is developed in meditation (Chapter 10) or progressive relaxation (Chapter 4), for example.

- ✔ **Repetition of certain phrases that invite relaxation into your body:** The phrases you recite are about creating a heaviness and warmth, a calm heart beat and breathing, a warm belly and a cool forehead.

- ✔ **Attention focused on a particular body part:** When you repeat the phrases, the idea is that you focus your passive awareness on a particular area of the body. Each time your mind goes to other thoughts, gently bring your attention back to the body part.

- ✔ **Remembering you are in control:** At any time during the autogenic training, you're in control. You repeat the phrases in your mind and you pay attention to the particular body part.

Autogenic training was originally designed to be acquired through a qualified trainer. For help in finding a qualified trainer in your area go to the British Augenic Society at www.autogenic-therapy.org.uk.

Practising autogenic training for relaxation

To practise autogenics, either make a recording of the script with all the phrases in it or, alternatively, you can memorise the phrases. If you practise from memory, begin with the first set of phrases. Then, once you feel confident that you know the first phrases, move on to adding the next set of phrases. Continue until you know all the phrases by heart.

Practise twice a day for about 20 minutes at a time. If you can't manage that much time, do one session a day, or spend less time on each session. You should begin to feel some benefit after a few weeks.

Practise either lying down on a mat or soft surface, or in a reclined chair. Repeat each phrase four times to yourself, slowly. As you breathe in say the first part of each phrase, and as you breathe out, say the second part. For example, 'My right arm' as you breathe in, and 'is heavy' as you breathe out. This training is composed of six phases. Do each phase for three days and then move on to the next phase. Eventually aim to do all the phases in one session. The phases are:

✔ **Phase 1 – heaviness:**

- My right arm is heavy ×4 (if you are left-handed, start with your left arm instead)

- My left arm is heavy ×4

- My right leg is heavy ×4

- My left leg is heavy ×4

- Both my arms and legs are heavy ×4

  To help you develop a sense of heaviness, imagine your limbs sinking into the grass in a sunny meadow or on a beach. You can even choose a hot bath or sitting in your favourite chair by a log fire. Use an image that feels relaxing. Once you have chosen a particular image, stick with it for the duration of the session.

  You can end this session and all the other sessions when you're ready by stretching your body gently in any way that feels good to you. Allow your eyes to open and look around for a few moments. Say to yourself, 'I am relaxed and yet refreshed and fully alert.'

✔ **Phase 2 – warmth:**

- My right arm is warm ×4

- My left arm is warm ×4

- My right leg is warm ×4

- My left leg is warm ×4

- Both my arms and legs are warm ×4

✔ **Phase 3 – calm heart beat:**

- My heart beat is calm and regular ×4

- I am at peace

✔ **Phase 4 – calm breathing:**

- My breathing is calm and regular ×4

- I am at peace

✔ **Phase 5 – warm solar plexus:**

- My solar plexus is warm ×4

- I am at peace

✔ **Phase 6 – cool head:**

- My forehead is cool ×4

- I am completely at peace

Developing autogenic practice

Once you've established yourself in the autogenic phases and are enjoying some sense of relaxation, you can move on to the next step where you introduce positive affirmations. After practising autogenics, you're likely to be in a more relaxed and open state of mind. You can use this time to state affirmations to yourself to help you to feel more in control of any issues or problems that are a source of stress for you. Keep the affirmations positive, short, in the present tense, and personal for optimal effect. Here are some examples:

✔ **My mind is calm and relaxed.** Use this if you suffer from anxiety.

✔ **I can deal with stressful situations.** Use this if you find yourself getting stressed easily.

✔ **I'm in control of my habits.** Use this if you want to quit smoking, for example.

Sussing Out Self-Hypnosis

The word 'hypnosis' comes from the Greek *hypnos*, meaning sleep. Hypnosis is best thought of as a form of deep relaxation through a passive focus. In this state of mind you are more susceptible to accept positive self-statements.

Hypnosis is probably the least understood of all techniques in this book. This is probably due to stage shows where people under hypnosis start barking like a dog, or are immediately attracted to the next person they see. Many people think that when people are hypnotised they lose control. This has been shown to be untrue through research – actually hypnosis makes you feel more in control over your symptoms. You can be hypnotised in many ways but you can't really be hypnotised if you don't choose to be. So in a way, all hypnosis is self-hypnosis!

Self-hypnosis can be used in two ways for relaxation:

✔ You can use self-hypnosis to access a state of deep relaxation. This engagement of your relaxation response helps to reduce the symptoms of stress-related illness and can help to break the cycle of chronic stress.

✔ You can use self-hypnosis to make better choices or improve your self-image so that stress is better managed. For example, you can encourage yourself to quit smoking, exercise more regularly, eat more fruit and veg, or feel more confident when at work.

Because you hypnotise yourself, it is an especially useful way to relax as you don't need to find a hypnotherapist.

Self-hypnosis engages the relaxation response, like many other relaxation techniques in this book. This relaxation is achieved by focusing on positive, calming affirmations. The affirmations can also be used to overcome any other problems or issues in your life and are more effective in the relaxed state of hypnosis.

Some people use the word 'trance' when talking about states of hypnosis. Trance just means a state of mind where you're both focused and relaxed. For example, day dreaming is considered to be a trance. Watching a good film is another example of a trance, where your attention is absorbed in the action but if there was any kind of emergency, you'd immediately notice. You can also go to get some extra popcorn if you wish! Hypnosis is a bit like that – a focused and yet relaxed awareness. In this state of mind you are more open to positive suggestions.

Hypnosis works by helping you to focus on feelings of calmness and peace. You are therefore not distracted by thoughts about your problems and feel more tranquil.

Self-hypnosis can be used on a daily basis for about 10 minutes or so to help you to relax.

Here are some of the benefits of self-hypnosis:

✔ Greater ability to relax

✔ Pain relief

✔ Healing from injury or surgery more rapidly or effectively

✔ Overcoming anxiety in particular situations, such as when you're flying or in a lift

✔ Breaking habits

✔ Reducing the nausea of chemotherapy

If you have any kind of medical condition, see your doctor before engaging in self-hypnosis.

In July 2008, a woman in the UK, 67-year-old Bernadette, managed to undergo knee surgery with no pain relief or anaesthetic – just the power of self-hypnosis. Although most people would feel excruciating pain if undergoing this keyhole surgery, Bernadette showed almost no sign of pain. Scientists believe she achieved such a deep state of relaxation through self-hypnosis that her pain signals were blocked. She came out of the surgery smiling and saying 'I didn't feel any pain.'

Practising self-hypnosis

Begin by deciding what you hope to achieve from self-hypnosis. You want to feel more relaxed I assume, but in what situation in particular? Think about something that is troubling you that you'd like to feel a bit more relaxed about. The clearer you are about what you want from self-hypnosis, the more effective you'll find it. Maybe you want to overcome your tension headaches, or want to be able to respond more calmly when your children misbehave.

After you decide, think about what sort of affirmations you may like to say to yourself in the self-hypnosis – positive self-statements to make you feel better.

1. **Find a quiet place.**

   Switch off your mobile, turn on your answering machine and let others know that you don't want to be disturbed for the next 15 minutes or so.

2. **Sit down on a relaxing chair and loosen any tight clothing.**

   Ensure you're sufficiently warm and comfortable. Close your eyes if that feels more comfortable.

3. **Start with some deep belly breathing.**

   Each time you breathe out, let yourself have a sense of letting go. Then just notice your own natural breathing. Each time your mind wanders off to other thoughts or concerns, gently guide your awareness back to your breathing.

4. **Scan your body from the top of your head to the tips of your toes and allow your body to relax as best you can.**

   As you move your awareness from one body part to the next, allow the tension to drop away from your body. Imagine each part of your body becoming heavier and at ease. Combine these thoughts with soothing images like water washing away the tension or a golden light moving through your body, releasing the stress. Choose an image that works for you.

5. **Begin to give yourself suggestions to help you to relax more deeply.**

   You can use phrases like 'I'm getting more and more relaxed,' or 'Every time I breathe out, I'm feeling more and more calm and relaxed.' Or you could say 'My whole body is getting heavier and heavier as I feel more and more sleepy. . . more and more relaxed.

6. **Imagine yourself at the top of a set of ten steps that lead to a peaceful and relaxing place.**

   Allow the stairs to be of any design and material you find beautiful. Imagine yourself going down the steps. With each step you take, invite yourself to feel more and more relaxed, more and more calm. When you get to the bottom of the stairs, imagine that you're arriving at a place that you find most peaceful and relaxing. Enjoy the tranquillity and serenity of this relaxing place, exploring it with each of your senses in turn.

7. **Once you feel very relaxed, use the affirmations you decided to use earlier.**

   You can go back to the relaxation phrases and intersperse them with your affirmations to deepen the effect.

8. **Once you're ready to bring the self-hypnosis to an end, you can imagine walking back up the stairs and counting from 1 to 10 as you do so.**

   As you walk up the stairs, say to yourself 'I'm feeling more and more refreshed, yet relaxed.' When you get to the top say 'I'm now fully awake and refreshed.'

9. **As with all relaxation exercises, make sure you get up slowly or you may feel dizzy.**

You can also use audio CDs or mp3 audio files to carry out self-hypnosis. For a list of popular websites that offer these hypnosis audios, visit www. relaxationfordummies.com/hynosis.

Some people like to use soft background music when practising self-hypnosis. Experiment to see what works for you. Be patient with the process. As self-hypnosis is working through your subconscious, you may not notice the positive benefit of regular self-hypnosis at first.

If you'd like to find a hypnotherapist in the UK, you could begin by looking on The General Hypnotherapist Register on www.general-hypnotherapy-register.com or British Hypnotherapy Association on www.hypnotherapy-association.org.

Trying a sample hypnosis script for relaxing through stressful times

You may find it helpful to have a script for engaging in self-hypnosis as it gives you a structured way to relax rather than trying to make it up as you go along. You can then focus on relaxation rather than trying to think of the right words to say to yourself. See the guidance in the section 'Using Guided Imagery or Visualisation' at the beginning of this chapter for tips on using scripts.

You can record this script or ask someone to calmly and slowly read the script to you. Sit in a relaxing chair or lie down, undisturbed, for about 20 minutes or so.

Sit or lie down and allow your eyes to gently close. . . take a deep breath and as you breathe, allow some of the tension in your body to just fall off your body. . . now take a deep breath into your belly, hold it for a few seconds, and breathe out slowly until your lungs are almost completely empty. . . see how your lungs naturally draw air into your body, filling your body with nourishing, clean oxygen. . . let go and allow your breathing to be natural once again. . . each time you breathe out, say to yourself 'relax'. . . each time you breathe out you feel more and more relaxed. . . Now I'm going to count down from 10 to 1 and with each number you become more calm and relaxed. . . .10. . . you're feeling relaxed. . . 9. . . you're getting more relaxed. . . 8. . . tension is dissolving from your body. . . 7. . . .your muscles are feeling limp and loose. . . 6. . . every muscle is relaxed. . . 5. . . your whole body is in a state of relaxation. . . 4. . . with every exhalation your relaxation deepens. . . 3. . . your whole being is relaxed. . . 2. . . you're filled with a feeling of relaxation. . . 1. . . you're now deeply relaxed. . .

Now when you're ready, imagine yourself feeling this same level of relaxation in a stressful situation. . . even though you are faced with something that normally makes you feel anxious, you're no longer overwhelmed by the stress. . . you deal with the situation calmly and in an efficient way. . . continuing to breathe smoothly and calmly. . . .with each out-breath you continue to feel calm and in control. . . you're body feels relaxed and your mind is calm and focused. . . .you're able to deal with the stressful situation and create a positive outcome without getting stressed. . . you're in control. . . you're capable of coping effectively. . . you use the relaxation techniques you've learnt to manage any stress that arises. . . you breathe deeply and dissipate any tension and anxiety. . .

Each time you breathe out, you're feeling more and more cool, calm and relaxed. . .

In a few moments, I'll count from 1 to 10, and with each ascending number, you'll feel more refreshed and alert. . . 1. . . feeling energised. . . 2. . . energy is filling your body. . . 3. . . you feel more and more awake. . . 4. . . a sense of alertness is filling your being. . . 5. . . more and more awake. . . 6. . . energised and refreshed. . . 7. . . calm yet alert. . . 8. . . you're ready to wake up. . . 9. . . you feel wonderfully refreshed and energised. . . 10. . . opening your eyes, awake and alert. . . connect back with the outer world around you, bringing a sense of relaxed alertness.

Using Music to Relax

Music gives a soul to the universe, wings to the mind, flight to the imagination, and life to everything.

Plato

Music is powerful. It can pick you up when you feel down or calm you down when you're stressed. Music seems to have an almost direct effect on emotions. Some experts believe that music with a calming beat is relaxing because it evokes subconscious memories of your mother's heart beat when you were in her womb – feelings of safety and warmth automatically soothe and relax you.

In this section, you can discover how to use music to help you relax, including how to select the right type of music for you, and some suggested ways of listening. This section also includes an explanation of music therapy, and how to find a music therapist in your area.

Discovering the power of music

Research has shown that music with a slower beat promotes a calmer, more meditative state of mind. Interestingly, the changes that take place go on to work even when you stop listening to the music – so the sounds make lasting, positive changes in the brain, after the music has stopped.

Breathing and heart rate are also found to slow down after listening to relaxing music. This slowing down is the hallmark of the relaxation response working you enter a more relaxed state of body and mind through listening to the calming sounds. The result is a more positive frame of mind and lower feelings of stress and anxiety.

Music can be used with all the relaxation techniques in this book to help deepen your experience. Experiment to see what works for you.

Music helps premature babies

An incredible study published in the *Journal for Music Therapy* found that by playing music to babies that were born prematurely or with low birth weight helped them to gain a healthy weight faster and leave hospital significantly earlier. The babies also appeared to show less stressful behaviour. The music they played to the babies included lullabies and children's music. This study demonstrates just one example of the healing power of music.

Using music to help you relax

If you want to help yourself feel more relaxed and calm, you need to choose relaxing music – no surprises there. However, everyone has a different taste so there's not one piece of music that works for all. What's relaxing for me may be stressful for you.

Here are some suggestions to help you maximise your musical relaxation:

- ✔ Go for a walk whilst listening to your favourite, calming music for 20 minutes or so. Allow your breathing to match the slow rhythm of the beats if appropriate. This technique is effective as you're combining music, exercise and deep breathing to relax.

- ✔ When choosing music go for a slow beat. If you find pieces with less than about 70 beats per minute, you'll help to lower your heart rate and feel more relaxed.

- ✔ Settle down in your favourite chair and put your headphones on. Listen to your chosen soothing music and let the sounds wash away your stresses. Listen to the music and the silence between the notes. Don't worry too much if you find yourself thinking about your worries – as soon as you can, just turn your attention back to the tranquil sounds.

- ✔ There are a lot of CDs available with the sounds of nature and this is a great way to relax for some people. If you're lucky enough to live in a place with access to nature and all the lovely sounds that go along with nature, that's a good way to relax. Sit or lie down and drink in the sounds of the birds, the breeze through the trees and other relaxing sounds of nature.

Using a music therapist for further help

Music therapy is an evidence-based way of using music to reduce your stress by a professional. Music therapy is not just used to experience relaxation but also for increasing wellbeing, reducing pain, expressing emotions, improving memory and concentration, and even to help with physical rehabilitation.

A music therapist assesses your physical, mental and emotional wellbeing through your responses to music and designs sessions to meet your needs or the needs of a group if you have therapy with others.

Each music session varies. Generally speaking, the sessions are quite active and you may be encouraged to use your own voice and a range of different musical instruments.

You may benefit from music therapy especially if you have mental health challenges, learning needs, Alzheimer's disease, other age-related conditions, substance abuse addiction, brain injuries, pain or physical disabilities. Expectant mothers can also find help through music therapy.

One of the main misconceptions about music therapy is that you need to like a particular style of music. This isn't true. Your particular situation, preference and goals help to determine the most suitable music for you. You also don't need to have any special musical ability. The therapy usually takes place in a sound-proof room to protect your privacy too.

Visit the British Association for Music Therapy on www.bamt.org for more information and to find a therapist near you.

Music can calm your nerves, literally

When a neuroscientist was undergoing spinal surgery, a thought struck him — what effect would relaxing music have on the brain of patients having this operation. So, using his own music player and headphones, he set up an experiment and analysed patients undergoing surgery for Parkinson's disease whilst awake. Most patients preferred melodic music for relaxation. The results found that the music reduced activity deep in the brain, and some patients even fell asleep during the surgery! So, the music helped to reduce the stress of a normally traumatic experience, lower blood pressure, reduce the need for medication and may even have resulted in faster recovery time and a shorter hospital stay.

Chapter 10

Meditation

● ●

In This Chapter

▶ Introducing meditation

▶ Exploring mindfulness meditations

▶ Discovering relaxation response meditation

▶ Trying out other meditations

● ●

> *Do not dwell in the past, do not dream of the future, concentrate the mind on the present moment.*
>
> Buddha

Meditation is a great way to relax. How many other activities do you know that you can do on your own, with no equipment, in almost any posture, at any waking moment of the day that offers scientifically proven stress relief and relaxation?

Meditation offers more than relaxation though. Meditation has been used as a practice for both spirituality and healing for thousands of years in many parts of the world.

In this chapter I focus on two non-religious forms of meditation that are accessible to everyone, regardless of faith – mindfulness meditation and relaxation response meditation. Both of these meditations have been well researched and found to effectively relax participants from a range of different ages and backgrounds. I explain how to prepare yourself for meditation, the way to overcome common obstacles and how to cultivate the right attitudes. I also include some alternative meditations like candle flame meditation and metta meditation.

If you enjoy simply looking at a sunset or a beautiful landscape, you've already had a taste of meditation.

Uncovering the Basics of Meditation

If you want to learn to drive a car, someone needs to tell you what the different pedals do before you head off on your first journey. In the same way, you need to discover the basic principles of meditation before you dive into your first experience of meditation. In this section I show you the basics of meditation.

Simply put, meditation is about focusing your mind. Meditation usually involves a certain posture, a passive attitude, a quiet environment and something to focus on. People use meditation not only for relaxation, but to overcome psychological issues, increase focus, and manage a chronic condition or to raise levels of health and wellbeing.

Most types of meditation have the following four key elements, which are, in order of importance:

- **A passive, friendly attitude:** Meditation involves accepting distracting thoughts without self-criticism or judgement. If your mind drifts, you just gently shift your attention back to your focus again.

- **Something to focus on:** Different types of meditation offer different things to focus on. For example, you may focus on the feeling of your breath, or on a word that you're silently repeating in your mind. Some meditations involve an open attention, where you focus on whatever thoughts or emotions are most predominant in your mind.

- **A particular posture:** Your posture is recommended to be relaxed, or in an upright, seated position. Most practitioners offer the choice of sitting on the floor, using a meditation cushion, or seated on a chair.

- **A quiet environment:** Although it's possible to meditate with lots of noise around, a quiet environment is best for beginners.

The words meditation, medication, and medicine don't only sound similar: They all share the same root meaning – all of them are about healing.

Seeing how meditation relaxes you

There is no question of going anywhere, arriving anywhere, or doing anything; you are there already.

Nisargadatta Maharaj

Ultimately, meditation is not something you 'do' as such. 'Doing' involves putting in a significant amount of energy to achieve an aim. Meditation is about letting go of trying too hard to achieve anything. Some describe meditation as a process of 'non-doing'. In that way, meditation is like relaxation.

Relaxation is not something you 'do' or 'attain', but a natural state when you stop trying to run away from the here and now.

Here are some of the ways in which meditation can relax you:

- **Meditation brings you into the present moment.** Meditation is about focusing your being in the here and now. Regrets about the past, and worries about the future, may be dominating your mind, not allowing you to relax. Meditation takes you back to the present.

- **Meditation changes your brain.** Meditation has been found to create more positive ways in which your brain operates. The parts of your brain associated with relaxation and wellbeing are strengthened, and the parts associated with stress and anxiety are weakened. Areas to do with emotional intelligence are also strengthened, so you don't react to others or your errors so easily.

- **Meditation untangles habitual patterns that cause stress.** Over the course of your life, you build up certain patterns of behaviour, ways of coping with different stresses and situations in your life. Until you begin to change those patterns, you find that you hold on to the same old attitudes and react in the same, engrained way to life's challenges. Your 'inner patterns' become automatic responses within you and are rarely undone simply by 'trying harder'. Meditation offers a different approach. Meditation offers your mind and emotions space to untangle themselves without you reacting to your concerns in your habitual way.

- **Meditation improves your relationship with yourself and others around you.** Meditation is an inner journey. You get to know yourself better. And through the course of time, you learn to really like yourself too. The more you, dare I say it, love yourself, the more potential you have to love others. In my experience with clients, as soon as they learn meditation and become more at ease with themselves, their close relationships flourish. You begin to create a positive energy within yourself rather than depending on others for inner nourishment. Your inner serenity naturally attracts others towards you.

- **Let's see what happens.** Rather than expecting to feel more relaxed or calm, just think of each meditation as an exploration – a chance to do the exercise and just be curious about how you feel – see what happens!

- **Failure as such doesn't exist.** Ultimately, meditation is a goal-less activity. You simply do the exercise and see what happens. Therefore, you can't fail. Even if you feel more stressed at the end of the meditation, just try to notice what caused the feeling rather than suppressing it.

- **It's normal to be distracted by thoughts.** If you expect meditation to empty your mind, you are going to end up frustrated. It's the nature of your mind to wonder off into other thoughts, so just expect that.

Finding the right posture for you

Not all meditations involve keeping your body still, but many of them do. If you want to meditate regularly, you need to consider your posture. Scientists have found that our posture has a big effect on our state of mind. Here are the key principles when it comes to finding the right posture, as well as some suggested postures that you could be in for your meditations:

- ✔ **Be comfortable.** If you feel uncomfortable in your posture, your attention is going to be repeatedly drawn to your sense of discomfort.

- ✔ **Keep your back relatively straight.** If your spine is not straight, you're more likely to feel both uncomfortable and sleepy. As meditation is about developing your attention, you're more likely to stay awake with your spine straight. Either sit on a chair or sit cross-legged on the floor. If you can't sit up for any reason, you can lie down on a mat or carpet. I show some suggested postures for meditation in Figures 10-1 and 10-2.

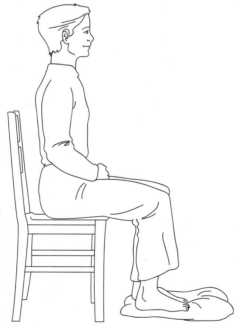

Figure 10-1: Keep you spine straight by sitting on a chair.

Choose the right time to do your meditation. Avoid meditating immediately after a meal as you may be too sleepy. Also, meditate in the morning or during the day rather than last thing at night. However, for some people, meditation is a great way to help them to sleep. If you use meditation to help you sleep, choose another time in the day to meditate too, to enjoy the full long-term benefits of meditation.

Figure 10-2:
Try sitting cross legged for comfortable meditation.

Understanding the principles of meditation

The flowering of love is meditation.

J. Krishnamurti

Following some key principles and having the right attitude to meditation makes you more likely to stick with it and reap the rewards of the practice. Meditation is quite a unique activity and if you're looking for instant success, you'll be disappointed. However, with a bit of time, even just a few weeks, you may notice yourself feeling significantly calmer. Consider the following principles and attitudes, which you will find helpful to cultivate:

- ✔ **Keep your back relatively straight.** You don't have to sit cross-legged on the floor to meditate. You can sit in any comfortable posture for most meditations, including lying down. Keeping your back relatively straight can make a big difference, helping you to stay awake and generating a feeling of inner confidence.

- ✔ **Expect your mind to wander on to other thoughts.** You don't have to stop your thinking. You have more connections in your brain than there are stars in the universe – you're bound to start thinking! Meditation leads to a different relationship to your thoughts, and often a side effect is fewer thoughts during the meditation itself. When you realise that you've been lost in a train of thought, gently guide your attention back to the focus, without criticising yourself. Mind wandering and guiding your attention back is what meditation is about.

✔ **Let go of your aims in meditation.** Meditation isn't just about relaxation – relaxation is a nice side effect of meditation. Meditation leads to insight and wisdom about yourself. Deep relaxation, both in the meditation and as a resilience to stress in day-to-day living, is a powerful long-term outcome of the process. Sometimes you feel more emotional, or frustrated, or it doesn't feel as if it's working. Other days you think, 'I've got it.' These are all just feelings and they come and go. Don't worry too much about how you feel and just keep practising regularly.

✔ **It's okay to feel emotions arising.** Sometimes meditation can release some emotions that you've been avoiding or suppressing. This can lead to further relaxation into your body over the long term and so is a helpful effect. Don't think you've got the meditation wrong if you start feeling emotional. And, remember, you can always stop the meditation if you feel too uncomfortable by simply opening your eyes and getting up.

✔ **Neither try too hard nor give up.** Use a balanced effort. If you try too hard to meditate, you'll get tired easily. If you don't put any effort in, you'll just fall asleep.

Think of meditation like training to run a race. You need to practise regularly to get better, and some days you may not enjoy it. Just because it's painful doesn't mean it's not helpful. So, with meditation, regular practice is the key. In the long term you do reap the rewards.

Discovering Mindfulness Meditation

Mindfulness is about cultivating awareness of the present moment with attitudes of kindness, curiosity and acceptance. Mindfulness has been shown to reduce stress, anxiety, depression, chronic pain and blood pressure and to accelerate the rate of healing from a range of medical conditions. The UK National Health Service recommends mindfulness for managing recurring depression.

Teaching mindfulness is one of my specialties. I like mindfulness because not only does it reduce my stress, but it also makes me more aware of my thoughts and emotions. I can practise mindfulness at any time and it helps me to appreciate the world around me. Being a scientist, I also like the fact that many research studies have shown the technique to be effective. For more on mindfulness, check out *Mindfulness For Dummies* by Shamash Alidina (Wiley).

In this section you'll discover how to practise five different mindfulness meditations of various lengths. By trying them out regularly you'll be able to determine if they help you feel more relaxed in the long-term.

Trying a breath meditation

Here's one of the most popular meditations in the world. It's called breath meditation or mindfulness of breath. It simply involves becoming more aware of the natural, physical sensation of your own breathing within your body. This seems to have a calming effect for people who practise the exercise everyday. Have a go for about five minutes or however long you wish to begin with.

1. **Find the right posture for you.**

   I explain this in the section 'Finding the right posture for you' earlier in this chapter.

2. **Close your eyes or let your eyes look softly downwards.**

3. **Make it your intention to stay relatively still for however long you plan to practise.**

4. **Take three deep breaths, breathing out for slightly longer than you breathe in.**

   This helps engage your sense of relaxation and also helps to focus your mind on your breath.

5. **Let your breath be natural and normal and simply feel the sensation of your breath.**

   You could feel the sensation of your breath around your nose, the back of your throat, chest, or in your belly, your lower abdomen. Feel your breath wherever you find the sensation is most predominant. If you feel uncomfortable to feel your breath, persevere if you can. You'll get used to it after a while.

6. **Each time you realise your mind has wandered off into other thoughts, ideas, images, worries or anything else, turn your attention back to your breath.**

   When you do so, take care not to criticise or judge yourself. Watch out for thoughts such as 'I can't do this right,' and, 'My mind is all over the place – this isn't for me.' These are just thoughts – don't take them to be true. Come back to feeling the sensation of your breath.

7. **After your allocated time is up, notice how you feel.**

   If you feel more relaxed and focused, great. If you don't, this is also extremely common, especially in meditation. Meditation is a long-term process and any sense of relaxation is a deep and powerful side effect that arises through regular practice.

Research shows that mindfulness actually rewires your brain in a positive way. This rewiring can be seen in brain scans after just a few weeks of daily practice.

Connecting with your senses mindfully

If you don't like focusing on your breath, or you want to try something different, you may like to try being mindful of your other senses. This is great fun and wakes you up to a totally different way of living from day-to-day. Rather than just constantly worrying about your personal issues and challenges, this is a way of opening up to the world around you. Paradoxically, by turning your attention to one of your senses in a deliberate way, you're better able to notice and manage your own inner thoughts and feelings positively.

1. **Sit or lie in a comfortable posture.**

2. **Connect with the sensations of your body as a whole.**

   Maybe you can feel the sensations of your feet on the floor or perhaps the weight of your body on the chair that you're sitting on. Feel the touch of your clothes against your skin if you can. And if you can't feel a particular sensation, that's okay – just notice the absence of sensation.

3. **Notice what you see in front of you.**

   Become aware of the range of different colours and tones. Remember that the experience of the colour blue, for example, is not the same as the experience itself. Notice the various shades of colour, the shape of objects and the sense of distance between you and the object. Allow the colours to enter your eyes rather than grasping the colour. Now gently close your eyes, or just move your attention to the next sense.

4. **Notice the scent in the air around you.**

   As you're naturally breathing in, become aware of the actual scent itself, rather than how you'd describe the smell. If you find yourself judging the scent with thoughts like, 'That's nice,' or, 'I don't like that,' notice these as just judgements and go back to the actual scent. Again, if you can't detect any scent, just accept that you can't – that's perfectly okay.

5. **Become aware of any sense of taste in your mouth.**

   You may be able to detect the after taste of a meal you've eaten. If there's no sense of taste that you can notice, just be aware of sensations in your mouth.

6. **Turn your attention to sounds.**

   Listen to the sounds you can hear in the room around you, even the sound of your own breathing. Maybe you can hear the sounds of people walking in the building that you're in, or the sounds of cars, planes or birds. Notice that you don't have to 'do' listening – sounds naturally enter your ears and your awareness picks up the sounds. Listen without labelling the sounds such as, 'Oh, that's a plane,' and, 'That sounds like the heating coming on.' If you can, listen to the pitch and volume of the sound, just as you would when listening to a piece of music.

7. Bring the meditation to a close by letting go of all effort to practise mindfulness and just 'be'.

Let go of all sense of 'doing' or 'trying' and just rest in your own inner sense of 'presence' or 'aliveness'.

This whole meditation can take up to 20 minutes. You can choose how much time you wish to invest in it.

Engaging in mindful sitting meditation

This mindful sitting meditation has been well tested and proven to reduce stress for most people if practised on a daily basis. It involves mindfulness in five stages – mindfulness of breath, body, sounds, thoughts and then what is called choiceless awareness. You can practise this meditation for as long as you wish, but often people spend about five minutes or so on each stage, so the meditation can take about 30 minutes. As a beginner, start with practising just one stage, and gradually add more stages as you become more proficient in the technique.

1. Begin with a breath meditation for about five minutes.

Read the section 'Trying a breath meditation' earlier in this chapter for full details.

2. Turn your attention to your bodily sensations.

Get a sense of your body as a whole as you sit there. Notice how the sensations flux and change, or stay the same, from moment to moment. Do this sensing of your body for about five minutes.

3. Open your attention to sounds.

Listen to the sounds around you as though you're listening to your favourite piece of music. Try not to label or judge the sounds. Do this listening to sounds for about five minutes

4. Turn your attention inwards.

Listen to your thoughts like you were listening to sounds. Avoid judging your thoughts. If you don't seem to have any thoughts, just listen to the silence in between. This is not easy. If you like, imagine clouds passing through the sky and place each of your thoughts on the clouds and watch them come and go. Do this listening to thoughts for about five minutes

5. Practise choiceless awareness.

Just be aware of whatever is most predominant in your awareness – it could be breath, body, sounds, physical sensations, thoughts or emotions. Continue for five minutes.

6. Bring your practice gently to a close.

Go about your everyday activities with a mindful awareness, rather than automatically rushing from one task to another.

This sitting meditation usually takes about 30 minutes but you can just start with doing the first five minutes and build it up by five minutes every week or so. Go at your own pace – don't force yourself too much. Enjoy the process if you can.

Practising a body scan meditation

This mindfulness meditation helps many of my clients to fall asleep. However, I also recommend that you use it in the morning or afternoon to train your mind to reduce stress and become more mindful.

The benefits of this mindfulness exercise include a greater awareness of your body enabling you to notice stress creeping up in your body, as well as a greater ability to focus your attention and an ability to move your attention from one object to another. The mindfulness of bodily sensations seems to naturally release tension over time.

1. Lie on a mat, the floor or your bed.

Allow your arms to be a little distance away from your body with your palms facing upwards.

2. Remember that mindfulness is about allowing things to be as they are, rather than trying to change yourself, or improve.

Remember that deep down, you're okay just the way you are.

3. Become aware of the sensation of your breathing in your belly area for a few minutes.

4. Move your attention all the way down to your feet.

Notice any sensations there. If you can't feel anything, just be aware of the lack of sensation. You're doing it correctly even if you can't feel anything.

5. Continue to slowly move your attention up your body.

From your feet go to your lower legs, then to your upper legs, hips, pelvis, buttocks, lower abdomen and back, chest and upper back, hands, arms, shoulders, neck, face, top of your head.

6. Be aware of each part of your body, together with the sensation of your own breathing.

Concentrating in this way deepens your awareness of each sensation.

7. **End the practice by imagining your breath sweeping up and down your body, filling each of your cells with nourishing oxygen.**

   Just rest, lying down, doing nothing for a few minutes before you get up. Avoid rushing into your next activity. Go about your day with a quality of mindfulness.

Your mind will lose attention and you'll think about anything and everything. That's okay. Just as soon as you notice, bring your attention back to the body scan. You may even feel a bit worse as if it's not working. Don't worry about that. Practise every day for a few weeks before you judge if this exercise is right for you.

Using regular mini-meditations

Many of my clients like mini-meditations best of all. Some call them life-changing. They are short, easy to do, and can be practised at any time of day when you have a few minutes to spare. The mini-meditations can also be practised when you feel overwhelmed with a difficult series of thoughts, emotions or bodily sensations.

Simply practising the mindfulness of breath meditation, described earlier in the section 'Trying a breath meditation', can be used as a mini-meditation.

In the inside-out mini-meditation, you begin by turning your attention inwards, and then expand your attention outwards. It's an ideal meditation at work when you have a few minutes spare, or are trying to calm yourself down before an important meeting or presentation:

1. **Find the right posture for you and switch off any possible distractions. Close your eyes if you prefer.**

   Take deep, slow in breaths and out breaths for 30 seconds.

2. **Turn your attention inwards and scan through your body, from the soles of your feet to the top of your head.**

   Let go of any excess tension if you can for about 30 seconds.

3. **Become aware of any emotions you detect within you.**

   If you can feel an emotion, notice where in your body you feel the emotion, if anywhere. See if you can just accept the emotion for about 30 seconds.

4. **Notice any thoughts that arise in your mind.**

   You may notice many thoughts or no thoughts at all. Your experience is correct, whatever it is. Just watch your thoughts for about 30 seconds.

5. **Turn your mindful awareness to your breathing.**

   Feel each in-breath and each out-breath, for about a minute. Alternatively, count five mindful breaths and feel each breath as you count.

6. **Turn your attention mindfully outwards to sounds.**

   Listen to the sounds around you, without moving. Just listen. You may have thoughts like, 'Oh, I need to call Michael about that report,' or 'I need to email Sue about lunch on Tuesday,' but just acknowledge and then ignore these thoughts and turn your attention to sounds. Just listen to sounds, without labelling, for about a minute.

7. **Gently open your eyes if they've been closed, and bring your attention fully to your surroundings.**

   To finish, think about something that you're grateful for to help you to move on in a positive, and hopefully, a little more relaxed, way.

This meditation takes about four minutes but can totally change your state of mind. And even if your state of mind doesn't change, being aware of your own inner thoughts and feelings is helpful.

Try to sit upright for the mini-meditation as you then send a signal to your brain that you're doing something different, rather than just daydreaming. Body posture has been shown to have a direct effect on your state of mind.

Exploring Relaxation Response Meditation

The relaxation response meditation is a well-tested meditation technique that's free of any particular religious creed, dogma, or belief. Dr Herbert Benson of Harvard University first came up with the term *relaxation response* when he tested people who practised transcendental meditation. Benson removed the religious roots of the technique that some people found questionable and found the method to be just as effective. He was then able to make the approach accessible to anyone.

See Chapter 1 for the low-down on the relaxation response.

When your body uses less oxygen, it's a sign that you're more relaxed. Oxygen consumption was found to be lower after three minutes of relaxation response meditation – as good as five hours of sleep. This suggests that deep relaxation can be achieved very quickly in meditation, even deeper than sleep.

Benson considered that a passive attitude is one of the most important aspects of meditation. Here are some of the thoughts that go with a passive attitude:

- ✔ 'I'll focus my attention on the word, but if my mind wanders off into other thoughts, that's part of the process.'
- ✔ 'I'm not going to try too hard. . . the relaxation will come by itself. I don't need to force myself to get relaxed.'
- ✔ 'If my mind wanders, I'll just think "Oh well" and turn my attention back to my focus.'

Choosing a relaxation response phrase

For the relaxation response meditation, you need to choose a word or phrase to use during the meditation. You can choose either a neutral word like 'one' or a word that has positive aspect to it, like 'peace', 'calm', or 'relax'. If you find a word or phrase soothing, your positive belief will reinforce the relaxation response.

If you have a religious faith, you may like to choose a phrase from your particular tradition that is meaningful for you.

Whatever phrase you choose, let the word be one you feel comfortable with. If you're filled with indecision, don't worry about what to choose, almost any word will suffice.

Trying the relaxation response meditation

Begin by reading through the instructions below and then have a go if you have time. After a few practices, you probably won't need these instructions. Start by practising for ten minutes, twice a day, and after a week increase to 15 minutes, twice a day, if you have time. From the third week, practise for up to 20 minutes, twice a day.

Experiments have shown that 10–20 minutes of this meditation, once or twice a day, lead to significant benefits.

1. **Find a quiet place to sit, in a comfortable posture.**

   You can lean against the back of a chair if you wish. If sitting isn't possible, you can lie down. Be comfortable, but not so much that you fall asleep.

2. **Let your eyes close gently.**

3. **Let your muscles relax as much as you can.**

   Scan your attention through your body, from your feet up to your head. If there's any tension still there that doesn't release, that's fine, you don't need to worry about that.

4. **Breathe through your nose if you can.**

   Each time you breathe out, recite your chosen word, phrase or prayer silently to yourself. For example, breathe in, breathe out and say to yourself 'calmmmm'. And simply repeat the process. Let your breathing be normal and natural. If your breathing slows down, don't worry – it's a natural effect of relaxation.

5. **Each time you lose concentration due to other thoughts, go back to saying the word silently to yourself.**

   Don't judge yourself. Be nice to yourself instead. Just maintain a passive attitude and allow the relaxation to happen by itself. You could just say to yourself, 'Oh well' and go back to your chosen word or phrase.

6. **To check whether your time for meditation has finished, have a guess and open your eyes to confirm.**

   I don't recommend using an alarm, as the noise may startle you.

7. **When your meditation time is up, stop repeating your chosen phrase.**

   Rest quietly with your eyes closed for a few minutes.

8. **Gently open your eyes.**

   Rest for a few more minutes, before you go back to your daily activities.

A passive attitude is the key to this exercise and probably all meditation and relaxation techniques. Being passive means having an attitude of, 'Let things be as they are.'

You can record how relaxed you felt at the beginning and end of the meditation in your relaxation journal (see Chapter 3) if you use one. You can also write about or illustrate your experience to explore what else you can learn about your capacity to relax through this meditation.

Exploring Alternative Meditations

Thousands of different types of meditation exist. By finding a meditation that you're drawn to, you're more likely to practise on a regular basis and enjoy the fruit of your efforts. In this section I describe a few more meditations that you may like to try.

Gazing at an object

I used to know an art teacher who practised meditation. However, he found that when he closed his eyes, his mind was filled with visual images that just distracted him. So, he always meditated with his eyes open. This prevented him feeling overwhelmed by dreamy imagery and helped him to focus.

You can try the meditations in this section if you like visual stimulation or want to try something different. They are ideal ways to develop a sense of both calm and focus.

Candle flame meditation

You can find many different ways to do a candle flame meditation. Here's one of them. This meditation is best practised at home – it doesn't seem to go down too well at work!

1. **Prepare your space.**

   Turn down any bright lighting and draw your curtains. You'll probably find this meditation easier to concentrate on in lower lighting.

2. **Sit cross-legged on the floor or cushion, or sit on a suitable chair.**

3. **Centre yourself.**

   Feel the sensation of your natural breathing for a minute or so, with your eyes closed.

4. **Light your candle and place either at eye-level or slightly below.**

   Get the distance right for you; too far away and you'll have difficulty focusing, and too close and you'll be overcome with the heat and smoke of the flame.

5. **As you light the candle, think of this meditation as a chance to shed light in your inner world and bring a quality of warmth and cosiness, just as a candle does.**

6. **Fix your gaze on the candle flame.**

   Let your attention rest on the visual flame itself.

7. **Each time your mind wanders off, without criticising yourself, bring your attention back to the flame.**

8. **If your eyes begin to water, close your eyes.**

   You'll see an impression of the flame behind your eyelids. Focus on that image. After the image fades away, open your eyes again.

9. **After ten minutes or so, bring the meditation to a close.**

   Notice how you feel as you go about your normal activities.

Imagine breathing in a sense of light and peace as you breathe in, and breathing out any stress or tension as you breathe out.

If your eyes hurt when you do candle flame meditation, it's better to avoid it, just as a precaution. Try the flower meditation below instead.

Flower gazing meditation

You can practise this meditation indoors with a flower on your desk or outdoors in nature. If you don't have a flower available, you can even try the practice with a picture of a flower on a photo, computer screen or phone. Not quite as effective, but better than nothing.

1. **Sit in a comfortable posture.**

   Turn off any potential distractions.

2. **Place a flower in front of you, at a comfortable distance so you can see it.**

3. **Take a few deep breaths to centre yourself.**

   Begin looking at the flower.

4. **Notice the colours, shape and the way the flower stands.**

   Look at the flower as if for the first time. The idea is to look at the flower itself, rather than to think about the flower. Imagine you're a child that doesn't know what the flower is called and doesn't know the name of its features. Look with awe and curiosity if you can – it's an amazing creation of nature.

5. **After ten minutes or so, slowly bring your attention back to your surroundings.**

You don't have to use a flower. You could look at a plant, a tree, or almost anything. The idea is to focus your attention on the object. Each time your mind wanders off into other thoughts, bring your attention back in a friendly way.

Trying metta (loving kindness) meditation

Metta is an Eastern term for loving kindness or friendliness. In this meditation practice, you use words and phrases to develop a sense of kindness towards yourself and others. This feeling is strongly associated with relaxation and so is an ideal way to both relax and ensure that you're resilient to future stressful situations. There has been a lot of exciting research recently on this type of meditation, which has been proven to have many positive long-term benefits – it improves relationships, makes you feel happier and protects you from stress.

Here's a metta meditation. You don't need to be able to do all the stages right away. Just move through the guidance at your own pace:

1. **Find a suitable posture for you.**

   You can sit or lie down. Take particular care to ensure you're comfortable and warm and feel secure for this meditation. You can either have your eyes closed or gently open.

2. **Turn your attention to the feeling of your breath.**

   Take a few deep breaths, down into your belly if you can. Now return to natural breathing.

3. **When you're ready, move your attention to the area of your heart.**

   Notice any feelings or sensations here.

4. **Allow words that you most desire for yourself to arise from the area of your heart.**

   Choose something long-lasting and that you would wish for all beings. Here are some examples:

   'May I be peaceful.' 'May I be relaxed.' 'May I be happy.' 'May I be free from suffering.'

5. **Let your phrases softly resonate within your being.**

   Say the phrases softly to yourself, with a sense of warmth and affection. If no feelings arise, that's fine. Your intention is the key.

6. **Bring to your awareness someone you care about.**

   Recall a good friend or someone inspiring. You can either imagine the person if you find that easy, or get a sense of their presence. Then use your phrases in the following way:

   'May you be peaceful.' 'May you be relaxed.' 'May you be happy.' 'May you be free from suffering.'

7. **Follow Step 6 for a neutral person.**

   Think of someone you may see regularly but have no particular like or dislike of.

8. **Follow Step 6 for a difficult person.**

   Think of someone you have trouble getting on with or just don't like.

9. **Imagine all three people and yourself and wish them all loving kindness using your phrases.**

   Try to send equal amounts of loving kindness to all, including yourself.

10. **Expand your sense of loving kindness to the whole universe.**

    You may be able to get a sense of loving kindness radiating out from your being, or visualise rays of positive energy from your heart area. Wishing all living beings, the whole of nature, peace and happiness.

11. **Bring the meditation to a close by spending a few moments feeling your breathing.**

You may not feel any emotion when you do the metta meditation. That's okay and a common observation. As long as you bring an attitude to kindness and use the metta phrases, you'll gain some benefit. Through regular practice you may occasionally be able to feel some warmth and affection.

You can spend the whole metta meditation on one phase if you want. For example, you can send metta to your friend or yourself for the whole meditation. The easier you make the meditation for yourself, the more you get out of the process.

Chapter 11

Spirituality and Prayer

- -

In This Chapter

▶ Exploring what prayer and spirituality mean for you

▶ Discovering ways to find inner peace through prayer

▶ Understanding the importance of spirituality to feel calm and grounded

- -

Every one who is seriously involved in the pursuit of science becomes convinced that a spirit is manifest in the laws of the Universe – a spirit vastly superior to that of man, and one in the face of which we with our modest powers must feel humble.

Albert Einstein

*B*efore you roll your eyes and skip to the next chapter, I encourage you to take some time to look through this chapter, especially if you feel sceptical. By 'spiritual' I don't necessarily mean soul or God or a need for organised religion. And although prayer is traditionally directed towards a higher power, even if you're an atheist you can still experience feelings of connectedness, wonder, awe or humility. I call these experiences spiritual. If you're more religiously inclined, you may find some of the ideas in the section on prayer helpful, and they may help lead you to a deeper sense of relaxation and ease of being.

If you have no deeper experience of life beyond your normal everyday activities and feel a sense of dissatisfaction with life, spiritual relaxation may be your answer. Perhaps you have a feeling of emptiness or a sense that something is missing in your life. You may be in a happy relationship, have a lovely family and wonderful friends, and yet you feel anxious or unhappy in some way. Try some of the different exercises in this section and see what effect they have. Even just reading and reflecting as you read may create a helpful shift within yourself.

By spirituality I mean either a religious experience with God, or a human experience of intense emotions such as awe, wonder, peace, joy or connectedness. You don't need to be religious to experience spirituality – you just need to be alive and open to something beyond your everyday routine.

Creating Spiritual Relaxation

We aren't human beings having a spiritual experience. We're spiritual beings having a human experience.

Teilhard de Chardin

In this section I clarify what I mean by 'spirituality' and explore ways to tap into this part of your human nature to find some peace and calm in your life.

Spirituality means different things to different people. At its heart, spirituality is about your connection to yourself and others, developing your own personal values, and searching for meaning and purpose in your life.

For some people, spirituality is to do with religion, prayer, God, meditation, faith and a higher power. Other people find spirituality through art, nature, charity work or even a secular community.

Defining spirituality

Spirituality is about natural human experience. The following examples of spiritual experiences have been identified by the Royal College of Psychiatrists in the UK, who think that spirituality is an important part of mental wellbeing.

Spirituality is an experience of:

- A deep sense of meaning and purpose in life
- A sense of belonging
- A sense of connection of 'the deeply personal with the universal'
- Acceptance and a sense of wholeness

All these experiences are natural human feelings that don't necessarily need belief in a particular religion.

When you face a difficulty in your life, such as the death of a loved one, you are hurt emotionally. The various relaxation exercises in this book may help you manage the stress to a certain extent, but without a deeper understanding of what the event tells you about life and death, healing cannot take place.

The word 'heal' originally meant 'to make whole'. Difficulties in your life may have made you feel fragmented or broken. Spirituality offers practices for you to re-embrace your inner sense of wholeness.

Spirituality recognises that life has its ups and downs, and that's the way it is. To resist challenges, to see them as problems to be constantly avoided, leads to a life lived with fear and insecurity. A deeper understanding of life, of the inevitability of change, results in a more peaceful and accepting state of mind.

All religions involve spirituality, but spirituality is not limited to religion. As a human being, you can have a range of different spiritual experiences without any religious belief.

Discovering the benefits of spirituality

Greater spirituality leads to relaxation and a sense of wellbeing in four main areas. Before you practise some of the spiritual exercises in this chapter to develop and deepen your inner experience of your own spirituality, consider some of the benefits of this inner connection:

- ✔ **Greater spirituality gives a higher sense of self-confidence, self-esteem and self-control.** If you see the way in which you connect to the greater whole, you feel more secure in who you are. This security leads to more positive feelings about yourself.

- ✔ **Greater spirituality encourages healthier recovery from loss.** One of the biggest challenges you face in life is the loss of a close relationship. Spirituality can help you to see this loss in a different light, in a way that strengthens you rather than just leaving a painful vacuum. You see the loss as a chance to reflect on the good times of the past and to really value what you still have in the present.

- ✔ **Greater spirituality leads to improved relationships.** Relationships are about connection. And so is spirituality. You develop a stronger and more positive relationship with yourself, those around you and with God, nature or the universe.

- ✔ **Greater spirituality lets you accept inevitable difficulties of life.** Through having a deeper meaning in life you are able to see beyond the immediate difficulties you face. For example, if you have arthritis in your knee, you may see this as an opportunity to learn to be mindful with a painful sensation, and grateful that the rest of your body doesn't have the same disease.

All of these benefits lead to a greater resilience to the inevitable stresses that you face as you journey through life. In a way, spirituality is simply a different way of seeing life other than you as a tiny human being fighting to survive in a dangerous world. Your difficulties become a series of lessons to discover what life is about, and to seek opportunities to connect with the more important things in life. Pleasant moments are a chance to be grateful for your good fortune.

Secular spirituality through mindfulness

One of the reasons I became a teacher of mindfulness was its all-encompassing secular approach to wellbeing and, if you want it, spirituality. Mindfulness offers a set of techniques, as well as a way of being, that helps you to relax, to understand your emotions, and even reflect on your personal identity. For some people, mindfulness meditation is a way of tuning in to their spiritual selves without any need for joining an organised religion or belief in God. For others with religious beliefs, mindfulness offers a way of deepening their connection with a higher being. After all, the word religion comes from the Latin *religare*, meaning 'to reconnect'. Perhaps that means to connect with your own wholeness, or the greater whole, which we call the universe.

Exploring your spirituality

It is possible to explore your own spirituality through doing a writing exercise. In this section you can try reflecting on a series of deep questions that help to clarify your innermost values and beliefs. This makes a useful starting point in your journey towards a more meaningful, satisfying and relaxing life.

To do this exercise, plan to have about an hour or so to complete. The more unhurried you are, the more you'll enjoy the process and discover new insights. Turn off any potential distractions and use your relaxation journal (see Chapter 3) or notepad. Have a go at writing down the answers to the following questions. These notes are for you and no one else has to see them, so be totally honest if you can. If drawing, or some other medium, seems a more natural response for you, then go ahead and do that.

- ✔ In what ways are you spiritual or religious, if any?
- ✔ What has helped you through your difficult times in life in the past?
- ✔ What gives your life meaning or purpose?
- ✔ Consider your current problem or challenge. Could there be a spiritual solution to the problem? If so, what could that be?
- ✔ What, if anything, gives you hope?
- ✔ Are you worried about dying or death? Do you believe in an afterlife and, if so, what are your thoughts about it?
- ✔ Do you feel in any way connected with God, nature, creation or the universe? And if so, how? What does this connection mean to you?

After you finish writing or drawing your responses to these questions, reflect on how you feel about the experience. Do you feel like you know more about yourself and your spirituality? Try the exercise again in a month's time and see whether your responses differ; if so, reflect on what has changed for you.

Engaging in spiritual practices

There are two ways to live: you can live as if nothing is a miracle; you can live as if everything is a miracle.

Albert Einstein

Spirituality is about experience. Through practising spiritual exercises, you increase the possibility of enjoying a spiritual experience that leads to a deep insight about you and your place in the universe.

Try not to see the exercises as prescriptive and remember that you don't need to follow them to the dot. Spiritual practices that feel as if they are your own are more engaging and enjoyable. Always do what feels right for you, rather than feeling forced to follow my particular instructions. And keep an open mind for maximum benefits.

Looking at different spiritual exercises

Spirituality is a deeply personal experience and you will discover it in your own way. Begin by having some daily quiet time, some opportunity to read spiritual material, whatever that means for you, and making friends with others who share a similar spiritual outlook.

Spirituality is not something you either do have or don't have. You can develop your spiritual side with a range of different exercises and some of them are not that difficult.

See whether any of the following spiritual exercises appeal to you:

- ✔ **Make time to meditate or pray.** Prayer and meditation help you to connect with your inner self and develop a deeper relationship with yourself – a key aspect of spirituality for many people.

- ✔ **Be grateful.** Gratitude is an opportunity to reflect on how fortunate you are rather than just what's missing. Simply think of five things that you're grateful for each evening before going to bed. You can find out more about gratitude exercises in Chapter 13.

- ✔ **Let everything be your teacher.** This way of looking at life is considered as a spiritual attitude towards daily living. When you're faced with a problem, trying to see how you can profit from it can be helpful. For example, when you lose your job, it's so easy, and to a large extent understandable, to focus on the problem. But your loss of job can also be seen as an opportunity to make a fresh start in a brand new position. You may even be grateful for the chance to do something new and different.

✔ **Be intrinsic.** Some people are extrinsically spiritual – they're spiritual in order to make more friends or join a community. They also like to be seen as religious. However, research seems to suggest that people who are intrinsically spiritual – spiritual for the sake of personal meaning and inner motivation – enjoy greater benefits. Practise spiritual exercises, prayers and meditations because you think it's important rather than doing it mechanically to satisfy someone else.

✔ **Spend time enjoying nature.** Nature can be inspiring and beautiful. Being in nature reminds you of your connection with the earth. Reflecting on how your very ancient ancestors were, in a way, plants and animals makes you feel part of a huge family.

✔ **Explore your creativity.** Engaging in creative activities that you like, such as art, writing, cooking or gardening, evokes a sense of wonder and joyous unpredictability. You don't really know how things will turn out. The mystery of creativity has a mystical and awe-inspiring dimension to it. You may not always feel creative but, even once in a while, just trying to be creative is rewarding.

✔ **Read literature that encourages reflection, such as poetry and philosophy.** Explore different poets and philosophers. You can even join a poetry or philosophy club that leans towards spiritual reflection and discussion.

✔ **Listen to your intuition.** Sense what you need to do or say by tuning into your inner self. Focusing your attention in the area of your gut (gut feeling) may help, as this is where many people sense their inner voice of guidance.

Practising forgiveness

To forgive is to set a prisoner free and discover that the prisoner was you.

Lewis B. Smedes

When someone hurts you, feeling angry and holding a grudge against him or her is a natural response. But this kind of attitude is not helpful for your long-term health. Forgiveness is another way of dealing with the situation that has many benefits, including relaxation.

Everyone has had the experience of being hurt at some time. Perhaps a teacher at school always criticised you, or your partner always forgets your birthday. You're left with feelings of anger and frustration, but if you don't ever forgive, you continue to hold that pain within you. Holding on to the anger is like holding on to a hot piece of coal – you're burning yourself rather than the other person.

Forgiveness is a decision. You're deciding to stop holding on to thoughts of resentment and are seeing the situation from a different perspective. You're hurt, but you decide to stop thinking in a constantly negative way towards the other person. Forgiveness is about letting go and moving on. You may even develop feelings of compassion for the other person.

Forgiveness doesn't mean that the other person behaved reasonably. You can forgive someone's actions without believing that what they did was right. If you forgive your partner for forgetting your birthday, it doesn't mean that the forgetting wasn't important to you. You simply let go of what has already happened and give lots of subtle clues next year to help them! Through forgiveness you're choosing peace rather than bitterness for yourself.

One way of seeing this is to forgive the person, but not the act. So you may forgive John but you're not happy with what John did that day.

Here are some of the benefits of forgiving:

✔ Greater general feeling of relaxation

✔ Improved relationships

✔ Greater sense of wellbeing

✔ Lower blood pressure

✔ Reduced episodes of anxiety or depression

Here's how to forgive:

1. **Understand the grudge that you're holding is hurting you.**

   Although you may be thinking about how awful it was for the perpetrator to do that, he or she has probably moved on and is doing something else.

2. **List the positives of the perpetrator.**

   You've probably been focusing on the negatives and wrongs that the perpetrator has done. Now may be a good time to try to write down five positive things that have come from the event. Doing so isn't easy but may help you to feel a bit better and see things from another angle.

3. **See the bigger picture.**

   Although the situation may have been difficult for you, it may have given others the opportunity to help you, and feel better for doing that. So others gaining from the situation sometimes makes it a bit easier to forgive.

4. **Be kind to yourself.**

   Getting hurt by someone is painful and although there may not be any physical scars, the emotional pain can be even more difficult. So be nice to yourself and don't expect to be able to instantly forgive. Allow yourself time and space to feel the emotions and work through them in your own time.

184 Part III: Discovering Relaxation Techniques Using Your Mind and Heart

5. **Forgiveness doesn't mean you have to trust someone.**

If someone has behaved wrongly towards you, understand that the forgiveness is for you, not for them. You are freeing yourself from unnecessary hurt long after the incident has happened. If you have reason to believe that the person is not trustworthy and may hurt you again, either stay away from them or deal with them appropriately, including reporting them to authorities if necessary.

6. **Stop repeating the story in your head.**

You may find yourself replaying the past situation in your head again and again. This process isn't helpful and just makes the circumstance more painful for you.

7. **Tell the story from the other person's perspective.**

This technique is difficult but powerful. Imagine seeing the whole situation from the perpetrator's perspective. Try to think what their motives are, why they do the things they do, and behave in a particular way. Take this one step further and sit with a friend and tell them the story from your perpetrator's perspective. Changing your own way of seeing the situation helps you move towards forgiveness.

8. **Send good wishes.**

This powerful way of retraining your brain isn't easy. Each time you get a negative thought about the perpetrator, wish them well. You could think 'I hope they get their life sorted out soon' or 'I hope that they settle down and find some happiness'. Although offering good wishes may seem totally artificial at first, if you keep practising, you may even generate some genuine feelings. This sense of compassion is very healing for your own body and mind.

Nurturing loving kindness

This deep spiritual exercise is covered in Chapter 10 on meditation. Give it a try if you haven't already done so.

Volunteering your time

Volunteering for a particular cause obviously has benefits for the cause, but also offers a range of benefits for you.

When you volunteer, you tend to stop thinking about yourself and start thinking about others. Volunteering encourages connection with those around you and connection helps to ease stress and increase your feeling of relaxation. Spirituality is about meaning, purpose and relationships as much as anything else – volunteering helps to offer you all those things. You feel like you're making a positive difference in the world and you're bound to meet others and communicate in a positive way. Giving your time has been shown not only to relax you but also to boost your overall wellbeing.

Michael was a high-powered executive in his late 20s working in Los Angeles when he started losing his hair due to the tremendous stress he was under. He thought enough is enough, left his job and found part-time work. In the rest of his time, he signed up to volunteer as a tutor. He immediately began to feel better. A couple of years later he said 'I feel happier, get on more positively with my partner, and my hair isn't falling out any more'. He was only volunteering one afternoon a week but that made all the difference. Find out how you can do a bit of volunteering to see what effect it has on your life.

Using Prayer to Relax

Most major religions emphasise the importance of prayer. But what is prayer? And what's the purpose? And is there any scientific evidence to suggest that prayer helps you to relax in addition to any 'spiritual' benefit?

Prayer is usually a religious practice to create a communion with God or spirit. Prayer can be either individual or in a group setting. Prayer can also be not just words but a song, like a hymn for example. Prayer exists in many forms and can be directed to a deity, another person, or even an ideal. Prayers can be used for the sake of worship, help or guidance, to confess sins, or simply to express your thoughts.

You may have the idea that prayer needs to use complex words and eloquent language – this isn't true. Being honest and genuine is more fulfilling and enjoyable.

I have been exposed to a wide range of religious communities. My mother was brought up in a Hindu tradition, my father was raised in the Muslim tradition, and I attended a Catholic school. Due to this upbringing, I began to see the similarities and differences of different religions. However, I didn't think of myself as spiritual. I enjoyed science and felt the subject offered answers to pretty much everything, until I had a conversation with friends one summer's evening after lectures. From that moment on, I've always enjoyed reflecting on both scientific ideas and the possibility of a non-physical, universal, all-encompassing, 'intelligence energy' that pervades the universe and beyond. That's what I call God.

Appreciating the power of prayer

People use prayer and spirituality to cope with life's difficulties. The benefits include being more able to cope with stress, and higher levels of health and wellbeing. By praying you also see things as part of a bigger picture and stop trying to take complete control of your life. All your responsibilities are no longer on your shoulders alone – you have a sense of being able to ask for help, spiritually, if not socially, through others.

In this chapter, I focus on how praying helps you to relax rather than whether or not your prayer requests are fulfilled. This subject is beyond the scope of this *For Dummies* book, which is big enough already.

One major study reported by the BBC found that people who pray regularly are much less likely to suffer from anxiety and depression. Incidentally, those who prayed more regularly had significantly higher self-esteem too.

A different study by the National Institute for Health Care Research on Canadian college students found that those who connected with their ministries, and probably prayed more, had fewer doctor visits and suffered less from stress during difficult times. They also had more positive feelings and lower levels of depression.

Seeing how prayer and spirituality affect your brain

Scientifically speaking, prayer has an observable effect on your brain. This new brain science called 'neurotheology' looks at the relationship between your brain and religious or spiritual experiences.

During prayer, the part of your brain that deals with focus and concentration lights up with electrical brain activity. So the chances are that you become better at focusing in your daily life through regular prayer, and better focus means less stress.

However, with deeper prayer, things get very interesting. A part of your brain called the parietal lobes calms down when you have a 'spiritual' experience, such as deep connectedness or oneness with your surroundings. The parietal lobes use your senses to create your sense of self or individuality. So, if you're going to have an experience of connectedness or oneness, you need to let go of your feeling of separateness.

The result of these discoveries doesn't necessarily mean that all spiritual experience is in the brain, but does mean spirituality can be observed scientifically in this way. Scientists have looked at people with brain damage to the parietal lobes and they were found to be more spiritual than the average person.

Interestingly, if you have lower stimulation of the parietal lobes, you're less self-centred and more likely to think about others – a trait which is often considered a spiritual practice.

Prayer is about creating a connection with your God or other power or force. This connection can be through thinking, speaking or listening. You can pray in your own way, using words and a style that suits you. Just try to allow your communication to come from your heart.

Finding a time and a place to pray

You can pray as little or as much as you feel comfortable with. But remember, if you're interested in putting prayer into your life, you do need to make time for it. Most people lead busy lives and forgetting about prayer is easy. One great tip is to put prayer into your daily routine. You could pray first thing in the morning, last thing at night, or around mealtimes. Alternatively, you could be conscious of your connection with God, a higher power, or whatever you pray to, throughout the day, and that is your prayer. During emotional and difficult times you may like to pray to help you get through your problems without feeling you're completely on your own. Prayer is a powerful way to get through times of despair.

In terms of location, you're not bound by any set rules unless you're following a particular religion. You might like to dedicate a place in your home for praying, with a few pictures or maybe some flowers and a place to light a candle or incense. Others prefer to just pray by their beds. Experiment and see what works for you. You could even pray on the bus to work, whilst walking to the station, or in the checkout queue. Just see what feels right for you.

Preparing to pray

Your preparation for prayer depends on your religious belief, if you have one. You may need to wash your hands and feet, have a shower or bath, sound a bell, lay a mat on the floor, or face in a specific direction. Do what feels right for you. If you're praying in your room and are surrounded by clutter, try taking a few minutes to clear a space. A physically clear area helps you to feel mentally and emotionally clear too. You could also do a short relaxation technique like deep breathing (see Chapter 5), yoga (see Chapter 7) or mindful walking (see Chapter 6) just to prepare your mind for prayer. None of these activities is essential but some people find them helpful.

Learning how to pray

You can communicate your prayer in several ways. You could simply say a prayer silently, out loud, or even sing. You don't have to make up a prayer on the spot – you can use a book of prayer or one that you have memorised.

Here are a few step-by-step instructions if you've never prayed before or want to try something new:

1. **Prepare to begin praying**.

   Turn off any potential distractions.

2. **Get comfortable.**

   Unless your particular religion dictates otherwise, sit or kneel, or choose any posture that you feel comfortable with. Make things easy for yourself, especially if you're praying for the first time in ages. Your eyes can be open or closed.

3. **Communicate.**

   You can communicate with your God, or a higher power, through thought or out loud. Just move your attention to your heart area and be totally honest if you can.

4. **Ask for guidance or support.**

   You can communicate about your current life situation and any challenges you're facing. You can ask for help. Remember to ask with a sense of humility. You can also ask a particular question that's in your mind and then listen for any subtle responses, either now or later.

5. **Think of others.**

   You can also pray for others, which is a nice way of thinking of other people rather than just yourself. You may find that praying for others deepens your experience and you can combine these prayers with some personal thoughts and requests for guidance or support as well.

6. **Express gratitude.**

   Use the opportunity to give thanks for what's going well in your life. This act of gratitude helps to deepen your sense of connection and increases your sense of wellbeing too.

7. **End the prayer.**

   End your prayer in a way that feels right for you. You can end with a word depending on your religion, or by bowing or making a religious sign in the air with your hand. Alternatively, you can remain quiet for a minute or so and enjoy the peace of your connection with a higher power.

In a nutshell, think of prayer as a chance to humbly ask for help for yourself or others, and a chance to express gratitude.

Trying a prayer for relaxation

One of the most common ways people deal with stress is to pray for help. Through prayer, people do find some peace and relaxation. Here's an example of a prayer you may use for helping you to relax through stressful times. You can fill in the dotted line with whatever is worrying you or of concern at the moment.

> *Dear God, I'm going through a difficult time in my life at the moment, and I'm feeling very stressed. The level of stress is high for me. Please help me find strength to get through this difficult time. You have been a solid support for me during the hardest times in my life, and I know you will help me to find a way through this one somehow. My main worries and concerns are. . . With your loving help I shall do my best to deal with the situation, in a way that's good for me and those close to me.*

I'd like to thank you for all the good things in my life like. . . Thank you for all you do for me and provide for me, even when I don't feel relaxed or at ease. And thank you for listening to me God. Here's another prayer you may like to try:

> *Dear God,*
>
> *Help me get through the stress of today*
>
> *So that I can feel a bit more relaxed tomorrow.*
>
> *I know that you give me challenges to help me learn and grow,*
>
> *And I know in my heart that you only want what's best for me.*
>
> *Please assist me to remove the barriers that prevent me*
>
> *From enjoying the beauty and peace of your creation to the fullest.*
>
> *Can you offer some advice and guidance to me now or later? Thank you!*
>
> *I also pray for all the people around the world who are suffering*
>
> *Through lack of food, shelter or any other reason.*
>
> *Help them to find some peace and joy dear God.*

Chapter 12

Managing Your Mind

In This Chapter

▶ Exploring well-researched mind techniques to reduce stress

▶ Discovering the power of positive but realistic thinking

▶ Understanding how to solve your problems to help you relax

 Be master of mind rather than mastered by mind.

Zen proverb

If you want to relax but don't enjoy techniques based on relaxing your body, you may want to consider ways of relaxing by managing your mind. Several well-proven techniques exist to help you get back in the driving seat of your life. I describe some of these approaches in this chapter. I recommend you try them out if you have excessive stress – you may learn skills to last you a lifetime.

For me, the relaxation techniques based on the approaches in this chapter work better than more physical approaches to relaxation. I have always had a fascination with psychology, philosophy, neuroscience and mindfulness disciplines that explore the world of thoughts and feelings. However, you may be different and that's perfectly okay. I suggest you give each technique at least a few goes and then settle into an approach that naturally suits your temperament. Everyone's different – do what works for you.

Using Cognitive Behavioural Techniques to Relax

Cognitive behavioural techniques come from a well-researched form of therapy called cognitive behavioural therapy, or CBT.

CBT helps you change your thinking (the cognitive bit) and the way you act (the behaviour bit). Using CBT techniques can help you feel more relaxed.

Unlike many other therapies, CBT focuses on the present rather than on resolving the past, offering ways to make you feel better rapidly.

CBT is helpful for reducing stress and many mental health issues. Regular use of CBT techniques can make you feel more relaxed and resilient to future stressors.

Breaking problems into five areas

CBT works by breaking down your problem into five key areas: your situation (the event or circumstance preventing you from relaxing), your thoughts, your emotions, your body sensations and your actions. I show the connection between these five areas in Figure 12-1.

Figure 12-1:
Diagram
showing
relationships
between
situation,
thoughts,
emotions
and actions.

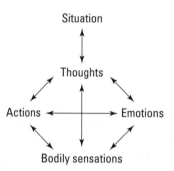

CBT reduces your stress by encouraging you to think differently or act differently:

- ✔ **Think in a more helpful way.** If the way you're currently thinking about a situation is negative and unhelpful, CBT helps you make your thoughts more helpful, leading to more manageable emotions, body sensations and actions.

- ✔ **Act in a more helpful way.** CBT encourages you to act in a different way in order to change your thinking and feelings. For example, if you feel low and think negatively, the best thing may be for you to go for a walk – this action helps to lift your mood and makes you feel less stressed. Your thoughts then become more positive and hopeful.

The following short exercise is designed to show you that the way in which you think about a situation affects how you feel and act.

*Imagine you plan to meet your friend in a coffee shop at noon. You turn
up a few minutes early, buy a drink and sit down, waiting for your friend
to arrive. The time continues to tick by and noon comes and goes, but your
friend doesn't turn up. Notice what you think and feel about this situation.
You continue to look at the clock and time goes to 12.15 p.m., 12.20 p.m.,
12.30 p.m. Still no sign of your friend. What do you think? What do you feel?
What do you do?*

If you think, 'My friend doesn't care about me' you probably feel low and
don't speak with your friend for a while. If you think, 'I hope my friend's
okay,' you feel concerned about your friend and try to contact him or her.

Consider the following quote:

Men are disturbed not by things, but by the view which they take of them.

This is a quote from the Greek philosopher, Epictetus, about 2,000 years ago.
The insight he had is often quoted in CBT sessions.

Your thoughts have a very powerful effect on how you feel. Although you
may be convinced that your life situation is the cause of your stress, actually
your thoughts also play a big part. If you didn't already know this, you may
find this insight alone life changing.

Situations themselves don't cause stress in your life. It's what you *think*
about the situation that causes the stress. Research shows that the way you
act, and even your body posture, can impact on how you feel about a challenge in your life.

An easy way to feel better is simply to sit up straight and ease off the frown
on your face. You then trick your brain into thinking you feel better, and you
actually do begin to feel better.

Understanding your mind with the ABC model

The ABC model is an easy way for you to understand CBT. The letters stand
for the following:

A – Activating event: The situation that causes you stress.

B – Belief: Includes the thoughts that go through your mind during the
situation or what you think about the situation afterwards.

C – Consequences: Your emotions and the actions that you take.

This ABC model is often recorded in a form like the one below. The idea is that you complete the form yourself after experiencing a challenging situation in your life. Each column represents the activating event, the belief and the consequence. By completing the form, you become clearer about the reasons why you feel the way you do. Later on you'll learn how to change your thinking to make you feel less stressed too.

Table 12-1 shows an ABC model on a form for someone who feels anxious about their upcoming exam.

Table 12-1	An Example of an ABC Model		
Activating event	*Belief/thoughts*	*Consequences*	*Action*
I have a maths exam next week.	I'm going to fail. I haven't done enough revision. I hate maths.	Feel anxious.	Go out with friends to avoid stressful feeling.

Table 12-1 breaks down a stressful situation, in this case someone's upcoming maths exam, into thoughts, emotions and actions.

Table 12-2 shows an example of a slightly different form. In this case you have the situation (activating event) in the first column, and then examples of unhelpful and helpful thoughts about the situation. Each thought is followed by emotions, bodily sensations and actions. Unhelpful thoughts are thoughts that make you feel more stressed, perhaps unnecessarily. Helpful thoughts are thoughts that are more realistic, don't jump to conclusions and may make you a little concerned rather than anxious or stressed.

In Table 12-2 someone has filled in the situation with their initial unhelpful thoughts, followed by a more helpful way of seeing the situation.

Table 12-2	An Example of Unhelpful and Helpful Emotions	
Situation	*You arrange to meet a friend for coffee but he doesn't show up.*	
	Unhelpful	Helpful
Thoughts	He doesn't care about me.	Maybe he forgot accidentally – he's been very busy recently. I hope he's okay.

Situation	You arrange to meet a friend for coffee but he doesn't show up.	
	Unhelpful	Helpful
Emotions	Sad, low, frustrated.	Concern.
Bodily sensation	Weak, low energy.	No significant sensation.
Actions	Don't bother getting back in touch with friend for weeks.	Give him a call as soon as you can to check he is okay.

I often use this example when I teach groups. People in the groups are always amazed at the range of different responses by all the different participants. The situation is the same but the response is different.

So in the example shown in Table 12-2, a different way of thinking about the situation led to different emotions, bodily sensations and actions. Applying CBT techniques in your life enables you to find different ways of thinking about situations and so respond in more helpful ways.

Identifying stress-inducing thinking

Before you can change your thinking so that you feel more relaxed rather than stressed, you need to identify the kinds of thoughts you're having. You may find that you always think in the same habitual patterns, increasing your level of stress unnecessarily.

You may be thinking 'How do I actually know that I'm having unhelpful thoughts?'. Well, if you're feeling particularly stressed about a situation, the likelihood is that your thinking is unhelpful. Most situations that you feel stressed about may not be that serious – your habitual thinking patterns may be making you more stressed than you need to be.

Look at the common unhelpful thinking patterns in Table 12-3 and see if any of them seem familiar to you. Then, next time you feel stressed, see if you can identify what your actual thoughts are, and what type of unhelpful thinking pattern you are having, looking at the list below.

Table 12-3	Common Unhelpful Thinking Patterns	
Unhelpful pattern of thinking	**Unhelpful type of thought**	**Explanation**
Constantly worrying about the future.	Catastrophising or 'what if?' thinking.	When you're worried about the future, it's easy to begin imagining the worst that could happen. For example 'What if I lose my job?', or 'What if she's been attacked?'
Easily taking things personally.	Jumping to conclusions. Mind reading. Labelling.	When you're feeling vulnerable, you can easily take what people say in a personal way. You jump to negative conclusions, try guessing that what they're thinking is something negative about you as a person, and labelling yourself. For example, 'She hasn't phoned me today. She hates me (jumping to conclusions). I'm a bad friend (labelling)'
Only seeing the negative.	Ignoring the positive. Filtering.	You may have a tendency to only notice the negatives in a situation and ignore the positive. For example, if you're not good at maths, you may think you're not academic at all (ignoring your brilliance in English or Art). Or if someone says you didn't write a good article, you forget all the praise that others gave you (filtering out the positive and focusing on negative).
Seeing things in 'all or nothing' ways.	Black and white thinking. Perfectionism. Should thinking. Over-generalising.	You may have a pattern of polarised thinking. This can lead to wanting things to be absolutely perfect, and feeling a failure if they aren't. You may think in terms of 'shoulds' and when one thing goes wrong, you over-generalise as if everything will go wrong. For example, 'My son behaved badly yesterday. He's totally out of control (all or nothing). I should have been more strict (should thinking). He'll always be out of control (over-generalising).'

Learning to question your stressful thinking

To feel more relaxed in your life, you need to learn to question or challenge your stressful thinking, which are your thoughts that elicit your stress response.

Reflect on the last few times that you felt stressed? What was the situation? What were the kind of thoughts that were popping into your head? Write them down in the first column of Table 12-4. Then, looking at Table 12-3 see if you can roughly identify what sort of unhelpful thought you were having.

Remember, at first your thoughts may not feel as if they are unhelpful at all – they are just your thoughts. But if you want to reduce your stress using this well-proven approach, you need to just be open to the possibility that your thoughts may not be as helpful as you assume.

Fill out Table 12-4.

Table 12-4	Identifying Types of Unhelpful Thoughts
Thought	*Type of unhelpful thought*
e.g. I'm always late	All-or-nothing thinking

Now question your stressful thinking by asking yourself the following questions. Try to make your thoughts more positive and realistic:

1. Is there evidence to show this thought isn't true?

2. If a good friend had a similar thought in this situation, what would you say to them?

3. What's the advantage and disadvantage of thinking in this way?

4. How do you think you'd see this situation in a few months time? Or in a year?

5. What other ways are there of seeing this situation?

Now write down your more helpful thought.

Keep this new thought in a safe place so that you can refer to it regularly. Perhaps write it on a card that you can carry with you. Then, whenever you feel stressed at the thought of the situation, you can look at the card and your more helpful thought to put your mind at ease.

If you have high levels of stress, you may need to visit a professionally qualified cognitive behavioural therapist to help you. Visit the CBT register in the UK on www.cbtregisteruk.com to find your nearest, qualified CBT therapist.

Making Your Thinking Optimistic

A pessimist sees the difficulty in every opportunity; an optimist sees the opportunity in every difficulty.

Winston Churchill

Are you optimistic? Do you naturally look on the bright side of life? The meaning of optimism is more subtle than just thinking positively – it's a scientifically established way of looking at situations in your life that leads to physical and mental wellbeing. If you're a pessimist, you may like to read through this section to see if you can make yourself a bit more positive and thereby more relaxed.

I thought of myself as a very optimistic person, but when I did an optimism test, it showed there were several areas in which I classify as a pessimist. I was surprised at first as many of my friends thought of me as optimistic too. I began becoming more mindful of the times I saw circumstances in my life in a pessimistic way and used the exercises in this section to make my thinking more optimistic. I don't know if I now classify as highly optimistic, but I am far more aware of my thinking style when faced with a difficulty and apply the more positive framework to explain challenges in life.

I don't advocate blind optimism. Keeping a balance, depending on your circumstances, is important. If you are a passenger on a plane, for example, you probably don't want the pilot to be so optimistic that he decides to fly in dangerously bad weather.

Discovering the benefits of balanced optimism

Optimists tend to be more relaxed than pessimists. If you're an optimist, you expect things to turn out well and look for more positive things to happen in the future. You're more likely to take risks, which often lead to further positive outcomes.

Research shows that optimists make more efforts to relax when they are stressed compared with pessimists. Optimists take a proactive approach and use the kind of strategies that I describe in this book to keep relaxed. The fact that you're reading this book is probably a sign that you're optimistic to an extent – if you were a total pessimist, you wouldn't even bother trying to relax. So give yourself a pat on the back!

Traditionally, researchers thought of optimism as seeing the positive in everyday situations. Professor Martin Seligman, father of Positive Psychology (the psychology of positive human functioning) took a different approach. He looked at the way you explain your experiences, called explanatory style.

There are three ways of explaining your experience according to the 3Ps of optimism:

- ✔ **Permanent:** When things go well, optimists think the situation will last long-term. For example, if they manage to save enough money for a new home, they think 'I'll always have plenty of money to buy things I want,' rather than, 'It was just a good couple of years financially.' If things go badly, such as a relationship break-up, they think, 'S/he just wasn't the right one for me. I'll soon find my ideal,' rather than, 'I'll never find the right person.'

- ✔ **Pervasive:** Optimists think of positive events as bigger than they are, but when things go wrong, they're not so big. So if they receive a bonus at work, they think 'The reason is that I'm an excellent employee,' rather than just, 'The company had some spare money this time.' In negative situations, like losing a job, an optimist would think of a specific reason like, 'I've just not bothered working very hard recently,' rather than a bigger reason like 'I'm useless.'

- ✔ **Personal:** Optimists take the credit when things go well but don't blame themselves so much when things go badly. They take responsibility for their actions, but in a measured way. So if they organise a great party, they think, 'I did a great job putting it all together,' rather than, 'The people that came made it so much fun.' If things go badly, the optimist blames an external reason. So if they knock over a cup of coffee, they think, 'I did knock it over, but that cup was a bit unstable too,' rather than, 'I'm so clumsy. What's wrong with me?'

Problems don't last forever and aren't all your fault, so try not to think of them as bigger than they are.

Learning how to be optimistic

Seligman discovered three ways to become more optimistic. Read through these ways carefully and try one of them out each week over a period of three weeks. Notice which approach appeals to you and persevere with that approach. This is a way of becoming more optimistic and therefore healthier and more relaxed.

- ✔ **When a positive event occurs, notice what you think about the situation.** For example, if you manage to run farther than you have ever done before, think about how you achieved this through dedicated training (take it personally). Think about how running farther has a positive impact in other areas of your life (you'll be fitter, more attractive and feel better overall). Think about how you'll continue to run farther because you're a disciplined and fit person (stable).

- ✔ **Challenge your pessimistic thoughts with more optimistic ones by finding evidence that proves the pessimistic thought is untrue.** For example, you don't *always* talk too much, or just because your boss was rude to you, it doesn't mean it's your fault – maybe she just had a bad day.

- ✔ **Notice when the pessimistic thought is occurring and think 'Stop!'** Imagine a stop sign then distract yourself by thinking about something pleasant and relaxing. For example, you could imagine yourself relaxing on your favourite place, like a beach or beside a lake.

Optimism is about maximising your successes and minimising your failures.

Setting positive goals

> *It doesn't matter where you are coming from. All that matters is where you are going.*
>
> Brian Tracy

You may feel stressed because you feel lost. You are not doing the kind of things that you value. If you value watercolour painting but find yourself working in a bank, making no time for your passion, you may feel you're missing out. Or maybe you just feel like you're drifting through life without achieving anything of real value. If this is the case, then goal-setting may be just what you need.

Like many people you may think, 'How can I do what I want?' You may have all sorts of excuses for not setting goals. But these excuses are just negative thoughts popping into your head and may not be true. This kind of thinking is what I aim to challenge and question in this chapter.

Work through the following steps to begin journeying towards your goals:

1. **Carry out your favourite relaxation technique for five minutes to get you calmer and focused. Perhaps t'ai chi (see Chapter 7) or guided imagery (see Chapter 9).**

2. **Imagine you can have your ideal future.**

   What would that future look like? You've been given a magic wand and can have whatever you desire in the future – what would you have? Don't think about how you'll get there – just dream. Where do you live, what do you do, who do you live with and how do you spend your free time?

3. **Write down five specific long-term goals that you imagine achieving in your ideal future.**

   For instance, you can consider ones for health, relationships, personal development, vocation/career and living space. You may find this exercise scary or silly, but that's a good sign – it means you're stretching your limits and challenging your mind.

4. **For each goal write down the tiniest step that you can take, either today or in the coming week, that would move you towards your ideal goals.**

   Be specific. Think of something that you can do easily, otherwise you'll feel more stressed if you can't achieve the goal. Here are some examples: for health you may aim to walk for ten minutes every day. For relationships you may ensure you finish work on time this week so you can spend quality time with your partner in the evening. For personal development, you may decide to read this book every morning before leaving for work. If your goal is about your career, you could get in touch with a colleague in a senior position to see if they're willing to mentor you.

5. **Before you start thinking that you'll never achieve these goals or that this exercise is a waste of time, have a go.**

   Try achieving the small, manageable goals first and see how you feel afterwards. Keep an open mind and try the exercise before you judge it.

6. **Tell someone who is supportive and whom you trust about your goals.**

   Having the support from friends is tremendously powerful.

7. **Reward your progress.**

   Give yourself a treat for achieving the smallest goals. Every step, no matter how small, is worthy of self-congratulation and reward rather than ignoring them or, worse still, self-criticism for a slow rate of progress. Some examples of rewards include a new e-book reader, a gorgeous new haircut or a night out at the theatre with your friends.

When you set goals, try to follow the SMART mnemonic – make your goals:

Specific: Be clear about what you want to achieve.

Measurable and meaningful: Choose a goal that is clear when you achieve it and a goal that is meaningful for you rather than anyone else.

Attainable: Don't set goals that you are unlikely to achieve. Set small, easy-to-achieve steps. If you can't achieve your goal, break it down further into something attainable.

Rewarding: Go for goals that are positive and make you feel great having achieved them. Then you'll feel less stressed and more relaxed.

Time-bound: Set a date by which to achieve your goal – if you don't, you may never get round to doing it.

For example, instead of saying 'I want to work for myself,' you could set the goal 'By 1 August 2015, I want to own and run a bookshop in central London.' Don't worry, you're allowed to change your goals along the way, just be as specific as you can along the way.

Move towards positive results rather than away from negatives. For example, try saying 'I want to finish reading *Relaxation For Dummies* and do one relaxation exercise every day for the next two months,' rather than, 'I must be less stressed and anxious.'

Don't try to achieve too much in too short a period of time. Too many goals that are too far out of reach cause stress rather than relaxation. As always, keeping a balance is the secret.

Creating self-confidence step-by-step

Self-confidence is an attractive quality. You may envy a business colleague at work who seems cool, calm and collected whilst delivering a presentation, or your sister who isn't scared of applying for a new job that you'd love to do.

Self-confidence isn't about arrogance – a confident person sees themselves as equally valuable as any other human being – no less or more important than anyone else.

If you think you're lacking in the confidence department, work through the following steps. It's not a quick fix and you may need support along the way, but the rewards are great and well worth the effort in the long run.

1. **Write down all your achievements to-date.**

   Take your time and start with what you reckon are your most significant achievements. Think about tests that you've passed, times that you have helped someone out, been a good friend to someone, looked after a pet, learned to use some form of technology, brought up a child, completed a report or project. Stick the piece of paper up on the wall or somewhere you can read over it often. Enjoy the success you've had already.

2. **Write down your strengths.**

   Listing these won't be easy. Ask a good friend, colleague or family member to help you out – others find it easier to see your strengths. For example, you may be good at organising, planning, getting friends together or finishing work on time.

3. **Set some meaningful and attainable goals for your personal and professional life.**

   See the section 'Setting positive goals' earlier in this chapter for some help in this area. The gradual achievement of goals you value will begin to build your self-confidence.

4. **If you find negative thoughts popping into your head, use mindfulness (Chapter 10) or the cognitive-behavioural techniques in the section 'Using Cognitive Behavioural Techniques to Relax' earlier in this chapter to help you manage them.**

   Finding, and getting rid of, negative thoughts is common and part of the process.

5. **Build your skills.**

   Think about what you need to learn to help you achieve your goals and go out and learn it. You can learn from books, audio books, courses (online or in the real world) and workshops. Contact your local adult education college or local library for help.

6. **Begin taking small steps to achieve your goals.**

   Make sure your goals are achievable and see if you can take one small step each day to achieve them. As you achieve your goals, your confidence rises. You'll feel excitement and find more energy rather than stress and anxiety.

7. **Set yourself more challenging goals if you want.**

8. **Practise gratitude.**

   As your confidence builds, keep things in balance and perspective by remembering all the things you have in your life already. Thinking about what you already have helps to prevent possible over-confidence and promotes humility – a healthy, relaxing and welcome characteristic that helps improve your relationship with others too.

If you need help with discovering your strengths, visit `www.relaxation fordummies.com/strengths` for links to websites that help you discover your strengths for free.

Over-confidence can be just as unhelpful as under-confidence. Ensure you work towards finding the optimal level of self-confidence for you.

Using Problem-Solving Techniques to Relax

Never let a problem to be solved become more important than the person to be loved.

Barbara Johnson

If your life is full of problems, you probably find it difficult to relax. You may find yourself worrying about your problems, with the same thoughts circling round your brain. Some relaxation techniques may give you temporary relief, but solving the problem is the best approach if there is an answer. Even taking steps towards solving the problems gives you some relief.

In this section I help you improve your problem-solving skills using the following five-step approach:

1. Identify the problem.

2. Come up with possible solutions.

3. Choose a solution.

4. Break down the solution.

5. Try out your solution and review how it went later.

Identifying the problems causing stress

Sometimes you may not be sure exactly what your problem is. The secret is to write down the problem. The problem may have been going through your head for days, if not weeks. Writing the problem down has the effect of taking it off your head and outside of yourself, relieving a bit of the stress straight away, which is good news!

So, for example, you may write your problem as: 'I don't have enough money for the rent this month,' or 'I don't know how I'm going to finish the report by next Monday.'

If your problem is totally outside of your control, think about what you can control. Worrying about something you can't control will never solve the problem – instead use your favourite relaxation technique to take your mind off the worry, like guided imagery explained in Chapter 9 or deep breathing described in Chapter 5.

Coming up with solutions

Write down as many solutions as you can. Don't try to be completely realistic here – you can write down some crazy solutions too which helps to engage your creative brain to eventually come up with the right solution. You can even time yourself for five minutes and see how many solutions you can come up with, as a little challenge. The idea is to try and bypass the critical part of your brain by just writing down everything. You may feel uneasy doing this initially, but do persevere. Who knows, you may even begin to find the process fun thus improving your ability to come up with novel ideas.

Consider the following questions to help you:

- ✔ What would your best friend suggest to you now?
- ✔ What have you done in the past in a similar situation?
- ✔ Who can help you to solve this problem?

Choosing a solution

Using your list, choose the best solution. Take your time to make the best choice for you. You can try listing the pros and cons of each possible solution to help you decide. If you still can't decide between a set of possible solutions, just choose one. You can always try one of the other ones if this one doesn't work.

One of the following questions may help you to choose a solution:

- ✔ Which solution is most likely to work, realistically?
- ✔ Which is the simplest solution that appeals to me?
- ✔ Which is the easiest solution for me to do, that'll work?

Breaking down the solution

Breaking your solution down into easy-to-manage steps helps make your solution more 'doable'.

Let's say your problem is that your son is not behaving at home and your solution is to teach him how to behave well. By breaking down the procedure, a possible route to follow is:

1. Talk to my friend to see which book she suggests that I read on behaviour management.

2. Go to the bookshop and buy the book.

3. Read the book and make notes.

4. Book local parenting class.

5. Attend parenting class regularly.

6. Try out the different strategies to see which one works best.

Trying your solution and reviewing the outcome

You need to work through the steps for your chosen solution. Take your time to help maximise your chance of success. Be aware of any excessive negative thoughts about your achievements and gently focus your attention on working through your steps instead.

How I help people turn stress into relaxation

As a mindfulness-based stress management consultant, when a client calls me or books a consultation and says 'I'm stressed! Help me feel more relaxed. What shall I do?' the first step I take is to identify the cause of my client's stress. If the stress is due to a particular problem I start with an initial period of relaxation like deep breathing, and then we work through the problem-solving approach to find a solution. If the stress is due to a particular negative thought pattern, I may use techniques like mindfulness and sometimes CBT approaches to make them more aware of their thoughts, and then change their relationship to thoughts. I always look for opportunities not just to reduce the stress, but ways to increase wellbeing – greater wellbeing is associated with a greater sense of relaxation. I also set home practice – relaxation or mindfulness meditation CDs to listen to on a regular basis. You can try this yourself. Think about what is causing your stress and then decide what approach to take to begin to relax. Then go step-by-step towards greater relaxation.

After you work through all the steps, review your progress. Ask yourself whether you've managed to solve your problem. If not, don't despair! You can do the following:

✔ Look back at your possible solutions. Is there a different solution you can try?

✔ Try to think of some new solutions – you may now have a different perspective having tried one solution.

✔ Can you ask for some help from someone, or try a combination of different solutions?

See the whole problem-solving approach summarised in Figure 12-2.

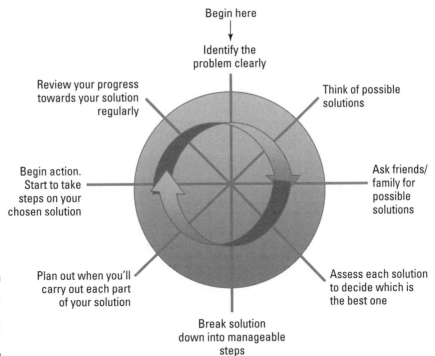

Figure 12-2:
Problem-solving circle.

Chapter 13

Improving Your Attitude

. . . .

In This Chapter

▶ Feeling the power of gratitude

▶ Discovering why play and humour are seriously important

▶ Finding ways to reduce self-criticism and increase self-compassion

. . . .

*I*n this chapter I talk about three attitudes or skills: gratitude, self-compassion and playfulness. In my opinion these attitudes are some of the most important of all mindsets to cultivate a happy and successful life, and such a life is imbued with a sense of relaxation and stress resilience.

Attitudes are like your spectacles through which you see the world and yourself. If your glasses are filthy, no matter what you look at, you see dirt. When you choose to do so, you clean your glasses and suddenly everything is much clearer. Using the exercises recommended in this chapter you start to see the world around you much more clearly too with hope, optimism and warmth.

I am wary of sounding cheesy or uncomfortably optimistic but I have found in my own life the transformative effect of cultivating healthy attitudes. Thinking of things that I am genuinely grateful for, cultivating a sense of warmth and kindness towards myself and looking at life circumstances in a light-hearted way all positively shift my mental and emotional gears. And scientific evidence shows that cultivating these skills would benefit you too.

Developing Gratitude

> *When it comes to life, the critical thing is whether you take things for granted or take them with gratitude.*
>
> GK Chesterton

Gratitude is a highly valued attitude to living, in all the world's major religious traditions. Relatively recently, science has also begun to grasp the tremendous health and wellbeing benefits of a grateful attitude.

Learning the benefits of being grateful

If you're generally a grateful person, you're more likely to be happier and more relaxed about the ups and downs of life. Thinking about things I'm grateful for every day has changed my life for the better. Here are a few reasons to adopt a grateful attitude:

- **Gratitude reminds you of the positives in your life.** Your brain has evolved to focus on dangers and negative situations. Gratitude helps you to turn your attention to what's going well.

- **Gratitude reminds you to thank others.** People are important and they do a lot for you. A genuine little thank you from time to time brings lots of warmth into almost any relationship. A quick e-mail, call or word of thanks makes them feel happy, and that'll make you feel better too.

- **Gratitude makes a stressful situation feel better.** If you have a hard time at work, for example, you may have forgotten the benefits your job offers – the regular salary, the friendship of colleagues, the pension scheme, the medical insurance and the way your income helps you to rent your flat or pay your mortgage. Be grateful you have work and grateful for the challenges it offers.

- **Gratitude helps you focus on what's really important in life.** Most people find they reflect on their family, their home, their friends and their pet. In other words, the things that really make them feel happy. In the midst of a stressful life, you can literally get into a 'tunnel vision' and only focus on the negative objects of your stress. Gratitude dissolves the tunnel, so you look at the big picture, shifting your perspective and feel more at ease.

Research in a controlled experiment by Professor Emmons of the University of California and Professor McCullough of the University of Miami found the following characteristics of people who kept gratitude journals (which I cover in the section 'Using a gratitude journal to feel more relaxed' below) over a few weeks on a daily basis, for a few minutes each day:

- They did more physical exercise.

- They felt better about their lives as a whole, and felt less ill.

- They were more optimistic about the upcoming week.

Other research by the University of California identified that gratitude helps people attain their personal goals, greater alertness, enthusiasm, determination and energy. People practising daily gratitude were more likely to help someone with a personal problem. A 21-day daily gratitude challenge gave people more energy, more positive moods, greater connection with others, more optimism about their lives, and even better quality and longer sleep. Even children who practise gratitude report having more positive attitudes about school and home.

This morning I walked to my local coffee shop. My mind turned to all the work I need to complete and deadlines I had to hit. Fortunately, after about a minute, I caught myself in the unhelpful thought pattern. I challenged myself to think of ten things that I'm grateful for. I thought of the sunshine and the fact that my legs are working, my supportive friends and family, my exciting projects, my ability to smile and my high energy levels. By the time I'd finished, I was in a totally different state of mind. I felt far more relaxed.

Try naming ten things you're grateful for next time you go for a walk and notice how you feel more relaxed at the end.

Finding ways to be grateful

> *Reflect on your present blessings, on which every man has many, not on your past misfortunes, of which all men have some.*
>
> Charles Dickens

It's all very well knowing the benefits of gratitude, but you need to know some practical ways of being grateful on a regular basis. Below are five proven, easy ways to get you started on the road to gratitude. Have a go at them all at some point and see which ones you'd like to continue to use on a daily basis:

- ✔ **Say thank you.** Say 'thank you' when someone helps you out. Even the small things count – someone holding open a door, a bus driver issuing you a ticket, or a waiter bringing you your meal. Look the person in the eye and genuinely mean it.

- ✔ **Write a gratitude letter.** Think about someone who has helped you in your life and you haven't properly thanked. Then write them a letter of gratitude for all they have done for you. Just doing that is beneficial. You can take it further by meeting up with them and reading the letter out to them – this isn't easy for most people, but if you can do it your level of wellbeing is boosted for months, which makes you more resilient to stress and thereby more relaxed, and more often.

✔ **Go gratitude dating.** Make a date with your partner specifically to express gratitude to each other. Try eating dinner, going for a walk or doing some gardening together, and simultaneously express gratitude to each other.

✔ **Use creative expression.** If you're an artist or like photography, for example, use your creativity to express gratitude. You could create a collage with things in your life that you're grateful for. Enjoy being creative and grateful at the same time.

✔ **Generate a handful of gratitude.** I love this one. Each time you find yourself in negative mode, worrying or feeling down, try to cultivate a handful of gratitude. To do this, think of one thing you're grateful for, for each finger and thumb. You can count them physically on your hand to make sure you get all ten. Don't worry if you find this difficult at first. You're training your brain to be more grateful, and at first your brain will resist. Just do your best and, remember, any small thing counts no matter how seemingly tiny and insignificant.

Using a gratitude journal to feel more relaxed

I would maintain that thanks are the highest form of thought, and that gratitude is happiness doubled by wonder.

GK Chesterton

A gratitude journal is one of the best ways to cultivate gratitude. The physical act of writing your blessings helps to make them more concrete, and you've always got a record of positive words to refer to when you need something to lift you. Additionally, the very act of creating a journal itself has been proven to be a relaxing and stress-relieving process too.

Follow these steps to get you started on the road to creating a gratitude journal:

1. **Choose a journal.**

   You can treat yourself to a beautifully designed new journal, or if it doesn't bother you, any kind of notebook is suitable. If you're like me, you could use your laptop to journal your thoughts of gratitude each day in a simple document. Nowadays you can even get 'apps' on your mobile phone that remind you to be grateful on a daily basis.

2. Choose a writing style.

You could either write a paragraph each day, exploring all that you are grateful for, or you could list five or ten things each day. I prefer the latter – decide or experiment to see what works for you.

3. Journal regularly.

Pick a time of day to journal your thoughts and stick to it if you can. Then you're more likely to get into the gratitude habit. For most people, morning or evening time is best. The nice thing about evening gratitude journaling is that it improves your sleep and therefore has a positive impact on the whole of the next day.

Try not to be grateful for exactly the same things or people every day. Flex your mental gratitude muscles and see if you can think of a few different reasons to be grateful.

Discovering Laughter, Humour and Play

The human race has only one really effective weapon and that is laughter.

Mark Twain

If you were fortunate enough to have been brought up in a safe and loving household, and with good health, then laughter and play would have come to you naturally. But you may no longer find yourself playing around and laughing so much – you're an adult now in the serious business of surviving. These qualities that you normally associate with children are tremendously powerful ways to reduce stress and feel more relaxed, sometimes in the most tense of life situations.

If you don't naturally laugh and have a serious outlook, see if any of the tips in this section appeal to you. You may discover an easy way to be a little bit more light-hearted, and small baby steps of positive change make all the difference. In fact, small steps are the only realistic way towards positive change so look out for little improvements in your outlook and praise yourself for them.

After graduating from college and completing teacher training, I spent several years teaching in different schools all over London. I could tell what it would be like to work in a school by the atmosphere in the staff room. In some schools, usually the most challenging ones to work in, I would hear the most laughter – that was a good sign. The teachers managed their stress through jokes and banter. Without this outlet, the tension from the lessons they taught would build and build. The laughter was like a pressure-relief valve and made for an enjoyable teaching experience, both for teachers and students.

Bringing on the benefits of laughter

Laughter has a hugely positive effect on your level of relaxation. You also get a lift in mood, an energy boost and a greater ability to solve problems creatively. All these effects feed back to make you feel less stressed.

Relationships have one of the most powerful effects on your level of relaxation. Relationships can both make you feel more relaxed if they're going well, and more stressed if they don't. Laughter and playfulness is to relationships as oil is to an engine – they make things run smoother, especially if they're in the right place!

Here are some of the physical benefits of laughter:

✔ Boosts your mood by reducing stress hormones and increasing the level of health-inducing endorphins.

✔ Improves the level of oxygen in your brain, lowers blood pressure and strengthens your immune system.

✔ Gives your abdomen and even your shoulders a good internal workout, leaving your muscles more relaxed.

Here are some of the mental benefits of laughter:

✔ Puts your life situation into perspective, thereby reducing feelings of depression and anxiety.

✔ You see things in your life as a challenge rather than a threat.

✔ Improves the quality of your relationships and so level of optimism and positivity.

✔ Laughter turns your attention away from challenging emotions like anger, sadness or guilt.

Finding opportunities to smile mindfully

Sometimes your joy is the source of your smile, but sometimes your smile can be the source of your joy.

Thich Nhat Hanh

The above quote by a popular Zen master has been shown to be true by scientists. Using the muscles you use when smiling can lift your mood. This effect is because your brain works out if you're happy by checking in with your smile muscles. Your facial expression and emotions are linked in a feedback loop.

Recent research at Cardiff University used special Botox injections (Botox is used in cosmetic medicine for treating a range of issues like wrinkles or uncontrolled blinking) preventing participants from frowning. The participants reported feeling more cheerful and less anxious.

When you feel stressed, your breathing becomes more rapid and you're more likely to frown. But you have some control over both of these aspects of your body. So, by putting a fake smile on your face and slowing down your breathing a bit, you begin to feel more relaxed. Try it right now for a minute and see if it works. Rate how you feel before and after the minute.

Using laughter as a relaxation tool

Seven days without laughter makes one weak.

Mort Walker

Although research is still relatively limited, all the signs point to laughter as being a powerful tool for increasing your level of relaxation. Positive psychology, the science of wellbeing, identifies 24 human character strengths such as creativity, forgiveness and social intelligence. Humour is classified as one of 24 human strengths that people can possess, showing how highly humour is valued according to psychologists. You can now even join a laughter club, sometimes called laughter yoga, where you meet others and do laughter exercises. I tried attending once – it was funny.

When I feel stressed, I sometimes use laughter to relieve the tension. I usually go to YouTube and type in 'funny' or 'comedy', and away I go. After ten minutes of watching funny videos, I feel more relaxed, uplifted and energetic. I also feel more creative in my writing and coaching when I smile.

Try some of the following to inject some humour into your life:

- ✔ **Pretend to be happy.** The fake feeling soon becomes real. Whilst not easy for some people to do, the old saying 'fake it till you make it' does hold true. Even a pretend laugh seems to have similar benefits to a real one, and sometimes turns into real laughter too. Try imitating a really funny laugh, or make silly laughter sounds.

- ✔ **Entertain yourself.** The entertainment industry is a huge industry for a reason. Comedy on television, radio, films, and the theatre always attracts large audiences. Make time to enjoy some entertainment in your life.

- ✔ **Spend time with funny, light-hearted people.** By being with happy people you're socialising, a powerful way to relax in itself, as well as sharing jokes and laughter – an attractive combination. Happiness has been well documented to spread from person to person – it's catchy.

Spend time with happy people and you're pretty much guaranteed to feel better.

✔ **Move the conversation towards fun.** When talking with others, ask them if they know any good jokes, or tell them one of your funny stories. Sometimes, things that go slightly wrong in your life make the most humorous stories. See if you can exchange funny stories till tears come to your eyes.

✔ **Play with your children.** Children are masters of playfulness and fun. Spend time with these experts! You'll feel better and your relationship with them will improve too.

Using playfulness in communication

Playfulness and humour can improve your relationships and lead to deeper levels of relaxation and greater resilience to future stressful situations.

Here are three key principles to keep in mind:

✔ **Use laughter to express joy, not to cover up emotions.** When you laugh with your partner or another person, just check from time to time that you're not covering up deeper emotions that actually need addressing. For example, if you feel annoyed that your partner spends all her free time watching television but you just laugh it off when talking about it to a friend, you may be using laughter to cover up the problem that needs addressing.

✔ **Make sure that you're both laughing.** Whilst pretty obvious, you may find that you're laughing subconsciously on your own. You do need to be careful when using a playful approach in communication. If you're laughing but your friend doesn't find the situation funny, you make things more difficult. Ensure both parties are in on the joke.

For example, if you like playing with your partner's hair, and doing so makes you laugh, but your partner finds it annoying, then you're better off stopping, even though you're having fun. Small irritations just add up to big frustrations. Think of a joke you would both enjoy together – that would bring you both closer.

✔ **Make peace using playfulness.** The feeling of peace is associated with relaxation. If you're in conflict with someone, you're unlikely to be feeling at ease. If appropriate, consider using laughter to diffuse the tension. This approach isn't easy to do in the heat of the moment, but you can plan for it. For example, if you're having a hard time with your partner, and nothing seems to work, try doing a relaxation exercise like deep breathing for a few minutes before you next meet. Make a conscious decision to try to diffuse any potential tension with a joke or comment that you know your partner finds funny; perhaps something that you noticed at work, or a comment made by your child. Laughter has the magical ability to diffuse conflict and bring some peace into a relationship.

Practising Self-Compassion

Self-compassion is about being kind to yourself. If you're like many of the clients I work with, you probably criticise yourself for what are actually perfectly forgivable mistakes. Perhaps you don't even know that you've got a harsh, negative inner-judge, always looking for slight imperfections to jump on you. This self-criticism leads to a greater feeling of stress and anxiety.

By developing greater self-compassion using the exercises in this section, you'll learn powerful ways to treat yourself with the respect that you truly deserve – one of the greatest gifts you can give yourself.

Before you begin thinking you can't do it, I've got news for you: you *can* do it, because many people *just like you* have gone from being tremendously unkind and negative to themselves, to living a life of greater ease and wellbeing. You won't find the path easy, but then again, most things of value are challenging and well worth the journey. You brain can be made to be kinder to itself through regular self-compassion exercises.

Self-compassion is a skill you can learn.

Understanding self-compassion

Self-compassion is about treating yourself in the same way you treat your friends or family.

You may find the term 'self-compassion' too soft or airy-fairy. You may think 'this is all well and good, but I've got real problems here. I don't have time to mess about being nice to myself. If I don't get on with things, everything will be a real disaster.' What I'm saying is that you can achieve whatever you want in your life *more effectively* with self-compassion. Just as children are motivated more effectively through encouragement, you can motivate yourself in a more positive and enjoyable way through self-compassion.

As I show in Figure 13-1, self-compassion is made up of three components according to Dr Neff, Professor of the University of Texas, a key researcher in the field:

- ✔ **Self-kindness:** Being kind to yourself, particularly at times of difficulty.
- ✔ **Common humanity:** Seeing your own experiences as part of a shared experience with all human beings rather than as isolated incidents.
- ✔ **Mindfulness:** Being aware of difficult thoughts and feelings without identifying yourself with them.

Self-compassion is not about being soft or overly self-indulgent. Actually, self-compassion leads to greater resilience and inner strength as you nourish your inner being with the food of self-compassion.

Figure 13-1: Triangular diagram of the three components of self-compassion.

(Triangle diagram labelled: Self-kindness at top, Self-compassion in centre, Common humanity at bottom left, Mindfulness at bottom right.)

Discovering the benefits of self-compassion

Research into self-compassion is promising. An article in the *New York Times* on self-compassion highlighted that not only do people who score highly on self-compassion have lower levels of stress, they also have lower levels of depression, and are happier and more optimistic. If you find that you eat too much or too little when you aren't relaxed, there is preliminary evidence to suggest self-compassion can help with weight management.

One of the main reasons you may not want to practise self-compassion is because you believe you are being self-indulgent. Self-discipline doesn't come from self-criticism but from encouraging yourself.

Measuring your self-compassion

In this section I offer you a simple way to assess how self-compassionate you are. Use the result as a base from which you can gently and kindly begin building your capacity for self-compassion. Remember, if you get a low score, there's no need to berate yourself – this is common and you're one of the few people in the world that has actually assessed their level of self-compassion, so you could congratulate yourself for that.

I have simplified a self-compassion scale developed by Raes, Pommier, Neff and Van Gucht and published in the scientific journal *Clinical Psychology and Psychotherapy*. For a link to Dr. Neff's work and scales, go to `relaxation` `fordummies.com/self-compassion-scale`.

Please read each statement carefully before answering. To the left of each item, indicate how often you behave in the stated manner, using the following scale:

Almost never				Almost always
1	2	3	4	5

1. I try to be understanding and patient towards those aspects of my personality I don't like.

2. When something painful happens I try to take a balanced view of the situation.

3. I try to see my failings as part of the human condition.

4. When I'm going through a very hard time, I give myself the caring and tenderness I need.

5. When something upsets me I try to keep my emotions in balance.

6. When I feel inadequate in some way, I try to remind myself that feelings of inadequacy are shared by most people.

Now add up your scores.

Average scores tend to be around 3 for each one. So, as a rough guide, if your score is 6–15 you are low on self-compassion, if you got 16–20 you are moderately self-compassionate and 21–30 you are high on self-compassion.

If you are moderate or low on self-compassion, try some of the exercises in the following section.

Trying self-compassion exercises

In this section I show you some self-compassion exercises for you to try out. These exercises have been used in experiments successfully. Start with the exercise that you think you can do most easily, and after a couple of weeks, try the second easiest. Work your way through the exercises in this way.

Self-compassion writing exercise

In this writing exercise, you are invited to reflect on aspects of yourself that you're not happy about, and then imagine how a wise and kind friend may soothe your disappointment with yourself by explaining that you're human and it's okay to be imperfect and make mistakes. Take your time to work through the exercise.

1. **Find something to write on. Keep it private if you want.**

2. **Reflect on the fact that everyone has some aspect of themselves that they don't like.**

   That's part of what it means to be a human being. Think about your own life, and consider what aspects of yourself you feel insecure about – something that makes you feel 'not good enough'. This aspect can be anything such as your physical appearance or perhaps something happening at home or work.

3. **Write about how you feel about this inadequacy.**

   How does this lack of perfection make you feel – sad, frustrated, angry? The idea is to write about your emotions as they are rather than as you want them to be. Don't shy away from your true emotions but don't over-indulge and magnify them either.

4. **Put your pen down for a minute and read what you've written.**

   Don't judge or criticise what you've expressed.

5. **Imagine you have a very wise, kind and accepting friend.**

   Think of someone who is unconditionally loving and compassionate. Someone who knows all about your background and all the issues you have. Imagine how this wise and kind friend accepts and understands these inadequacies you've written about and still feels great love and care for you.

6. **Write from the perspective of this wise and kind friend.**

   Explain that the difficulty or inadequacy of yours is not entirely under your control. Your genes, your upbringing and the environment you grew up in all played a part in this area. Your friend would remind you that you are only human, and like all other humans, you have strengths and weaknesses. Consider what this friend would say from the perspective of unconditional love and acceptance of you as you are. What ways would your friend empathise with your critical judgement of yourself? If your friend offers some ways to help you, how would they make that suggestion with limitless kindness and total acceptance?

7. **When you've finished writing that compassionate letter back to yourself, put it down for a few days.**

   When you're ready, read it back to yourself. Allow the compassionate words to fall deep into your heart. Notice the sense of acceptance and kindness that the letter offers you. Feel the kindness in your being if you can. See if you can give yourself permission to feel love and be accepted just as you are. Self-compassion for your innermost being is your deepest need and birthright.

Self-compassionate encouragement and motivation

You may think that self-criticism is an effective way of motivating yourself. However, research has shown that children are far more effectively motivated through praise and positivity rather than criticism. The same counts for you.

1. **Reflect on an aspect of yourself that you self-criticise, hoping that the criticism will help you to change.**

   For example, you may criticise yourself for being overweight, or shy.

2. **Notice how you feel when you criticise yourself.**

   Perhaps you feel frustrated or sad.

3. **See whether you can feel some compassion for yourself, for the emotional pain that you experience through the self-criticism.**

4. **Now imagine what a supportive friend or wise and kind mentor would say to you to encourage you in a positive way.**

   See whether you can think of the most supportive statement your wise friend could say to you.

Self-compassion journal

Journaling is a therapeutic and relaxing process for many people, once they make the time to sit down and do it. When you have a few minutes at the end of the day, reflect on any moments of difficulty that you experienced during the daytimes when you were self-critical or judgemental, or when you experienced physical or emotional pain. Now consider the three aspects of self-compassion (mindfulness, self-compassion and common humanity) and use them to generate some sense of self-compassion. For example, if you had an argument with your partner:

- ✔ **Mindfulness:** Notice any feelings of sadness and frustration within you, and accept them as best you can. Write about the feelings.

- ✔ **Common humanity:** Write about how most couples have disagreements. Note how, as a human being, you can't be perfect and nor can your partner, for example. Think about any other reasons for the argument, such as missing lunch and so becoming irritable.

- ✔ **Self-compassion:** Jot down some words of kindness for yourself, such as 'Hey I got carried away – that's bound to happen sometimes. It doesn't make me a bad person. It takes two to tango – we share the blame. I'll treat myself to a hot bath tonight and that'll help and be a bit of kindness to myself.'

Treating yourself

Life is difficult sometimes. Treats can help boost your wellbeing and help you feel better. I use the word 'treats', but actually they're essential ingredients to recharge your batteries. I give some suggestions below to get you started. You can create your own list and keep it handy – whenever you're having a tough day, full of self-criticism and self-judgement, take the list out and offer one to yourself.

- ✔ A little of your favourite food (chocolate?!) without feeling guilty.

- ✔ A hot bath, massage, facial or some kind of treatment.

- ✔ A visit to your local coffee shop with a friend.

- ✔ A gentle walk in your local area.

- ✔ Dancing or karaoke night.

- ✔ Go on holiday for a couple of days or longer.

In the future, any time you notice that you are criticising yourself to try to get moving, work through this exercise. Motivate yourself with words of encouragement and with a calm inner voice. Imagine your wise inner advisor speaking to you. Positive encouragement is a far superior motivator compared to negative self-judgement.

Self-compassion doesn't lead to self-centredness. Self-compassion takes the opportunity of suffering within yourself to develop kindness and connection.

Performing a random act of kindness

Kindness is my religion.

Dalai Lama

Last month I was in Barcelona on my way to my grandad's cremation in Malaga, Spain. I walked into a fruit and veg shop and picked up a tangerine and went to pay for it. The owner and shopkeeper looked at my one tangerine, smiled and said 'Just take it for free. Enjoy.' Shopkeepers don't normally say that! I smiled and said I'll pay for a few more if I like this one. I did like it so took a couple more. Again, he said the same thing. I still remember the incident and it makes me smile to write about it now. His random act of kindness is etched in my memory and though the money issue was small, the effect was great.

A random act of kindness is an action of generosity performed to either cheer someone up or to make the world a better place to live in. By doing an act of kindness on a daily basis, you're creating a win-win situation. You feel good for being kind, and the other person feels cared for and special. What more do you want?

Being kind is relaxing because you're not just thinking about yourself and your problems. Your attention is going outwards and you feel good about yourself. You create an underlying thought like 'I'm good' or 'I'm nice!' With that underlying thought arises positive feelings that lift you. You can't feel good and overly stressed at the same time. You displace the stress with a positive emotion like joy. Even if you feel just slightly better you're moving in the right direction.

Here are a few random ideas to get you started:

✔ Help a friend out. Give them a call to see how they're doing and see what you can do to help them.

✔ Write a note, poem or song for a loved one.

✔ Give someone your favourite inspiring book or CD.

✔ Tell someone who has served you a meal or sold you a ticket how excellent their service was.

✔ Pick up litter from your local park – you're being kind to the environment.

✔ Smile and say hello to a stranger – strike up a conversation if you can.

✔ Pay for the person behind you in a queue.

✔ Give away something that you own today.

✔ Invite your neighbours over for a snack.

✔ Leave flowers on the doorstep of a friend with a little note.

A random act of kindness is about doing something without expecting anything back.

Part IV
Everyday Relaxation

The 5th Wave
By Rich Tennant

"This procedure should help you relax. We're going to surgically remove the coffee cup from your hand."

In this part . . .

In this part, the art of finding moments of relaxation during the day are revealed. You discover how to relax at home, and sneak in some much-needed relaxation at work. You can also find tips on sleeping well in this part.

Chapter 14

Finding Ways to Sleep Serenely

. . . .

. . . .

A good night's sleep can make a world of difference. You feel energised and refreshed after a restful night's kip. Sleep is so routine that you may not even think about it. But if you don't sleep well, you probably feel anything but relaxed – dragging yourself around to do your chores is a huge effort and you may be irritable, snappy and agitated.

You're not alone if you have insomnia. Most people have trouble sleeping at some point in their life. You may be worried or excited, which can affect your sleep.

Your daytime rituals can make a huge difference to your nightly rest. By doing the right activities during the day and evening, your chance of falling asleep increases. In this chapter I offer tips and suggestions to help you nod off each night.

Understanding Sleep

People who say they sleep like a baby usually don't have one.

Leo J. Burke

Giraffes sleep for an average of only two hours a night. Pythons sleep for about 18 hours. Most people are somewhere in between.

Sleep is essential for your brain to function. Just as your body needs food to function properly, so your brain needs sleep to work properly. After a sleepless night you may feel the effects of sleep deprivation – poor speech (you start talking nonsense), poor memory (you leave your keys at home) and lack of creativity (your greatest idea is to hit your head with a pillow).

Sleep occurs in cycles that keep repeating through the night. You have two main types of sleep – non-REM (rapid eye movement) sleep and REM sleep. You probably wake up for one or two minutes every couple of hours as you go through your sleep cycle. You may not remember these short moments of being awake unless you're anxious or a noise disturbs you.

- ✔ **Non-REM sleep:** Non-REM sleep comprises the following four stages:

  Stage 1 pre-sleep: You probably know what this stage feels like. You're half awake and half asleep at the same time – you hear a slight noise and you jolt awake. You may experience sudden jerks in this stage, caused by the part of your brain that deals with movement being stimulated. Sometimes you get the feeling of falling with these bodily movements.

  Stage 2 light sleep: This is the first stage of a 'true sleep' state. This light sleep stage lasts for up to 25 minutes. Your heart and breathing rate slow down during this stage.

  Stage 3 deep sleep: You don't wake up easily in this stage. If you do wake up, you take a few minutes to reorient yourself to the world around you.

  Stage 4 very deep sleep: In this state other people have great difficulty waking you up. This part of sleep is important and you wake up refreshed if you've been in this state for some time during your sleep.

- ✔ **REM sleep:** REM is the part of your sleep where most of your dreams occur. In REM sleep your brain is highly active, your heart rate goes up and your breathing becomes more rapid. Your muscles are usually very relaxed. After this stage, you normally go back to stage 1 of non-REM sleep.

Getting the right amount of sleep

The amount of sleep you need depends on your age. Here's a rough guide:

- ✔ **Babies:** About 14 hours every day up to 12 months old.
- ✔ **Children and teenagers:** About 9–10 hours every night.
- ✔ **Adults:** About 8 hours a night.
- ✔ **Older adults:** About 8 hours a night, but many adults over 65 years old are light sleepers.

There's no 'right' amount of sleep. If you feel sleepy during the day, you probably need more sleep.

The symptoms of several sleepless nights include:

- You find it hard to make decisions or to concentrate.
- You feel tired or fall asleep during the day.
- You feel depressed or worry about your lack of sleep.

Many people are injured or killed due to drivers falling asleep at the wheel. If you feel sleepy, don't drive or operate heavy machinery.

Discovering your sleep profile

Many people have taken the Epworth Sleepiness Scale. For more information see www.epworthsleeinesscale.com. The scale is a worldwide standard way of measuring daytime sleepiness and so help to determine if you're getting enough sleep.

How likely are you to doze off or fall asleep in the following situations, in contrast to just feeling tired? The situations refer to your usual way of life in recent times. Even if you have not done some of these things recently try to work out how they would have affected you. Use the following scale to choose the most appropriate number for each situation:

0 = no chance of dozing

1 = slight chance of dozing

2 = moderate chance of dozing

3 = high chance of dozing

Situation	*Chance of dozing (0–3)*
Sitting and reading	
Watching TV	
Sitting inactive in a public place (e.g. a theatre or a meeting)	
As a passenger in a car for an hour without a break	
Lying down to rest in the afternoon when circumstances permit	
Sitting and talking to someone	
Sitting quietly after a lunch without alcohol	
In a car, while stopped for a few minutes in traffic	

Now add up the scores for each situation, to get a total score. Compare your total score with the following list:

1–6   Congratulations: you get enough sleep

7–8   Your score is average

9+   Consider whether you're getting enough sleep, improve your sleep hygiene or visit your doctor

If you do have a high score, find more advice by going to the website www.nhs.uk and searching for insomnia. A good book on the subject is *Overcoming Insomnia and Sleep Problems* by Colin Espie.

Preparing to Sleep

Sleep that knits up the ravelled sleave of care

The death of each day's life, sore labour's bath

Balm of hurt minds, great nature's second course,

Chief nourisher in life's feast.

William Shakespeare, Macbeth

If you have trouble sleeping, this is the section for you. Poor sleep preparation and night-time habits could be the main reason why you're not getting the amount of sleep you need. Here I suggest some simple things that you can put in place to invite more sleep into your life. The suggestions include how to prepare for sleep and how to ensure your bedroom environment is conducive to a full night's rest.

Using wind-down time

Life is complicated. You may be busy with work, family or socialising, preventing you from sleeping at the same time every night. But if you're an insomniac, you need to make the extra effort to sleep at the same time every night, and have an evening ritual to wind down. If you ensure that you relax rather than stress yourself out each evening, you're more likely to sleep better and wake up more refreshed. Here are some sleepy tips to make sleep your best friend:

✔ **Have a warm bath to get you to the right temperature for sleep.** Don't make it too hot, or you may sweat and feel uncomfortable.

✔ **Write down your worries and concerns.** Try making a short to-do list each evening before you sleep, so your mind doesn't need to worry about the things you need to do.

✔ **Read a book.** Try something that isn't too stimulating.

✔ **Listen to relaxing, soft music, or a relaxation CD.** This is a matter of personal taste so experiment to see what works best for you.

✔ **Do some slow gentle yoga or t'ai chi stretches.** For ideas, see Chapter 7.

✔ **Make a list of things in your life that you're grateful for.** Include the reasons that you're grateful. This exercise is proven to increase the quality and quantity of sleep. Practise this every night before sleeping.

Creating a relaxing bedroom environment

Your environment has a direct effect on the quality of your sleep. A noisy, messy room with light coming through the curtains is not going to do you any favours. It doesn't take too much effort to improve your bedroom environment, and once it's done, you just need to maintain it. Make falling asleep easier for you by trying the following tips:

✔ **Keep the noise down.** How noisy is your bedroom at night? Although some people claim that they can't sleep without noise, evidence suggests that the more noise there is at night, the lower the quality of sleep. If you can't prevent the noise of barking dogs or traffic through the night, try playing soothing music, wear comfortable earplugs, or use a white-noise machine. I sometimes use an app on my mobile phone to play relaxing music at night that automatically switches off after about 10 minutes.

✔ **Create an association of sleep with your bed.** Do this by ensuring you only use your bed for resting (and other fun activities) and not working. If you work on your bed, your mind may keep you awake thinking beds are for working rather than sleeping.

✔ **Ensure that you're comfortable.** If you wake up with an aching back or sore neck, you may have an issue with your mattress or pillow. Experiment with mattresses of different levels of firmness to see what suits you. If your mattress is too soft, your body will sag and your back will ache. If your mattress is too firm, your hips and shoulders will be under pressure. If possible, replace your mattress every ten years.

✔ **Lights, temperature, sleep!** To make your bedroom sleep-friendly, make the room as dark as possible. The glow from a computer screen or a street light beaming through your curtain can interfere with your sleep pattern. Use heavy curtains and switch off all the lights. The ideal temperature for sleep is around 18° C (65° F). Keep a window slightly open if your room needs the ventilation.

Figure 14-1 shows a summary of all the key actions you can take to help you to sleep.

Make bedroom cool, dark and quiet.

Avoid drinks that contain caffeine, especially in afternoon or evening.

Exercise regularly, but not in the late afternoon or evening.

Tips to help you sleep

Go to bed at the same time every night so your body gets used to a routine.

Have a bedtime routine such as having a warm bath, listening to relaxing music or reading a book sends a signal to your body and mind to prepare for sleep.

Avoid heavy meals just before going to sleep.

Figure 14-1: A spider diagram of tips to help you sleep.

You spend almost a third of your entire life sleeping. You may as well try to make yourself as comfortable and relaxed as possible during this time.

Dealing With Insomnia

Insomnia is either difficulty in getting to sleep in the first place, or not being able to stay asleep long enough to feel fully rested. Insomnia can result in you feeling irritable and tired, with difficulty concentrating.

Most people have trouble sleeping at some point or other. Women tend to have more difficulty sleeping than men. As you grow older, your chances of having insomnia tend to increase.

Investigating causes of insomnia

If a man had as many ideas during the day as he does when he has insomnia, he'd make a fortune.

Griff Niblack

Six main reasons exist for insomnia. By glancing through the following reasons, you may get an idea of the cause of your insomnia and be able to work out a solution. If not, and lack of sleep is affecting your daily life, you should visit your doctor.

- ✔ **Stress:** You could have guessed this one. Yes, stressful events cause insomnia. Sometimes insomnia continues even when the stressful event is over. The reason is that you begin to identify yourself as a bad sleeper. Stress doesn't have to be related to a heavy workload or relationship issues – something as simple as a noisy bedroom may be a cause of stress.

- ✔ **Food, drink, alcohol and cigarettes:** Eating too much or too little in the evening can cause insomnia problems, as can drinking too much fluid or consuming alcohol. Nicotine is a stimulant, so smoking before bed may keep you awake; as the night goes on, you may even experience nicotine withdrawal symptoms, reducing the quality of your sleep.

- ✔ **Irregular sleep routine:** If you do shift work, or have a baby that wakes you up at night frequently, your internal body clock gets confused, which can lead to difficulty sleeping.

- ✔ **Physical illness:** You may have a physical condition that causes insomnia. This could include heart disease, asthma, chronic pain, Alzheimer's or Parkinson's disease, hormone problems, arthritis, incontinence or enlarged prostate. See your doctor if you suspect that this is the case.

- ✔ **Mental health issues:** Mental health issues affect about one in four people in any one year. If you have issues with your mental health, you're more likely to have issues with sleep. Mental health issues include depression, anxiety, panic and bipolar disorder.

- ✔ **Medication:** Various medications affect your sleep, such as antidepressants, medication for high blood pressure or hormone replacement therapy. Check the label with your pharmacist or doctor if you think that the medication you are taking is causing your sleep problems.

According to the Royal College of Psychiatrists, sleeping tablets don't work for long; they cause tiredness and irritability the next day, gradually lose their effectiveness requiring the need to take more and more, and are addictive. If you've been taking sleeping tablets for a long time, see your doctor to discuss the possibility of reducing your intake gradually.

Overcoming insomnia

People who snore always fall asleep first.

Anonymous

Insomnia is not something you have to just accept. Even if you've been suffering from lack of sleep for a long time, some of the suggestions below may just work for you. For some people just one change can make all the difference – for others, they need to make a combination of positive changes before they notice any improvement. Give the following suggestions a try and see what happens:

- ✔ **Get exercising:** Regular exercise has a huge amount of benefits, one of them being better sleep – as long as you don't overdo it. Avoid exercising late in the evening as you'll stimulate your brain, which isn't good for sleeping. Check out Chapter 6 for lots of good exercise ideas.

- ✔ **Relax:** If your mind is highly active during the day, your incessant thoughts may prevent you from sleeping. Try practising slow, abdominal breathing every night (see Chapter 5 for the low-down on breathing techniques), listen to a relaxation CD, or try any of your other favourite relaxation techniques. Simply getting a massage or having a hot bath may help.

- ✔ **Stop trying to sleep:** If you don't fall asleep for some time and begin to feel annoyed or frustrated, stop! Leave the bedroom and do another calming activity, such as reading a relaxing book or working through a simple puzzle. When you feel sleepy, go back to bed.

- ✔ **Make your bedroom sleep-friendly:** Keep your bedroom for sleeping, not a high-tech, space-age entertainment zone. Televisions, computers and mobile phones stimulate your brain, which can have a negative impact on your sleep, impacting on your whole day. If you have to have these items in your bedroom, see if you can resist using them for a few hours before you sleep.

- ✔ **Think about what you drink:** Don't drink caffeinated drinks after lunch. Caffeine is a stimulant and may keep you awake or reduce the time you spend in a deep sleep. Caffeine can even affect your sleep after ten hours. Instead of drinking a cup of coffee in the evening, try a soothing herbal tea – there's a wide range of choice nowadays so see what you like.

 Drinking alcohol is okay in small quantities in the evening. But alcohol makes you urinate more, so if you drink too much you may wake up and need a wee in the middle of the night. Drinking alcohol also makes you more likely to snore – snoring reduces the amount of oxygen reaching your bloodstream, meaning you feel less refreshed in the morning. If you drink alcohol every evening and have trouble with sleep, maybe now is the time to reduce your alcohol intake.

- ✔ **Eat properly:** The adage 'Eat breakfast like a king, lunch like a prince and dinner like a pauper' makes sense. If you eat a heavy meal in the evening, your digestive system has to work hard, preventing you from sleeping properly.

 Serotonin is an important brain chemical that affects your sleep cycle. If you feel very hungry in the evening, stick to carbohydrates like bread, pasta and cereal, which help to release serotonin into your bloodstream, improving your sleep.

Tyramine is a chemical found in some foods that releases stress hormones into your bloodstream. Avoid foods that contain tyramine, such as aged cheese, soy sauce, some wines or cured meats like sausages or pepperoni as these release chemicals that stimulate your brain.

To reduce late-night stomach callings, try eating a snack that combines both carbohydrates and tryptophan (a protein that helps produce sleep-inducing serotonin in your body), such as a peanut-butter sandwich, a bowl of sugar-free wholegrain cereal, or a small piece of fruit with some herbal tea.

✔ **Be regular:** Humans are creatures of habit. Try to go to bed and wake up at about the same time every day. If you have a night when you don't sleep very well, get up at your regular time rather than messing up your body clock by having a lie-in.

✔ **Cut out long daytime naps:** If you feel sleepy and fancy a nap in the afternoon, go for it, especially if your boss doesn't mind or doesn't notice. This has been found to have a useful relaxation effect. But if you sleep for more than about 20 minutes you go into a different sleep stage and may feel worse when you wake up. You're then more likely to have trouble sleeping at night.

✔ **Keep a sleep diary:** You only need to spend a few minutes each night and morning filling the diary in, and you are likely to find patterns that help you to identify the kind of behaviours that affect your sleep quality and quantity. For example, you may notice that when you drink hot chocolate at night, you always sleep for two hours less, or a morning run results in a deep sleep. Here's what to put in your diary:

- When did you go to bed?

- What and when did you eat?

- What and when did you drink?

- Did you have any naps? When? How long?

- Did you do any physical activity, including things such as gardening and walking? When? How long?

- Did you have any caffeine, alcohol, nicotine or other drugs? When? How much?

- What does your bedtime routine consist of?

- How did you feel during the day as a whole today?

- How well do you feel that you slept?

- What did you do when you weren't sleeping (did you get up? Did you do some meditation in bed? Did you just toss and turn?)

- Total number of hours slept approximately?

If you're finding your lack of sleep is having a negative impact on your daily routine, see your doctor. You may have a sleep disorder and your doctor may be able to offer you treatment – there are many different options nowadays. It's much better to talk to a professional rather than suffer on your own.

I recently had a client who asked for help with her insomnia. She had been tested by doctors and found to have no physical reason for her lack of sleep – they put it down to stress. She was a busy, high-powered businesswoman who worked in the city. She told me that she liked her work but had always lived slightly 'on edge' and 'tense'. She had followed all the normal advice to prepare herself to sleep, like avoiding drinking stimulants, not watching television, or using the computer for the last few hours before sleep, eating the right foods, and exercising. And yet, each night, she found herself tossing and turning in bed all night. Through our conversation I discovered that she was trying too hard to sleep. She kept in control of everything, and she wanted to be in control of her sleep. As I explained to her, ultimately sleep is about letting go of control. Sleep comes when you stop trying to do anything, including trying to 'do' sleep. If you ask most people who fall asleep easily, what they do to help them to sleep, they usually say 'nothing'. Sounds frustrating, but ultimately the only way to fall asleep is to do nothing, or at least stop trying to sleep. Through practising a mindful approach to sleep I taught her mindful and relaxation exercises. She began to accept her insomnia. The battle of trying to sleep eased off through daily mindfulness and relaxation exercises. She learnt to ease off her control. Lying in bed, she became aware of her thoughts and gently practised some mindfulness or other relaxation strategies without trying to sleep. And then the sleep came.

Chapter 15

Discovering Relaxation at Home

. . . .

In This Chapter

▶ Overcoming common barriers to relaxing at home

▶ Looking at ways to create an oasis of calm

▶ Eating foods that encourage a stress-resistant life

▶ Finding quick, powerful ways to relax using your senses

. . . .

He is the happiest, be he king or peasant, who finds peace in his home.

Johann Wolfgang von Goethe

The average Westerner spends about 14 hours a day at home. That's over half your life! You sleep for a decent chunk of that time, but that still leaves about a quarter of your life awake at home. If high stress levels are an issue for you, finding ways to relax at home makes sense.

In this chapter I offer a range of ways for you to discover relaxation in your own home, from eating the right foods, to communicating effectively with your partner. Even if you live out of a suitcase, in this chapter you'll find some nifty ways of keeping your cool.

Relaxation is a necessity rather than a luxury. Cars need fuel to work. Lights need electricity to shine. You need rest from excessive work otherwise you'll probably burn out from chronic stress and that's not a nice place to be.

Breaking Down Barriers to Relaxation at Home

Depending on your life circumstances, your home may be a quiet sanctuary away from the hustle and bustle of everyday life, or a place where you need to be 100 per cent focused and on the job to prevent the next disaster.

Whatever your circumstances, you may identify with some of these common ways that home becomes a stress generator – relationship issues with your partner, raising children and managing financial pressures.

Enjoying your relationship with your partner

If you're in a relationship, this can be both a source of great joy and relaxation, and a source of conflict, stress and fear.

If your relationship causes you stress, you probably need to take some action to prevent things deteriorating. In this section I point you in the right direction and begin easing the stress.

Follow these steps to begin dealing with relationship stress:

1. **Stop blaming each other.**

   If you and your partner have problems, you probably blame your partner and your partner blames you. Try to reach an agreement that you both share some joint responsibility. Avoid sentences like 'Your problem is. . . ' and replace them with 'I' statements, such as 'I feel hurt when you. . . '

2. **Find time to talk.**

   You both need time to work things out. No matter how busy your life is, are you willing to damage the relationship further just because you can't make time to be together? Relationships are about spending time together. Managing time is about managing priorities, so try to put your relationships as high as possible on that priority ladder if you want to be together. Relationships matter.

3. **Communicate with respect.**

   When you communicate with each other, are you polite? Often, after some time in a relationship, respectful communication seems to disappear. Saying 'That was a delicious dinner, thank you,' doesn't take too much effort. Say 'Please could you mow the lawn today?' rather than 'It's been two weeks since you cut the lawn. You're lazy. You've always been lazy.' A little bit of courtesy goes a long way.

4. **Have an evening out and dress up.**

   Remember when you first dated? You may have made more of an effort to look nice for each other. Try the same approach again – small changes can make a big difference. Wear that new perfume, iron your shirt and make an occasion out of an evening together.

5. Socialise with friends.

If you spend time with the same friends that you were with when you first went out with each other, they may ease the tension and remind you of the good times together. Reminding you reawakens latent positive memories of why you got together in the first place.

6. Listen to each other without interruption.

You may feel that every time you try to make your point heard, your partner interrupts. But maybe you interrupt your partner too. Try using the five minute rule. Listen to your partner for five minutes without interrupting. Then swap, and you have a go at talking. You'll feel much better for being heard. After half-an-hour, agree that you're going to stop. You could also try mindful listening. When your partner's speaking, notice all the judgements and arguments that pop into your mind as he/she speaks, and let them go – just listen while your partner speaks, otherwise you end up listening to yourself, not to them.

You can also keep the following principles in mind when developing your relationship, to avoid relationship stress:

- **Life has its ups and down.** If you expect things to go well all the time, you're going to be disappointed. Everyone has different ideas about friends, family, finances and raising children, for example. So you'll have disagreements. And when your mother-in-law makes life difficult, you both feel the stress and patience levels will plummet. Accepting that life is always full of change and the challenge is managing it effectively helps – resisting challenges and seeing them as inconvenient and unfair difficulties causes greater suffering.

- **Remember to compromise.** Relationships are built on give and take. You can't always have your own way. If you want the TV on and your partner wants the TV off, you both need to agree on a solution. If you make 'winning' your goal all the time, you're going to make the relationship more difficult. When coming to a resolution of an argument, remember to start sentences with 'I' rather that accusing with the word 'you'. And notice if you often drag old arguments into the mix – stay with the issue at hand.

- **Physical touch is important.** Research suggests that human touch releases hormones associated with the feeling of affection and care. Holding hands, hugging, and kissing take very little time but helps to subtly strengthen your bonds with each other. Remember to be sensitive to your partner's needs. Develop physical intimacy in whatever form you're both comfortable with.

- **Keep interests beyond your relationship.** Develop other friendships. Don't depend on your partner for support all the time – you can end up putting too much pressure on them. You have a range of needs, as does your partner. If you like fishing and your partner prefers dancing, you can both meet your needs with different groups rather than dragging each other along. Creating some space in your togetherness prevents the relationship becoming stifled.

If you experience physical violence from your partner, report it to the police or seek professional advice immediately.

Coping with financial pressures

If you have a growing financial debt, no amount of relaxation alone is going to solve the issue. However, carrying out relaxation techniques whilst dealing with the debt issues may help to keep your stress levels down. This can aid in keeping your mind clear so you can make the most effective decisions, rather than being panicky and indecisive.

Here's some advice from a UK government agency on dealing with personal debt:

1. **Make a list of what you owe.**

   Include a list of who you owe money to, and how much you owe to each person or organisation.

2. **List your debts in order of importance.**

   For example, your mortgage repayments are probably more important than your credit card repayments, as your home is at risk if you don't pay your mortgage. Other high-priority debts may include rent and utility bills.

3. **Create a personal budget.**

   Make a list of all your spending and income every week or month. This total is your budget. You can then see areas where you can save money, and work out how much of your priority debts you can afford to pay.

4. **Get advice.**

   Contact an independent financial organisation to give you advice on managing your debt and how to contact your creditor (those you owe money to).

5. **Talk rather than avoid.**

   Get in touch with all the organisations to whom you owe money. Be careful that you don't end up getting advice from a dodgy advisor who ends up making you pay even more than you need to. Instead, talk to an advisor at your local Citizen's Advice Bureau, who can help you for free. Find your nearest local bureau by looking at www.citizensadvice.org.uk.

Worrying and getting stressed out about a lack of money won't solve the problem. If you catch yourself worrying, stop and write down your worries. Then take action if necessary. If you genuinely can't do anything about the problem, talk to someone who can help. Communication helps you to relax in this situation whereas stress could just make you ill, making the problem worse. Keep taking those small steps forwards.

Dealing with children's behaviour

One of the main reasons you may have difficulty relaxing at home is the demands of your children. In this section I offer some thoughts on managing one of the key causes of stress when raising children – behaviour.

- ✔ **Accept that your child will challenge you.** If you think your child will behave well all the time, and always do as you say, you're bound to set yourself up for stress. As children grow up, they learn to assert their independence and most challenge the authority of their parents. This challenging can take the form of arriving home late, answering back and not doing as they're told. You don't have to just accept the behaviour, but you do have to accept that it'll happen.

- ✔ **Communicate effectively.** Try not to shout when you talk to your child. Use explanations and reasons for doing things when you can. This is especially important in the teenage years when boundaries get tested more frequently.

- ✔ **Let minor issues go and focus on the positive.** Try to focus on praise and reinforce positive behaviour rather than picking on minor issues. Both you and your child then feel more relaxed. Focusing on poor behaviour can make your child's behaviour worse, as you start to give your child your attention only when they behave badly.

- ✔ **Use distraction.** If your child is locked into a bad mood or negative attitude, try distracting them by saying something like 'Shall we pop to the park and you can play some football there'?

- ✔ **Discipline the action, not the child.** If your child does something way beyond the line, you may need to impose a sanction. But make clear that it's the behaviour that you were not happy with, not them as a person. In this way you deal with the issue and don't knock your child's inner confidence. For example, say, 'Your behaviour was disgraceful because you didn't respect those people, Jonny,' not, 'You're disgraceful, Jonny.'

- ✔ **Be specific with praise.** Rather than just saying 'Well done,' be specific. Say what you like about your child's actions, such as 'I really liked the way you cleared the table without me having to ask you. Well done, Sarah!'

✔ **Set some rules and routines.** Having set times to wake up, eat and do homework makes life easier and less stressful for you and your child. Be firm about sticking to the routine but be prepared to do some negotiation as your child reaches early to mid-teens and becomes more independent.

✔ **Repeat statements to avoid arguments.** If you ask your child to do something and they try to engage you in an argument, simply keep repeating your statement, calmly and firmly. Use this 'broken record' technique so that you don't have to constantly think of reasons and arguments for everything. 'It's homework time, Nicola'. 'But I need to. . .' 'I said it's homework time, Nicola.'

Finding Relaxation at Home

A house is made of walls and beams; a home is built with love and dreams.

Author Unknown

Your physical environment can either be conducive to encouraging relaxation or stress. The way the place looks, the temperature and pollution levels, the sounds and scents all impact on how you feel. You can make feeling relaxed more likely by creating a physical environment conducive to rest and rejuvenation.

Creating your space for relaxation

You may like to dedicate a corner or, if you have the space, an entire room to relaxation. The benefit of this is, as soon as you step into that area, your body and mind associate the physical area with relaxation and you begin to let go of stress immediately. Here are some suggestions for your little space of relaxation, where you can use your relaxation techniques from this book:

✔ Clear your area of clutter.

✔ Have some pictures, statues, flowers or plants that help you feel relaxed when you look at them.

✔ Use an oil burner to disperse essential oils or incense sticks, whatever you prefer.

✔ Have some comfortable cushions, blankets or a favourite chair. Pick whatever makes you feel warm and relaxed.

✔ Play some relaxing music.

Your space of relaxation doesn't have to be in your home. It could be in your garden or a favourite place outdoors.

Share pictures of your relaxation space online on www.relaxationfor dummies.com/my-relaxation-space and have a look at what others have done.

Getting organised at home to unwind

If you're constantly rushing about, struggling to find things when you need them, or forgetting to pay important bills, you probably know that you need to get organised. An organised lifestyle is a great way for you to relax as you can take action and see the positive results, as can everyone else.

Here is a simple five-step approach to get your home more organised and a place to be proud of:

1. **In a notebook write down all the rooms in your home.**

2. **Go into each room and write down all the problems you notice.**

   Include areas of disorganisation. For example: 'Bedroom – lots of clothes on the floor in corner, two big piles of books on the desk, two boxes of disorganised paperwork.'

3. **Write down why these problems exist.**

   For example: 'The clothes are on the floor because the laundry basket is downstairs. We have disorganised paperwork because when we get new mail we don't deal with it there and then but just put it in the box.'

4. **Work out solutions to the problems.**

   Some may be simple, such as 'Buy a new laundry basket.' Other solutions need a bit more thought, such as 'Ensure new bills go into a special in-tray or deal with them when we open them. Give responsibility for other mail to partner or older child.' Other solutions may involve talking to other family members. For example, 'Tell Frank that he needs to put his books back after he finishes studying.'

5. **Take action!**

   Carry out the solutions you have written down. Focus first on the areas that you think are most important. Don't rush things but don't try to avoid them either – just go step by step.

Clearing out clutter to help you unwind

Clutter causes stress. All the bits and pieces remind you of all the work you have to do. Or perhaps you see things from a Feng Shui point of view and believe that the clutter prevents the positive flow of energy through your home. Either way, unnecessary clutter isn't helpful. It's a low-level stressor that constantly irritates you without you knowing it. Think of it like a bucket with a hole in it – no matter how much you do, the energy is gradually seeping away. So, take a small step today, as small as you want, and begin the journey to a clutter-free environment.

Here are some extra tips for getting yourself more organised:

- **Have fun.** Getting organised doesn't have to be boring. You could listen to your favourite music as you vacuum, clear your wardrobe out with your friend, and sprinkle in a few of your special dance moves as you put things back in their place.

- **Treat yourself.** You're probably not getting organised because you find it hard, boring or difficult. If you do manage to make a start, give yourself a treat – your favourite snack, a hot bath or a night out at the movies.

- **Set time limits.** Setting time limits helps ensure that you don't spend too much, or too little, time on organisation. For example, you may plan to spend two hours every Saturday morning working through your list of things to do to get more organised. Or you could spend just 15 minutes every evening, before sitting down to watch TV.

- **Get your family involved.** If you don't live alone, ask for help from others. Avoid extra stress and conflict by discussing the situation calmly in a meeting. Get each person to agree their roles, and check up on them every day or week. Try offering them rewards for keeping things tidy if you think that would work.

- **Hire extra help.** If you don't have the time to get organised, but do have the money, then consider paying someone to get your place organised. You may even save money in the long run, as you'll live in a more relaxed environment and have space for new ideas and see new opportunities.

Gardening for relaxation

Gardening is a great way to relax. Finding time to connect with nature, allowing your hands to get dirty in the soil, smelling the flowers or the grass, is often therapeutic and calming. The fresh air and the sunshine themselves are a relaxing aid. The whole experience of gardening draws your senses into the present moment and done in a mindful way (see Chapter 10) your chattering mind begins to calm down a little.

The other great advantage of gardening is the physical activity it provides. Exercise is a well-proven stress reliever – by doing a little bit of digging, planting, weeding and mowing, you're giving yourself an all-body workout. Just remember to have a little stretch before you start – injuries aren't relaxing!

The aim of this section is to share the relaxing benefits of Gardening. If you're interested in finding out how to actually garden, look out for *Gardening For Dummies* by Sue Fisher, Michael MacCaskey and Bill Marken (Wiley).

As a youngster, I used to love gardening. I had a lot of energy, and after going out cycling with my friends and having watched some TV, I began to feel restless. Then one day I discovered the joys of gardening. I used to dream about getting high-tech lawn mowers that could makes stripes on our lawn, like in a professional football stadium. I read books about growing different types of flowers, made hanging baskets, and even attempted to make a rock garden. That didn't go quite so well. When I went off to secondary school, I lost the habit and am only now beginning to rekindle my interest. Although I'm busy nowadays, I'm prioritising hobbies and activities like gardening to help me stay centred and relaxed – a stressed-out relaxation expert just doesn't look right!

Here are a few suggestions if you're gardening for the first time:

- ✔ **Start small.** As you're using this time to relax, don't try to think too much about the outcome. Focus on one corner of your garden, or start with tending pot plants.

- ✔ **Take frequent breaks.** If you tire yourself out too much to begin with, you're less likely to continue. In your break, remember to drink plenty of water to hydrate yourself.

- ✔ **Garden regularly.** Spending a whole day on the garden and then not touching the area for a few weeks isn't so effective. Little and often is the key.

- ✔ **Breathe.** If you find your thoughts going to worries and concerns as you garden, take a couple of deep breaths and then gently rest your attention on your breathing. After a few moments, turn your attention back to nature. Check out Chapter 5 for more on breathing for relaxation.

Cooking your way to relaxation

Like gardening, cooking is a sensual experience: you use your hands and you get in touch with nature through the food you prepare. I can think of few greater pleasures than taking the time to cook a delicious meal with care and attention, and then share the meal with close family and friends, fully tasting and enjoying each bite.

Again, this section is about cooking in a way that helps you feel more relaxed. If you actually want to ensure what you cook is tasty, then I'm not the one to ask. Instead flick through *Cooking For Dummies* by Alison Yates and Bryan Miller (Wiley) for inspiration and some delicious recipes.

Consider these two key tips that offer a way to enjoy yourself as you cook, rather than feel like you're constantly rushing to get food on to the table. Try them out by finding some extra time to cook, perhaps on the weekend to begin with.

- ✔ **Experiment for creative relaxation.** Although you may start cooking by following recipes, try experimenting. By allowing yourself the chance for things to go wrong a little, you also set up the chance for your cooking to come up with something new and scrumptious! Just like any adventure, when you make something up, you never know what will happen, and that's half the fun. Consider making time to do this kind of cooking – it's relaxing and fun, my favourite combination!

- ✔ **Use mindful cooking to calm your mind.** Try giving full attention to the kneading, chopping, frying and sizzling. Look at the range of colours in the food, enjoy the scent as you chop the fruit or vegetables, delight in the contact of your hands with the food you're preparing. You can even take time to listen to the food as it boils, sizzles or simmers on your stove. Concentrating on the look and sounds of your cooking makes the process more relaxing and keeps your mind off the usual worries and concerns.

Getting a pet to help you relax

Sometimes the world seems a big, scary place. You don't know who to trust or what to do. Coming home to a friendly cat purring or dog wagging her tail can make a huge difference. Suddenly you feel as if there's someone who cares about you and misses you, even if they're not a human. Humans can be terribly complicated anyway – animals are simple in an innocent way and don't judge you like other people may do. This attitude is incredibly liberating.

As you may have noticed, I like my science, and had a look at the evidence to show the relaxation benefits of owning a pet. Here are a few I liked:

- ✔ Several experiments have shown that looking at aquarium fish lowers blood pressure.

- ✔ A study on New York stockbrokers found that owners who spent time with a dog or cat had a drop in high blood pressure in a way that was even more effective than drugs!

✔ Pets may reduce stress more than humans can. In a recent study, the participants were given a stressful task to do, and split into two groups. One group had their supportive friend or partner with them, and the other had their pet. The pet owners were more relaxed than those with their supportive friend or spouse.

Pets help you to stay relaxed for a number of reasons. Here are a few of them:

✔ Pets offer enjoyable company. In this way, pets reduce the sense of loneliness and isolation. In one study in a nursing home, the residents felt less lonely when visited by a dog alone, rather than a dog together with a human friend. Even the researchers were surprised by the result. Less loneliness means a greater feeling of relaxation.

✔ Having a dog encourages you to go out regularly for walks, making you exercise. And exercise almost always leads to greater relaxation and resilience to future stress.

✔ Having a pet encourages you to socialise. For example, when you take your dog for a walk, you're more likely to talk to other people along the way and strike up a conversation. These small social interactions have a powerful stress-relieving effect.

✔ Pets help reduce depression. In a large study on the health benefits of pets, researchers examined people with HIV/AIDS. If the participants owned a dog, they were significantly less likely to have depression.

Enjoying a relaxing bath

Lots of people like to use a bath to relax. If you don't have a bath, try taking a long, hot shower instead. Here are some tips to make your bath nice and soothing:

1. **Prepare by ensuring your bath is clean and put some nice, clean towels on a radiator or somewhere warm.**

   Turn off all your phones and let everyone know you're busy and not to be disturbed please!

2. **Have something nice and comfortable to wear when you get out of the bath.**

3. **Arrange and light some scented candles in the bathroom to give a soothing glow and pleasant scent.**

4. **If you want, play some relaxing music.**

   Keep the player well away from the water – electricity and water are a dangerous combination.

5. **You may also like to enjoy a warm, caffeine-free drink.**

   If you have alcohol, for safety reasons make sure you don't overdo it.

6. **Fill your bath at the right temperature.**

   Too hot or cold and it won't be relaxing.

7. **Add a few drops of your favourite essential oil.**

   You could try contrasting the scent with that of the candles for a deeper relaxation experience. Alternatively, bath salts are a good choice. Epsom salts are popular for relaxation.

8. **Gently climb in.**

   If you have an inflatable pillow on which to rest your head, go ahead and use it.

9. **If you're into facial masks or putting cucumber slices on your eyes, now's the time to do it.**

10. **Enjoy the sensual experience of the bath.**

    Think that you have nothing else to do and nowhere else to go right now. Just enjoy the moment and be grateful to have the time and space for this experience.

11. **When you're done, gently dry yourself.**

    Slip into the robe or clothes you prepared and treat yourself to another warm drink before reading a book, watching a nice film (choose something relaxing!) or going to bed.

Trying a Relaxation Diet

You are what you eat. If you eat and drink things that increase your level of stress, then you're making life more difficult than necessary.

Most people have difficulty controlling what they eat. However, by reading this section, at least you have the knowledge about the kind of foods that encourage relaxation. And then, with a bit of willpower, you can begin to make tiny, baby steps towards meals that help you to feel at ease with yourself rather than anxious and stressed.

The great thing about preparing healthy food is that the actual act of cooking can help you relax too, as I explain in the section 'Cooking your way to relaxation' earlier in this chapter.

Eating food to encourage relaxation

Your nutritional intake affects the kind of chemical swirling in your blood stream. If you eat the right foods, you'll be able to encourage a natural relaxation effect. The wrong food will make it more likely that your stress response kicks in unnecessarily. In this section, find out which foods will make you feel more at ease.

Here are some foods that help you to chill out:

- **Avocado:** recommended by the NHS due to its high levels of potassium.

- **Broccoli:** Contains lots of folic acid, which is said to help reduce stress.

- **Celery:** Has a range of benefits including reducing blood pressure.

- **Dark chocolate:** I bet you're pleased to see this one on the list. Try taking a small piece and letting it slowly melt in your mouth and enjoy each moment. See if you can get chocolate with at least 70% cocoa.

- **Dried apricots:** They contain high levels of beta-carotene, which pro-tects your heart.

- **Green tea:** Contains lots of theanine, which helps generate a relaxing feeling by calming your mind.

- **Hot chocolate:** Helps you to generate a feeling of warmth and comfort, easing tensions from the day.

- **Milk:** A glass of milk raises serotonin levels, a brain chemical that helps you to relax. Turkey meat also offers the same effect. Finally, something that reduces stress for those who celebrate Christmas with a traditional meal!

- **Nuts:** These are great for keeping stress at bay. They contain lots of magnesium, which tends to keep the stress hormone cortisol in check. Walnuts and pistachios also help reduce blood pressure.

- **Salmon sandwich:** This contains omega 3, helping your brain to operate effectively. A better functioning brain creates relaxation.

- **Spinach:** A portion of spinach contains almost half your daily needs of magnesium, a stress-buster.

- **Sugar:** A spot of sugar on the tongue helps you to feel better. It also decreases the level of stress-inducing hormones in your bloodstream. Sweet potatoes are another very good option because they also contain lots of carbohydrate, beta-carotene and fibre, ensuring your blood sugar doesn't spike up.

- **Wholegrain bread:** Contains complex carbohydrates, which increase your level of serotonin, encouraging relaxation. Oats are also a great option too, lowering your chance of heart disease.

Eat small meals regularly, rather than big meals followed by hours of no food. Grazing (eating small quantities of food, regularly) helps to keep your blood sugar level fairly steady. If your blood-sugar level goes down too much, you indirectly generate stress.

Avoiding nutritional habits that cause stress

Now that you know the kind of foods that help you to relax, you can also ensure that you know the kind of nutritional habits that actually cause stress. Some of them are fairly obvious, but not all. This section lists the habits to avoid:

- ✔ Caffeine in the form of too much coffee, tea or soft drinks increases the level of the stress hormone cortisol. Caffeine offers a temporary 'high' but that is soon followed by a 'low'.

- ✔ Skipping meals is easy to do when you're feeling stressed, but leads to a drop in your blood sugar, causing your body greater stress. Make meal-times a priority otherwise you end up eating too much, too little or the wrong food. Eat in a mindful way, giving attention to the taste and colour.

- ✔ Lack of water is very common nowadays and prevents your body and brain from working properly. You feel edgy, irritable and snappy. Drink water before you feel thirsty – by the time you feel thirsty, you're already dehydrated.

- ✔ Avoid fast foods as these generally contain excess fat, sugar and salt, which aren't conducive to a healthy, relaxed lifestyle.

Eating mindfully to relax and enjoy

You may be in the habit of rushing your food, like most people. Mindful eating is about slowing down and really tasting each morsel, appreciating the flavour and being grateful to have food available for you to eat.

Have a go next time you have a bit of time to eat.

1. **Turn off all distractions, including phones, TV and the internet.**

   Avoid reading newspapers and magazines too – just make it you and your meal.

2. **Look at your food.**

   Notice the colour and shades. Notice the quantity of food. Check in to see how hungry you actually feel at the moment.

3. **Smell your food.**

   Become aware of the various aromas. Are you salivating now?

4. **Take a spoonful of food, place it in your mouth and slowly chew.**

   Become aware of the flavours and textures. Savour each morsel. Don't put anymore food into your mouth until you've finished this one mouthful.

5. **Continue eating in this mindful way.**

   Be grateful to have access to such beautiful food when so many have to go without food altogether. You could also reflect on the sunshine, rain and number of people involved in making this food available. For example, rice would need to be harvested, cleaned, packaged, transported, sold and stored, involving thousands of people.

The secret of mindful eating is to connect with your senses rather than letting your mind wander off for too long. If you start to eat quickly and automatically again, try not to beat yourself up about it. Just notice, and come back to mindful eating.

Using Your Senses to Relax

Your senses offer a quick and effective way of relieving your stress and feeling more relaxed. Stress is often caused by your own thinking. So any way of disengaging your thought pattern leads to relaxation. Your senses are a gateway to the present moment and take you out of your head with all its thoughts, worries and concerns. In this section I offer you the chance to experiment and find the right combination of senses that relax you most quickly and deeply.

Choosing the right approach for your stress

You react to stress in a unique way. So, you need to find the right approach for you. You may react to stress in one of these ways:

- ✔ **Emotional high:** You feel agitated, angry and irritable. You'd relax most easily with a sense that calms you down.

- ✔ **Emotional low:** You feel low, depressed, disorientated, spaced out and want to withdraw. You'd most benefit from a sense that uplifts and stimulates you.

✔ **Emotional high and low:** In other words, like having the accelerator and brake down in a car simultaneously. You don't get anywhere – you freeze. You need a combination of both stimulating and calming approaches to deal with your stress and feel relaxed again.

I can't predict which sense or stimulation will uplift you and which one will calm you. Everyone is different. By looking through the section below, experiment to see what works for you, remembering how you react to stress as explained above.

After you find the way you react to stress and the most effective way of relaxing through the use of your senses, you have a skill that you can use for a lifetime.

Serene sights

If you know yourself to be a visual person, this technique is for you. You don't even have to be able to see something directly – you can visualise. Here are some ways you can use your sense of sight to help you to relax:

✔ Look at something natural, like a tree, your garden or a plant.

✔ Gaze at a photo of a loved one or your family.

✔ Imagine your favourite peaceful place. See Chapter 9 for guided imagery exercises.

Calming scents

You need to choose the right scent depending on how you react to stress. If you need energising, choose the invigorating scents. If you need calming, go for the soothing smells. Experiment to see which scents work for you.

Scientists stressed out some poor lab rats and found that those who were exposed to linalool, a chemical in lavender, citrus, basil, birch and other plants returned to almost normal levels of stress.

Here are some examples of ways to access scents when stressed:

✔ Have a flower that gives off a pleasant scent at home or in the office.

✔ Carry a little bottle containing your favourite scent for relaxation, such as lavender.

✔ Burn some incense sticks in your home. Choose a scent you like.

✔ Use a scented candle when you can.

✔ Lightly smell your delicious meal before you begin eating it.

✔ Get some fresh air outside by walking or gardening.

Essential oils

An essential oil is a natural product taken from a single plant. There is growing evidence that essential oils are beneficial for stress relief, as well as other conditions. Peppermint is helpful for relieving fatigue and lavender helps to reduce insomnia. Essential oils enter your body through your skin or by inhaling. You can inhale essential oils using various devices or techniques like a diffuser, dry evaporation (a few drops of essential oil on some cotton wool), steam (a few drops in a bowl of steaming water) or as a spray (diluted in water). To prepare essential oil, you need to dilute the oil with a carrier such as vegetable or nut oil, or water at a concentration no more than 5 per cent. That's about one teaspoon of carrier for every five drops of oil. For massage, use no more than 1 per cent concentration. Essential oils are generally safe. You just need to be sure you've diluted them sufficiently, and check the label, as some essential oils can be used for inhaling but are not so suitable for massage. A small portion of people are allergic so use with care for the first time. If in any doubt, or for more support and guidance, speak to a professional qualified aromatherapist.

Relaxing tastes

Every time you pass food or drink into your mouth, you have an opportunity to relax. If you're eating under stress and mindlessly, not only do you end up compounding your stress, but you can put on weight needlessly.

To begin working towards ending this cycle of stress-eating, try eating one meal a week in a mindful way, looking carefully at each morsel, and fully tasting each bite.

Here are some things you could easily try during the day:

✔ Chew a piece of gum and really notice the sensations.

✔ Eat a small piece of fresh fruit.

✔ Drink a cup of herbal tea.

✔ Savour a piece of dark chocolate.

✔ Suck on a mint.

Soothing touch

For many people touching is a powerful way to get into a relaxed state. Try to find which method works for you. Some of these touch techniques don't have to be used just when you're stressed – they can also be used to deepen your feelings of relaxation. Then you're better prepared when the next stressful event comes along.

Here are a few ideas to get you started:

- ✔ Give yourself a self-massage (see Chapter 8).
- ✔ Gently stroke your dog or cat.
- ✔ Turn your attention to the sense of contact of your feet with the ground.
- ✔ Have a little soft toy handy to touch.
- ✔ Squeeze a tennis ball or a special stress ball.

Listening to chill out

If you generally like to use music to relax, use the sense of listening to explore further ways to relax. Have a look through these suggestions and see if any of them appeal:

- ✔ Use a *singing bowl* to generate a relaxing tone (also involves touch and movement). This is a metal bowl which makes a harmonious tone when resonated with a small wooden stick. It's probably easiest to buy online or at a local mind, body, spirit festival perhaps.
- ✔ Listen to some relaxing music.
- ✔ Try having some little bells or wind chimes just outside that you can hear.
- ✔ Go for a walk and listen to the sounds of nature – the wind against your face, the rustling of the leaves and the birds singing in the trees.
- ✔ Sing, whistle or hum. Humming is my favourite one although it does cause stress to anyone I'm near so I need to be careful!

Moving for rest and rejuvenation

You may find it easier to connect with your senses when you are moving. This form of relaxation is particularly effective if you feel low and withdrawn when you're stressed – emotionally low. Movement, even though you won't feel like it, has a direct effect on your mood and encourages relaxation. Try these suggestions:

- ✔ Go for a walk around the block.
- ✔ Stand upright and stretch towards the sky, opening up your body posture.
- ✔ Jump up and down whilst forcing a smile.
- ✔ Do a few of your favourite dance moves (may not go down too well in your office!).
- ✔ Roll your shoulders and then move.

Developing Your Social Support Network

Some people feel the need to meditate or go for a walk on their own to relax, but other people crave social contact. But actually, for most people, socialising is a powerful way to better wellbeing. Even if you think you'd rather be on your own, some social contact with the right people can make you feel more relaxed and open. It's about striking the right balance.

The benefits of socialising regularly are powerful. The more research I read, the more I'm convinced of the tremendous benefit of being with others. For example, a paper published in the *British Medical Journal* followed almost 3,000 people aged over 65 for about 13 years. Who survived? Those who exercised most, or who had lower blood pressure? Actually those who socialised regularly through things like volunteering or just getting together with friends lived as long as those who spent the same time exercising. Many other studies in the past have agreed – socialising keeps you feeling more relaxed and results in a longer and happier life, generally speaking.

Humans are social animals. You are designed to socialise frequently. If you live on your own or don't see friends very often, I suggest you read this section to help you build up a social network and feel relaxed.

Discovering ways of making friends

Making friends is an active process – it doesn't just happen by itself. Ultimately you only need two or three really good friends. That's far more valuable than lots of friends that you're not close to. If you want to make new friends, here are a few tips to get you going:

- ✔ Sign up to an adult education class, gym or sports club – you'll then meet like-minded people.

- ✔ Volunteer – you meet other people and feel good to be helping those less fortunate than you.

- ✔ Use the Internet to get off the Internet! Nowadays there are online groups that actually meet up in your local area. Check out www.meetup.com for starters.

- ✔ If you're having a party, tell all your friends to bring along a few of their friends and suddenly you've got a whole new group of people to meet with, mingle and enjoy. You're also more likely to get on with them if they're a friend of a friend.

- ✔ Dogs are friend magnets. All those daily doggie walks in your local neighbourhood soon get you chatting to the friendly bloke down the road, who you'd never chatted to before.

Improving your social skills

A true friend is someone who thinks that you are a good egg even though he knows that you are slightly cracked.

Bernard Meltzer

To start and keep friendships there are a few simple guidelines you need to follow. If you do them, your friends will really appreciate it, and will be more likely to reciprocate. Here are the common-sense guidelines that can be easy to forget:

✔ **Say a genuine thank you.** By showing some appreciation you naturally begin to deepen the relationship through your gratitude.

✔ **Listen.** If you love talking then this idea is especially for you! Taking time to listen to your friends is always much appreciated and they are more likely to stay in touch with you.

✔ **Give space.** Don't overwhelm your friend with constant texts, calls, e-mails and visits. Give them some space to just be themselves.

✔ **Celebrate success effectively.** If your friends succeed at something, don't just say, 'Oh great.' Ask them how they felt when they found out and how they feel about the success now. Tell them how proud you are of them and plan to celebrate together.

✔ **Use the golden rule.** Treat others as you would like others to treat you. This is the rule of reciprocity – simple, yet far-reaching.

Chapter 16

Find Relaxation at Work

. . . .

In This Chapter

▶ Finding ways to relax at work

▶ Improving communication with your colleagues to ease stress

▶ Managing your priorities to achieve balance

. . . .

Three Rules of Work: Out of clutter find simplicity; from discord find harmony; In the middle of difficulty lies opportunity.

Albert Einstein

ork.

Does that four-letter word bring a smile to your face or send steam out of your ears? Work can be an incredibly fun place to be, but it can also feel like hell on earth.

If you're stressed at work, you're not alone. Workplace stress is a huge problem worldwide. Many surveys show workplace stress is one of the major causes of stress for many people. In the US, 40 per cent of workers claim their job is very, or extremely, stressful. In the UK, half a million workers report falling ill because of excessive work stress.

If you are excessively stressed, you're unhealthier, less motivated, more prone to causing accidents and less productive than you can be. Taking time to find ways to ease your stress and relax helps you get more work done, more quickly, and offers you the chance of a more balanced, pleasant lifestyle.

In this chapter I show you ways to manage your personal level of stress in the workplace. Finding some relaxation may not involve huge changes – just changing those aspects of your work that you can control to enable constructive changes. I invite you to try the suggestions to see if they work for you.

Google likes to relax

One of my specialities is corporate and organisational stress reduction. I achieve this in a range of ways, but often it includes mindfulness, and a secular approach that helps people to feel calmer and more focused. Sometimes I train staff so that they can go on to facilitate groups within the company. I train groups of employees working on the ground in executive mindful coaching. Mindfulness is about becoming more aware of your body, thoughts, emotions and other people around you. Research has shown that an eight-week course in mindfulness in the workplace leads to positive changes in the brain, better defence against illness, and

greater feelings of relaxation. These positive effects prevent employees falling ill due to workplace stress and a more mindful workforce is a more effective and happy workforce. That's why leading global companies like Google have lectures and offer classes in mindfulness to reduce the stress of their employees. Other approaches I recommend are lunchtime yoga or t'ai chi, massage, policies to encourage lower stress levels within the organisation, access to healthier food and exercise. More and more companies are beginning to see that stress has serious consequences for the whole organisation if not managed.

Managing Stress in Your Workplace

The level of stress in your workplace is not a fixed thing. You may have a lot of control over your job, so that you can change things easily. On the other hand, changing things in your job may be tricky. One person may find a job stressful because they find it too difficult, whilst another person may find the same job stressful because it's boring. To a certain extent, you need to try to find work that offers the right level of challenge for you.

Sometimes work is so stressful and intense that finding time to relax is almost laughable. But if you don't manage the stress and relax, your efficiency goes down, your health deteriorates and you make poor decisions. Here are some of the issues that you may face if you have chronic workplace stress:

- ✔ **Back problems:** Research suggests that back and shoulder issues are often stress-related.
- ✔ **Cardiovascular disease:** This is more likely to occur in people with demanding jobs over which they have little control.
- ✔ **Psychological disorders:** Depression and burnout have been found to be linked to high job stress levels.
- ✔ **Workplace injuries:** These are more likely if you are highly stressed.

A little bit of pressure at work is good for you. But when the pressure becomes too much, it becomes stress, which is bad for you.

You can choose from a range of methods to lower your level of stress, from personal relaxation techniques to having discussions with management about your workload. If you work for yourself, you may have even more scope for change.

Discovering the warning signs of workplace stress

I've suffered from job stress. When my stress levels rose, my shoulders became tense. I frowned. I wasn't interested in talking to others or joking around. I felt tempted to stop exercising and had a tingle in my stomach. I tried to focus but couldn't. I wanted to get through my mountain of work, but things just got slower. I often got a headache. I felt I didn't have enough time and saw my job negatively. I had thoughts of inadequacy – that I wasn't good enough.

The following are typical warning signs of excessive workplace stress:

- ✓ **Physical symptoms:** Muscle tension, headaches, stomach problems, headaches, fatigue.
- ✓ **Psychological symptoms:** Difficulties in focusing, short temper, low morale, sleep disturbance, feeling anxious, irritability, depression, unwilling to socialise, using alcohol or drugs.

When you feel that your stress is rising take a notepad out and jot down all the warning signs that you're experiencing. Watch out for these warning signs next time you're at work, and take a few moments to reduce your stress. Use a relaxation technique that works for you, such as diaphragmatic breathing (which I describe in Chapter 5), going for a walk, having a cup of tea or listening to some calming music.

You get more work done when you're relaxed rather than highly stressed. High stress causes poor decisions, more mistakes, ineffective communication, illness and possibly even premature death. Put some relaxation into your day.

Identifying the causes of workplace stress

To manage your stress at work in the long term, you need to deal with the causes of your stress. After you find out the cause, you can take appropriate action. Likely causes of workplace stress include the following:

- ✔ **Excessive workload:** You have more work than you can cope with.

- ✔ **Lack of control:** You don't have a say about how you do your work.

- ✔ **Lack of job security:** You're not sure whether you'll be working there next week.

- ✔ **Lack of support:** You don't have sufficient information and advice from either your colleagues or supervisor to help you achieve your work.

- ✔ **Poor change management:** Whenever a change takes place at work, you don't have the opportunity to engage and communicate.

- ✔ **Poor conditions:** You work in a physically uncomfortable environment.

- ✔ **Poor workplace relationships:** You don't have harmonious, positive relationships; instead, you may experience workplace bullying or harassment.

- ✔ **Stressful commute:** Your journey to and from work is difficult.

- ✔ **Unclear role:** You don't have a clearly defined role at work.

Go through the points above and write down which of those factors may be the cause of your workplace stress. Then either take action to reduce your stress in that area or talk to your manager. If you can't talk to your manager, seek advice from someone you know and trust. You can also see your doctor, the company's occupational health therapist or a professional counsellor.

According to Professor Cooper, a leading workplace stress researcher, control is the key to managing stress and feeling more relaxed. When you feel out of control, you feel stressed. Think about what's causing you stress at the moment and ask yourself 'How can I take a bit more control of the situation?' and then take action.

Finding ways to relax at work

If you want to use self-help strategies to reduce your own stress levels, usethe following acronymn – TER. It stands for talk, exercise, relaxation technique. I explain what this means below:

- ✔ **Talk to someone.** If you have a certain issue causing you stress at work, you need to talk to someone about it. Talk to your friend or partner, colleague or counsellor. You can even talk to your doctor. The worse thing to do is to keep the problem to yourself and try to solve it on your own. Then you are internalising the stressor, which is unhealthy.

✔ **Get physical.** Taking exercise is a powerful way to relax after work. Rather than bringing all your stress home with you, go off for a run, take a brisk walk, visit the gym or play a sport. By doing some form of exercise, you put things into perspective. As you begin to relax through exercising, you start to get more creative ideas and solutions to deal with the issue. Or at least you have some time to take your mind off things.

✔ **Practise relaxation techniques.** You can use a variety of relaxation techniques to help deal with your stress. This book has a guide to most of them, from meditation to yoga, or maybe just a simple 10-minute guided imagery exercise, where you sit down after work and imagine your favourite peaceful place. Doing this won't solve the problem that is causing your stress, but by getting into a relaxed frame of mind, you may be able to see the problem differently, like a challenge for example, or you may just be able to accept it and move on.

Getting organised at work to feel more relaxed

If you're disorganised at work, you're more likely to feel stressed. Being organised helps you to relax. The section that follows offers tips for you to begin taking control of your work by becoming more organised.

Try to put the following ideas into practice to bring some order to your work:

✔ **Break down the big tasks.** If you have a huge task that's causing you stress, break down the job into bite-sized chunks. For example, when I'm writing a book, I break down the project into chapters and then sub-chapters. I assign days to write each section and give it the right priority. Writing a section is much less daunting than writing a whole book.

✔ **Delegate!** You don't have to do everything. Think about what you can pass on for others to do. Let go of your desire to control everything. Control is important but you also need to let go of some things.

✔ **Keep things in balance.** More about this later in this chapter in the section 'Balancing the Demands of Work'. In a nutshell, all work and no play is a recipe for a bundle of stress. Make time to socialise, exercise, for quiet time, and time to get your creative juices flowing.

✔ **Manage your mornings and evenings well.** Ensure that you leave plenty of time to arrive at work so you don't start the day stressed out. Leave some time at the end of the day to plan the next day's activities and to tidy your workspace.

✔ **Prioritise!** This is the biggest secret of them all. Make a 'to do' list of all the things that need doing, either at the end of the day or before going to sleep, so it's not on your mind. Then, number them in order of importance. Start with the highest-priority job in the morning, which is often the one you don't want to do. However, once you've tackled it, the rest of your day will feel more relaxed. Put exercise and relaxation on your list too.

✔ **Say no when you can.** Agreeing to do everything will cause you to get overloaded. Practise saying no to people if you're taking on too much work. Start with things that are easy and work your way up to saying no to more challenging or demanding tasks whenever you can.

✔ **Take regular breaks.** Short walks, perhaps even some banter with the staff at the local coffee shop, offers exercise, a change of environment and some socialising. All great ways to relax quickly. Alternatively, if you're behind a desk, stand up every 30 minutes or so and have a stretch, a drink of water or a piece of fruit and maybe visualise a pleasant place. A little meditation would be great too.

In addition to following the above tips, treat yourself to an organised space. Organised means you know where everything is and can get to it easily. Keep your workspace tidy. At the end of each day, clear your desk – no excuses! A clear desk keeps a clear mind. You may have the idea that you're more creative around clutter, but this is very unlikely. Try keeping a clear desk for 21 days and see what effect it has on your work. Here are a few ideas to help you clear your work area:

✔ **Use a system to organise all your paperwork.** For example, have an alphabetical system for filing bills and receipts.

✔ **Give yourself some time every day to organise your space.** The end of the day is usually a good time for this. Time yourself, say for 10 minutes, and do as much as you can on a daily basis.

✔ **Put things in their place.** This is just a habit you need to get into. Don't just put things down randomly on your desk or dining table or wherever you work. After you finish with something, put it back.

Overcoming unhelpful work attitudes

I can't change the direction of the wind, but I can adjust my sails to always reach my destination.

Jimmy Dean

Work attitudes are not easy to change, but as you begin to gain confidence in your ability to relax, you can discover approaches to work that just compound your stress rather than reduce it. Humans are creatures of habit, and if you can begin to mould your working life towards positive attitudes, you offer yourself the chance to ease off some of the anxieties.

To determine whether your attitudes towards work prevent you from relaxing, ask yourself the following questions:

- **Are you a perfectionist?** This is a common ideal that causes a great deal of stress. Notice whether you try to do things perfectly. Remember: perfection is an unreachable goal, as things can always be improved. Try listing all the disadvantages for yourself and others of a perfectionist tendency. Focus on enjoying the journey rather than only the goal. See criticism as a chance to learn rather than something to avoid all the time.

- **Are you negative?** Getting dragged into a complaining mode when working can be so easy. This approach drains your energy. Keep things in balance by remembering to appreciate what's going well. Phone a positive friend, make an excuse to go for a walk when your colleagues are just complaining too much, and jot down some work things you're grateful for on a daily basis.

- **Do you try to control everything?** If you try to control everyone and everything at work, you set yourself up for a stressful career. Change the things you can and need to change, but also learn to accept the things that you can't change. In particular, you can't control other people. Be responsible for yourself and your own actions. Lack of control doesn't mean weakness – giving others responsibility is a strength.

  The 'Serenity Prayer' is a good one for this. It asks for 'the serenity to accept the things I cannot change; courage to change the things I can; and wisdom to know the difference'.

- **Do you think you're incompetent?** You may have a sense of incompetence and self-doubt about your work. You may often think that your work is inferior and judge yourself harshly. Boost your confidence by countering your own judgements. For example, if you think 'I'll never get this work done on time,' think 'I've always done it on time in the past. Let me break it down and do the project step-by-step.' I like to just do what I can and let my manager/client/interviewer decide if they like my work rather than assuming I'm doing badly. And even if the manager is unhappy about my work, that's just one opinion. Another manager may disagree entirely.

- **Do you try to please others all the time?** If you constantly think about others' opinion of your work, you may base your self-esteem on other people's judgements. You can end up worrying if your work is good enough and avoid contact out of fear of hearing a negative judgement. This behaviour can be linked to perfectionist tendencies. Deal with this problem by noticing this pattern of behaviour and become aware of thoughts like 'I mustn't make a mistake or others will find out I'm useless,' or, 'If I show her my work, she might think it's rubbish. That would be terrible.' Make your thinking more realistic by saying to yourself things like, 'It's okay to make mistakes. I'm a human being,' or 'If she doesn't like it, that's her opinion. I don't have to depend on her for my self-esteem.'

Trying other strategies to stress less and relax more

Having worked as a senior manager and school teacher at secondary schools for over ten years, I've picked up a few ideas for ways of managing stress. All of these ideas are echoed by the National Institute for Occupational Safety and Health in the US.

- ✔ **Crack a few jokes.** Some laughter and banter with co-workers can help you to relax during the day. Don't miss out on all the fun – take a few minutes to share a joke.

- ✔ **Distinguish between work and home.** Make a clear transition between your home life and work. Listen to music, do a relaxation technique such as guided imagery or self-hypnosis, pop into your local cafe or go for a walk.

- ✔ **Do it now!** Avoid procrastination. If you really can't stand the thought of doing a task, do it for just one minute. You'll probably feel like doing more once you've started.

- ✔ **Do your time and let go.** Only work for the time that you're paid to work. Then stop, leave your work behind and go home. You'll get much more done in the long run and feel more relaxed. If you can't do that, finish your work at your workplace and try not to take it home.

- ✔ **Don't accumulate rubbish.** Sort out your e-mail and incoming letters as soon as you get them – it only takes a few minutes.

- ✔ **Follow your internal clock.** Tackle your most challenging work at a time of day when you're most awake and alert. For me that's the morning, for you that may be the afternoon or evening.

- ✔ **Get enough sleep.** By working late you'll feel tired the next day and end up being even more inefficient. Give sleep a high priority, especially in the long term.

- ✔ **Tackle stress.** When you feel your stress levels rising, stop what you're doing. Write down what you can do to lower your stress levels, such as breaking down your problem, scheduling a break, going for a five-minute walk or challenging your negative thoughts with more positive yet realistic statements.

✔ **Try the one-touch paper rule.** As soon as a new piece of paper arrives on your desk take action, or bin it, or file it. Try to bin it if possible!

✔ **Visualise successful outcomes.** If you're worried about an upcoming event you need to deal with, visualise yourself in the situation achieving success. Then visualise the steps you need to take to be able to achieve a successful outcome. This visualisation process makes you more likely to follow the steps and relax more during the process.

Improving Communication in Your Workplace

The single biggest problem in communication is the illusion that it has taken place.

George Bernard Shaw

Whenever I ask managers and executives what is one of the key areas they need to improve, almost invariably they say 'We really need to have better communication.'

Communication takes many forms in the workplace, from e-mails and phone calls, to notices on a board, to conversations by the coffee machine. The word 'communication' originally meant to join, share or unite. So communication is about unity or bringing together.

In this section you can find out ways to improve your communication with your colleagues, to help reduce the chance of unnecessary conflict and to improve the quality of your working relationships.

Listening attentively

We have two ears and one mouth so that we can listen twice as much as we speak.

Epictetus

Listening effectively is a skill. And it's not easy. You are a good listener if you listen to what the other person is saying without spending that time trying to craft a clever and brilliant answer. The problem is that you may be trying to work out what you're going to say next and thereby missing the key point the other person is saying. So, through this half-listening, you can only be half-communicating. If you are both doing this, you may as well be talking to yourselves!

Sometimes the other person just wants to talk about their problem – they're not looking for a solution. If you half-listen and then start to offer solutions, that isn't meeting their need to just be listened to. Watch their face and body language when you offer a solution. If the body language seems defensive or irritated, stop giving solutions and just listen.

To improve your listening skills, try following these tips:

✔ Sit or stand with an open body posture rather than crossing your arms or looking away.

✔ Look the other person in the eye when they speak.

✔ By gently nodding from time to time, acknowledge that you are still listening and not day-dreaming. The other person is saying something that's important to them, so let them know that you're listening.

✔ Focus on what the other person's saying rather than your thoughts and responses.

✔ Avoid looking at other people, playing with your phone, etc. when the other person is talking.

Developing your communication skills

Communication is a skill, and you can develop your skill in communication. Here are a few principles to put in place to help improve your communication with others.

✔ **Assume understanding hasn't taken place when you communicate.** Check to confirm the other person has understood. Checking for understanding lies at the heart of effective communication. However, if your colleague acts defensively and says 'Of course I understood,' explain why you're checking, and that you don't mean to be rude or lacking in trust.

✔ **See communication as a game of tennis, not golf.** Talking is a two-way process, not one-way traffic.

✔ **Look for opportunities to praise rather than criticise.** Other people are usually far more responsive to positives rather than negatives.

✔ **Be open and honest, without being hurtful.** Criticising a person instead of their actions never helps.

✔ **Observe body language.** If the other person folds their arms or avoids eye contact, there may be an underlying issue that needs addressing.

✔ **Keep the balance right.** If something needs saying, go for it. However, don't speak just for the sake of speaking – consider whether what you have to say is fair, kind and useful.

✔ **Pause and reflect before responding.** If you automatically react with words, remember that you can't take them back. Better to take your time and answer in a way that helps to achieve the desired outcome of the discussion.

✔ **Remember, emotions matter, not just words.** Note the tone of voice of the other person. Noting their tone of voice helps you to pick up on their emotions. And when you're expressing your thoughts, adjust your tone of voice too. Avoid using an aggressive tone – it makes others defensive and shuts down effective future communication.

✔ **Avoid using e-mail or text messaging for sensitive issues.** You're much better off speaking directly with the person if possible, or on the phone as a second best. If you do have to use e-mails, consider using emoticons to express your feelings too. A little :) can transform the way a sentence is understood.

Resolving conflicts

Speak when you are angry and you'll make the best speech you'll ever regret.

Dr Laurence J. Peter

You don't need to see conflicts in a negative way. Conflicts are a natural part of any healthy relationship. You can't have two people agreeing with everything all the time – any disagreement is a conflict. The question is how to resolve the conflict. By dealing with the conflict positively, you deepen your respect for each other and the quality of the relationship.

When conflicts occur, the stress response gets switched on and neither you nor the other person feels relaxed. Turning on your primitive fight-or-flight mechanism does not help you resolve the conflict. Instead, use your favourite relaxation technique from this book, such as visualising a relaxing place, taking time out to go for a brisk walk or doing a mini-meditation.

Try the following tips to deal effectively with conflict:

✔ **Remember, conflict resolution is the aim.** If you're clear about your aim, you'll be more successful. The aim is to find a resolution, not to continue to argue indefinitely. Relationships are more important than any one minor work issue. Let go of your urge to be right and find a compromise. If Susan really thinks this new idea will work when pitching to the difficult client, let her have a go and you pitch your idea with the other client.

✔ **Listen effectively.** Remember to 'listen' with your eyes as well as your ears. Notice the body posture and tone of voice as well as the words they use. The non-verbal communication can tell you a lot more about what they really want to communicate. If your colleague says he doesn't mind that you didn't finish your part of the project on time, but with an angry tone, you may need to ask further questions or apologise.

✔ **Stay in the moment.** Be aware of any past hurts in a relationship and remember to let them go in the present moment. Just focus on resolving the present conflict rather than dragging up the past. By staying in the present, your listening skills will be more effective too. Dragging up the fact that your co-worker forgot to return an important call two months ago doesn't help.

✔ **Forgive!** You need to forgive to resolve the conflict. If all you're seeking is revenge, you just end up perpetuating the conflict, causing more hurt and greater lack of communication. Be willing to forgive to see the situation clearly. If your colleague forgot to deal with that client's needs before going on holiday, there's nothing you can do now. After talking about the matter, forgive them and move on.

✔ **Agree to disagree.** If you can't find a middle ground to agree on, let the argument go and move on. If the issue isn't major, you may as well save your energy for something more interesting and nourishing for you. If a colleague really wants to un-jam the photocopier even though he messed it up last time, let him do it – there's more to life than photocopiers.

Balancing the Demands of Work

Picture this: things are going well for you at work. You seem to be doing a good job and your manager is happy. Suddenly the opportunity comes up for a promotion. All your colleagues encourage you to go for it. It's a big role with a lot more responsibility, and as everyone seems to think you should go for it, you do. You get the job but it's a lot more demanding. Suddenly you have to get to work earlier and finish later and you're constantly interrupted by complaints and things going wrong left, right and centre. You get home late and continue to work. You work weekends. You argue with your partner and stop playing squash. You don't have time to see your friends. Suddenly your life is turned upside down. Work has taken over.

In this section I explore the idea of developing a healthier work–life balance.

 Avoid saying 'I don't have time.' That just causes stress. You have the same amount of time as Albert Einstein, Michelangelo, Mohandas Gandhi and Leonardo Da Vinci did. Instead, say to yourself 'I have other priorities at the moment,' or 'How can I find more time?' or 'I can do that after 22 July.' Using this kind of language makes you feel in control of your life.

Developing a work–life balance

A good work–life balance is a wide-ranging concept that includes a healthy prioritising between work demands (career, vocation, ambition, financial success) and life (family, health, pleasure, leisure, socialising, spiritual development).

Here are some ways to make small improvements to your work–life balance:

- **Choose your work carefully.** Everyone is different. One person may love to work as a brain surgeon, but another may prefer to cook meals in the hospital canteen. You have your own unique talents and personality, so try to choose a field of work that you like. Choosing work that you enjoy makes your work–life balance much easier to manage. Ideally you want a job you look forward to go to each morning, and come home with a sense of satisfaction. If you're in the wrong job or career path, consider taking steps to change. For careers advice, get help by visiting www.nextstep.direct.gov.uk – use that site to get help online, on the phone or face to face. Great books on changing career paths include *What colour is your parachute?* by Richard Nelson Bolles and *The work you were born to do* by Nick Williams.

- **Know when to start and stop working.** When you're at work, work. Work hard to finish on time. But when it comes to the end of the day, stop and give time to other important parts of your life, such as family, friends and fun activities. Success entails far more than your bank balance, your position at work or how well you're known. All these are transient. Think about what people may say at your funeral – they're likely to talk about the kind of person you were and your generosity, not how many people you trampled on to get to the top of your career ladder.

- **Be passionate, not greedy.** The true joy in work comes from fulfilling your passion rather than focusing only on financial outcome. If you do a line of work that you're passionate about, you're rewarded with money as you're providing a good service. However, focusing on money alone leads to anxiety and stress as your bank balance goes up and down. You come home feeling relaxed and content if you work with passion through the day.

- **Shift your attitude.** If you're overworked and stressed out, a small shift in attitude can make a huge difference. Several times I've made career choices that resulted in a drop in pay, but it was definitely worth it. I find doing a job just for the sake of it particularly difficult. I need something I believe in. If your home and personal life are suffering due to excessive work demands, consider whether moving to a less demanding or more interesting job is feasible.

- **Have personal goals.** Most workplaces these days demand goals and target-setting. This strategy works so consider balancing it with personal goals. Maybe you want to take up a new sport this year, plan for a round-the-world trip in a few years' time or have at least one family holiday every year. Complete a wheel of life to help decide which area of your life to focus on. See Chapter 3 for more on how to do a wheel of life. Set achievable goals, write them down and review your progress every week. See Chapter 12 for more on effective goal-setting.

✔ **See the bigger picture.** I had a little idea for a start-up company and got the ball rolling very quickly. I partnered with a few people, but eventually disagreements began to appear. I rushed in without sufficient discussion and reflection. I began to feel frustrated. Then I thought, 'Let's see things in the bigger picture.' To see the bigger picture, ask yourself 'Why am I doing this?' My answer was to offer relaxation skills to more people. With that obvious but clear goal I was able to go into meetings with greater clarity.

As the title of the book by the late author, psychotherapist and motivational speaker Richard Carlson put it: *Don't Sweat the Small Stuff. . .and it's all Small Stuff.* Ask yourself: How would the problem you're facing now appear in a month's time? Or a year's time? Alternatively, step back and see things with a bird's-eye view.

Learn from nature. The sun rises in the morning, there is a flurry of activity with the birds and bees working and singing away. When the sun sets, things calm down and it's time for rest. Electricity has led us to lose touch with this natural balance. Try living in balance with nature for a day, a week or even a lifetime. Remember there's a time to start and stop working.

Setting your priorities and perspectives

You're a human being, not a human doing.

Jon Kabat-Zinn

If you struggle to balance your work with the rest of the demands of your life, you're not alone. Many people are overwhelmed by all the things they need to get done, both at work and at home.

You may not be able to control the amount of time you spend at work, but you do have some control outside of work. Concentrate your energy on managing that time and using your energy in that time wisely.

Here are some tips to improve the 'life' bit of your work–life balance:

✔ **Put 'life' activities into your calendar.** When you plan your week or month, put friends and family into your diary. A date with your partner at the end of the week acts as something to look forward to and makes you feel better. Looking forward to an enjoyable activity can be just as much fun as the activity itself.

For example, when you meet with your friends, take your diary so that you can plan the next get-together. Or schedule a fun afternoon trip with your kids every Sunday afternoon.

✔ **Remember the small things count.** If you can't manage to leave the office early every day, try just one night every week. If you struggle to make time to go on holiday, take a break one weekend a year. Spend half-an-hour on your hobby every week. Don't underestimate the value of small changes.

✔ **Squeeze some exercise into your day.** Exercising gives far more than the time it takes. You'll feel more alert and focused at work and have more energy at home, for your partner, family, friends and fun activities. Try waking up earlier or using your lunch hour for a 20-minute brisk walk or run.

✔ **Increase nourishing and reduce depleting activities.** Make a list of all the activities you do in a typical day. Put the letter 'N' next to the nourishing activities that make you feel energised and happy, and the letter 'D' next to the depleting activities that sap your energy. See what you can do to increase the amount of time you spend doing nourishing activities and reducing the amount of time spent on depleting activities.

✔ **Reconsider your chores.** Decide whether all your chores are essential. If they are, consider paying someone to help you, doing your shopping online or asking your children to do certain tasks around the home. You can even team up with a friend and do each other's tasks – for example, taking turns to drop the kids at school.

✔ **Be efficient with your time.** Make a list of all the things you need to do in town and get them done once a week. Be creative and find other ways to save time. Here are some more time-saving ideas:

  • Turn off your phone and internet when you don't want to be disturbed.

  • Do things now if you can, instead of putting them off.

  • Delegate things for others to do rather than trying to do everything yourself.

  • Do the most important things when you are fresh and have the energy.

  • Learn to say no to people's request for your time. If it's difficult for you, start with saying no to small request and gradually build up.

Ask yourself 'How can I bring greater enjoyment into my life?' With all the busyness of life, you may forget to do things you actually enjoy. You'll feel much more relaxed if you spend some time doing what you love.

Part V
Managing Problems Using Relaxation Techniques

The 5th Wave   By Rich Tennant

"Of course I'll switch sides with you, but I don't know how that's going to help you sleep."

In this part . . .

In this part you'll discover ways of relaxing when you really need it: managing anxiety, panic, phobias, depression, chronic illness, anger and when facing burnout.

Chapter 17

Managing Anxiety, Worry, Panic and Depression

Stress itself is not an illness, but stress can cause serious illness if it is not managed effectively. Clinical depression and anxiety are the most common illnesses resulting from stress. These can vary from being mild annoyances to life-threatening conditions.

By catching the symptoms of stress early and using a range of relaxation techniques, you can protect yourself from having to deal with other health conditions. In this chapter I suggest a range of strategies for you to nurture your inner healing process.

The advice in this chapter is not meant to replace the recommendations of your doctor or other health professional. If you suspect you are suffering from high levels of stress, anxiety or depression, visit your doctor. Additionally, if you do have a health condition, check with your doctor before using the exercises in this chapter to make sure they are right for you.

My experience of stress

My first major experience of stress was when I was training to become a teacher. I had to go to university lectures, plan lessons, mark books, write assessments and learn how to manage a group of challenging teenagers. Work started early in the morning and continued late into the night. As the months passed, the pressure continued to build. Eventually, after a particularly tough day, I had to take action. I spoke to a senior teacher and readjusted my workload temporarily. The stress I was under made it difficult to concentrate and I'd lost my sense of humour. I began to prioritise exercising every day, made sure I had time to practise meditation daily and talked about any issues rather than bottling them up. Within a week the stress began to ease and I felt hopeful again. However, if I hadn't noticed the stress building up and continued to drive forward, or if my tutor hadn't been sympathetic, I could have ended up with a clinical condition. From then on I became fascinated with stress, stress management and relaxation strategies, for both others and myself.

Managing Worry and Anxiety

Imagine you're about to have an important interview. You can feel your heart beating and the sweat in the palms of your hands. All you can think about is the interview. You feel butterflies in your stomach. You worry about all the things that could go wrong, and the more you think in this negative way, the greater your anxiety gets.

Worry and anxiety are completely normal and natural human experiences. It's only when they are much stronger than you're used to or can tolerate that it becomes a problem. The good news is that anxiety disorders are treatable so you don't need to suffer in silence. Visit your doctor for advice and treatment and additionally use the exercises in this section if your doctor approves.

Understanding worry and anxiety

Anxiety is the feeling of fear. Anxiety is your body's automatic, natural response to a challenge. Although uncomfortable, anxiety is not always a bad thing. Anxiety helps to motivate you to take action to resolve a problem, to stay focused and motivated, and to avoid dangers.

If your feeling of anxiety is preventing you from achieving what you wish to, you may be suffering from an anxiety disorder. But there's good news! You can reduce your anxiety. In this section I offer you some relaxation-based self-help strategies to manage your anxiety and get back in charge of your life.

Discovering whether you have an anxiety disorder

If you have difficulty controlling your worries, you may have generalised anxiety disorder (GAD). Generalised anxiety disorder is a long-term anxiety over a range of issues in your life rather than for one specific thing. You could have GAD if you have the following symptoms, although this list is not comprehensive. Each individual is different:

Physical symptoms of GAD include the following:

- Tense muscles, aches, pain
- Problems with sleep
- Often feel tired
- On edge, restless, jumpy
- Stomach and digestive problems and nausea

Psychological symptoms of GAD include the following:

- Inability to relax or control anxious thoughts
- Feeling of dread or irritability
- Difficulty in focusing
- Feeling loss of control or fear of rejection

Research shows that GAD may be due to a combination of factors including:

- **Your life experience:** Very stressful life experiences, for example.
- **Your genes:** You may have inherited a tendency towards greater anxiety.
- **Your thinking style:** Your way of thinking may focus on the worst. You can change this.
- **Your body's biology:** You may have a chemical imbalance in your brain, for example.

If your anxiety is interfering with day-to-day life, seek professional advice. Treatment is effective nowadays and may include cognitive behavioural therapy (CBT) and medication.

Understanding why you keep worrying

Worry is like a rocking chair – it gives you something to do but it doesn't get you anywhere.

Van Wilder

Worrying can keep you up at night and drain your energy. You may have difficulty getting on with your activities and find yourself repeatedly thinking about the same thing.

Worries continue not only because you have lots of problems in your life, but because of the way you see worry itself. You see the process of worrying in either a negative or positive way, both of which perpetuate your worrying.

The negative side is your worry about the negative effects of worry itself. You may think that your worrying will never stop, that it is damaging your health and that you can't do anything about it.

The positive side is you think worry helps you to solve problems or prevents problems from arising in the first place. You think of worry as a form of protection.

The positive belief is the most unhelpful. If you think your worrying helps you, you have no reason to stop worrying. Your first step is to see worry as an unhelpful habit that you want to stop.

Avoidance is another way anxiety is kept going. For example, you get invited to a party but you don't go because you think you'll bump into someone from your past that you'd rather not. Or you get an interview but don't turn up because you're too nervous and think you won't get it. By avoiding the situation, you discount any possible positive outcome and keep the anxiety alive.

Helpful worry results in action. All other worry is a waste of time.

Trying self-help techniques for anxiety and worry

When I look back on all these worries, I remember the story of the old man who said on his deathbed that he had had a lot of trouble in his life, most of which had never happened.

Winston Churchill

There is a range of different approaches you can take to reduce your worry that have proven to be helpful. In this section, you will find a variety of approaches such as acceptance, looking after your health, isolating your worry time, trying relaxation techniques and more. Read through them all first of all, and then test them out. With some of the techniques, it may feel like your anxiety level is going up before it goes down – that's quite common so no need to worry about that too much.

Accepting uncertainty

The desire for certainty in the future is one of the key drivers of worry in the first place. You want to be in control of your future and to do that you worry to try and predict all possible outcomes – often the most unlikely and worst-case scenarios.

To overcome this worry habit, you need to accept that there is uncertainty in life. You can't be sure what's going to happen in the next minute, let alone the next week, month or year.

Ask yourself the following questions and jot down the answers in a notepad:

- **Can I be certain about everything?** A nice, simple question to start with. Think about it before you write your answer.

- **What are the advantages and disadvantages of accepting some reasonable uncertainty?** For example, you can worry less and enjoy life more. You spend less energy trying to control things and are freer. There are very few, if any, disadvantages. Write your thoughts down.

- **What uncertainty do I already accept?** For example, driving a car, or any kind of travel involves uncertainty. Every time you have a conversation, do some work or check your e-mail, you can't be sure what will happen. So, seeing that you already accept some uncertainty, you can learn to tolerate a little bit more uncertainty.

- **Just because you're uncertain, does that mean the worst will happen?** Think about any possible positive outcomes that could happen. You may associate uncertainty in only a negative way. But positives happen through uncertainties too.

- **Can you live your life with a reasonable amount of uncertainty?** Having answered the previous questions, you may now understand that it is reasonable to accept some uncertainty in your life.

Having reflected on the above questions, what are your thoughts? Record your experience and thoughts in your relaxation journal (see Chapter 3).

Looking after your overall wellbeing to manage anxiety

By taking reasonable steps to look after yourself, you help to keep anxiety and worry at bay. Go through the following list of ways to effectively take care of yourself, and if any of these are not being done, take some small action today or this week to begin putting them back into your life in some way:

- **Avoid nicotine and alcohol.** They make things worse, so either cut down or cut them out. Nicotine is a stimulant and raises your level of anxiety. Alcohol is a depressant and if you depend on it to calm you down, it can become the first step to addiction.

- **Eat well.** Make sure you start the day with a healthy breakfast, and avoid strict diets. Instead, eat a balanced diet and avoid sugary and excessively fatty foods. Cut down on stimulants, such as caffeine, as they increase your anxiety. See Chapter 15.

- **Get some sleep.** You may be short of sleep due to your anxiety, and lack of sleep can make things more difficult. Follow the advice in Chapter 14 to see if you can get some more sleep and thereby feel better.

- **Take exercise.** Aim for about 30 minutes of physical activity, five times a week. See Chapter 6 for ways to get your body moving.

- **Use your social support.** Talking to others can be very helpful. Keep in touch with friends and family that you get on with. Then, when you're really worried, a quick chat with them can do wonders. See Chapter 15 for building a social network.

Organising some 'worry time'

If you have lots of worries and end up worrying all day, set aside some time, maybe half-an-hour, to worry every day. Set a particular time and place to worry. You could also sit down and write or draw your worries down as they go through your head.

The rest of the day, don't worry. Say to yourself that you'll worry about that problem in worry time. Many people find that they run out of things to worry about when they actually try to worry, so your worry time may run dry. That's fine! Many of my clients like this approach.

Trying some relaxation techniques

This book is filled with a range of proven relaxation techniques that you can use on a daily basis to help you to calm your mind. Anxiety is turning on your stress response, and relaxation helps you to switch it off.

If you like to use your mind to relax, you could try meditation, visualisation or having reasonable, believable, positive thoughts. If you prefer to use your body to relax, you could do anything from deep breathing, to progressive relaxation, yoga or t'ai chi. See Chapters 4 to 13 for a range of different relaxation techniques for you to try out. See which ones work for you.

Challenging your worries and behaviour

Use the cognitive behavioural type techniques in Chapter 12 to question your worries and turn them into more reasonable thoughts. This can be a powerful way of overcoming anxiety and retrain your thinking style to be more positive yet realistic rather than just expecting the worst all the time.

Understanding anxiety better

For some people, just reading about and understanding anxiety helps to reduce its stronghold. Look for books recommended by your doctor or therapists and see if reading them helps you.

Using problem-solving skills

Your worries are probably due to certain problematic situations. By developing your skills to deal with your problems, your worries and anxieties reduce. See Chapter 12 for how to solve problems effectively and methodically to make you feel in control.

Dealing with Panic

Panic disorder is a sudden, unexpected surge of anxiety, making you want to leave the situation you're in.

The feeling of panic is a natural one. Everyone experiences the feeling of panic at some point in his or her life. This is normal when you're going through a particularly stressful time. However, if you suffer from a panic disorder you feel surges of anxiety regularly and without warning. In this section I help you find out more about panic and ways of dealing with it.

If you have a panic disorder, you should see your doctor before trying out any exercises in this book.

Recognising and understanding panic attacks

A panic attack is a combination of physical and psychological symptoms during which you may feel fear and anxiety.

Physical symptoms of a panic attack may include the following:

- Nausea
- Confusion, shaking, dizziness or hot flushes
- Chest pain and rapid heart rate, dry mouth or a feeling of choking
- Changes in your breathing
- Tingling or numbness in your fingers or toes, or sweating

Psychological symptoms of a panic attack may include the following:

- Feelings of detachment from your surroundings
- Fear of dying, loss of control or going mad
- Thoughts of fear or terror

Panic attacks usually last for 5–30 minutes. The attack usually peaks after about 10 minutes and then the symptoms start to reduce.

Having a panic attack feels like you're having a heart attack. The sense of fear you get from the idea that you may be having a heart attack adds to the panic. However, a panic attack is not dangerous. With time you can manage and control your sensations without them causing even more discomfort.

Panic attacks are quite common and not a sign of a serious physical or mental illness. One in ten people experience occasional panic attacks.

Research suggests that panic is due to a combination of physical and psychological factors. These factors may include the following:

- Difficult life experiences such as a bereavement or other traumatic event.
- Inheritance of tendency to panic due to your genes.
- Your fight-or-flight reflex being triggered too easily. This is essentially a strong version of your stress response. (For the low-down on the stress response, check out Chapter 2.)
- An imbalance of brain chemicals.

Using techniques to reduce panic

You can use various techniques to reduce your feeling of panic. However, remember you're doing this to ease the considerable discomfort. If you have the attitude that the panic is dangerous and that you *must* reduce the feelings, you may find that you have more difficulty in controlling your panic attack.

✔ **Breathe slowly and deeply.** By changing your rate and depth of breathing, you begin to turn down your stress response and turn up your relaxation response. Focusing on your breathing also gives you something to pay attention to, rather than just your uncomfortable feelings. Aim to breathe (in and out) about once every six seconds. The slower and deeper you breathe, the better. By breathing through your nose, you'll naturally breathe slower. Also, see if you can exhale for slightly longer that you inhale as this turns up your relaxation response further. Breathe deep down into your belly, your lower abdomen. Breathing using just your upper chest is a shallow form of breathing and not conducive to relaxation. See Chapter 5 for more on deep breathing.

✔ **Breathe into your cupped hands or a paper bag.** If breathing slowly and deeply doesn't seem to work for you, try cupping both your hands over your nose and mouth whilst you continue to breathe. Alternatively, breathe in and out of a paper bag. This makes you re-breathe your own carbon dioxide. When you're having your panic attack, you're over-breathing and losing too much carbon dioxide. Using the bag helps to rebalance the carbon dioxide in your body. After you feel a bit more in control, go back to breathing slowly and deeply as described above.

✔ **Carry an object with some personal meaning.** Looking at a little picture of a loved one, for example, may help to calm you by taking your attention away from your symptoms. You begin to turn on your relaxation response and ease your panic gradually.

✔ **Focus your attention on your surroundings.** By giving your attention to your surroundings, like the colours, sounds or textures, you're reducing your focus on the panic symptoms. You could even focus on the passing time on your watch.

✔ **Jog on the spot.** For some people, jogging on the spot during the panic attack can help to settle down symptoms. This may be because the symptoms are then associated with the exercise rather than anything else.

✔ **Stay where you are.** When you have a panic attack, if possible stay where you are rather than running to a place of safety. Rushing to safety is unhelpful and puts your panic in control rather than you.

✔ **Use peaceful place imagery.** Imagine or think of a place of calm and peace. Focus your attention on that image and place rather than your panic. You may need to practise this before you can do it during a panic attack. The image helps to soothe your stress response. I talk about peaceful place imagery in more detail in Chapter 9.

Fighting a panic attack is like pouring fuel on to a fire. Instead of fighting, try to accept your experience as best you can. Remember that the panic will end, and focus on it ending relatively soon. Reassure yourself that panic attacks are not harmful. Going from fighting to accepting is not easy, but with experience you can do it.

Looking at longer-term strategies

This section is about preventing panic rather than just coping when you get a panic attack. Most of the suggestions are the kind of things that constitute a healthy lifestyle. Look through the list below and check that you integrate the suggestions into your lifestyle.

- **Eat a healthy diet:** Caffeine, nicotine and alcohol can contribute to panic attacks. Try to eat a healthy, balanced diet. Unstable sugar levels in your blood can contribute to panic symptoms.

- **Learn about panic:** Having a better understanding of what panic is, and how panic works helps you to see it in a different light. Take time to research and read more about panic if you think that may help.

- **Take plenty of aerobic exercise:** Doing regular physical activity that makes you slightly out of breath, five times a week, for at least 30 minutes in total, is very helpful. Your stress levels go down and you release serotonin from your brain, lifting your mood. Check out Chapter 6 for lots of suggestions to get exercising.

- **Use preventive relaxation techniques:** If you have panic attacks, you may constantly have a sense of anxiety about when your next panic attack may happen. Use your preferred relaxation techniques on a daily basis to make you feel calmer. For example, try yoga, visualisation, massage or hypnosis.

Dealing with Phobias

Feel the fear and do it anyway.

Susan Jeffers

Almost everyone has a few irrational fears. You may be scared of spiders, looking down from a height or of flying in a plane. However, if you feel absolutely terrified at the source of your anxiety and find your day-to-day activities are disrupted by your fear, you may have a phobia.

Phobias are the most common form of anxiety, affecting about 10 per cent of all adults.

Understanding phobias

A phobia is an extreme fear of an object, place or situation. A fear becomes a phobia when your life is changed by it.

Simple phobias are fears of objects such as needles, snakes or mice. Complex phobias are associated with situations. Claustrophobia is a fear of an enclosed place such as a lift, plane or crowded area. A social phobia is an extreme fear of situations involving social interaction or some kind of performance.

Phobias can start in a range of ways. They can start in childhood, sometimes for no apparent reason, or after a traumatic event in your life. Trying to make sense of a feeling of fear can cause a phobia too.

When you experience the object or circumstance of your phobia, you begin to experience the symptoms of anxiety including a racing heart, sweating, shortness of breath, discomfort in your torso and feeling terrified, and perhaps embarrassed and out of control. Sometimes just thinking about the phobia can trigger these feelings.

You may be coping with your phobia by avoiding it, which is common. If your phobia, such as fear of a snake, is encountered rarely, this probably isn't so much of a problem. Your life isn't seriously affected by it (unless your partner has pet snakes). However, if you have a phobia of flying and need to travel a lot for work, you may have a problem. For example, you may decide not to go for a promotion due to your phobia of flying.

Avoiding and escaping the object of your fear increases your fear of it.

Overcoming phobias by gradually facing your fears

Facing up to your fears is one of the most effective ways of dealing with your phobia. The process is called *exposure* or *exposure therapy*. The process works by gradually and repeatedly facing your feared object or situation, staying in control and going at your own pace. In this way you learn to work through your feelings of anxiety until they dissipate.

If this process sounds too frightening to you, and you can't imagine being able to face your fear, don't worry. You need determination and courage but the process is controlled by you and what you can cope with in each step. So think about where you are at the moment with regards to this phobia and where you want to be. Then you can fit in as many gradual steps in-between; small steps of exposure to your fear. As you gradually and slowly work through the steps, you feel less anxiety in each step you are exposed to, and feel ready to face the next step.

As an example, think about Jane, who has a phobia of cats. Jane wants to be able to stay in the same room as a cat without panicking. Here are the steps she comes up with:

1. Think about cats.

2. Draw a picture of a cat.

3. Look at a picture of a cat.

4. Watch a cartoon with cats in it.

5. Watch a film with cats in it.

6. Look at a cat behind a window.

7. Look at a cat through a window and gradually open the window.

8. Look at a cat through a doorway.

9. Friend holds cat and brings it into a room next to the room I am in.

10. Friend holds cat and brings it into the same room as me.

11. Friend puts cat down in the same room as me.

Consider a phobia you wish to overcome, and try writing out a set of very gradual steps to take. Get some help from friends or family to work through the steps. Positive support can make all the difference.

Keep going. You need to keep doing the exposure exercises as often as possible. If you leave too long a time between exposures, your old fears may come back.

For more information on overcoming phobias, see the NHS website on `www.nhs.uk/conditions/Phobias/Pages/Introduction.aspx` or the MIND website on `www.mind.org.uk/help/diagnoses_and_conditions/phobias`.

Handling Depression

Depression is a serious illness. Depression is a very different experience from just feeling sad or upset. The condition is also called *clinical depression* and *depressive illness*.

If you have depression, you feel extremely sad. Depression lasts for weeks or perhaps even months, interfering with your day-to-day life and making simple tasks challenging.

Depression is a common illness, affecting about 1 in 10 people. Even children can get depression, and these days it seems to be affecting children at a younger age.

Depression is not a sign of weakness or that you're a failure. Depression is a real illness with real effects. It has nothing to do with being a failure.

Understanding depression and stress

There is no one cause of depression. Different people get depression for different reasons. For some it is due to a major stressful event, such as a bereavement, illness, job issues or divorce. Sometimes it is a combination of major stressors that together trigger depression, such as job issues followed by a divorce.

Other factors can also lead to depression. Personality traits, a family history of depression, after giving birth, being isolated from friends and family, illness and the use of alcohol or drugs – all can contribute to the onset of depression.

Depression is described as a 'downward spiral'. You may become ill and feel low, and then refuse to see your friends, making things worse. You stop doing all exercise and perhaps start drinking too much alcohol. All this leads to a downward spiral into depression.

Here are some of the physical symptoms of depression:

- ✔ Continual low mood
- ✔ Feeling anxious or worried
- ✔ Feeling guilty
- ✔ Feeling of hopelessness
- ✔ Lack of motivation and difficulty in making decisions

Here are some of the psychological and social symptoms of depression:

- ✔ Lack of energy
- ✔ Aches and pains
- ✔ Sleep difficulties
- ✔ Change in weight or appetite
- ✔ Slow movement or speech

If you've been feeling down for more than two weeks, go to see your doctor to discuss your symptoms and be professionally assessed. If your doctor thinks you're depressed, you may be offered the choice of cognitive behavioural therapy (CBT), drugs, graded exercise, or mindfulness-based cognitive therapy (MBCT), among other options. Don't suffer in silence – effective help is available.

Using self-help strategies for depression

In addition to any treatment that your health professional may recommend for depression, you may find the following self-help strategies beneficial. Remember to let your professional know what you're doing to check if it's okay.

Getting active

When you have depression, stopping all your usual activities is tempting. In fact, you need to begin to take steps to be active even though you don't actually feel like it. The motivation starts to arise afterwards.

For some people, exercise is just as effective as taking antidepressants. If you haven't exercised for a while, just try some gentle walking for as long as you feel comfortable. Nowadays, some doctors can even 'prescribe' exercise. You could then be offered the supervision of a qualified trainer free or at reduced cost, depending on where you live. Ultimately aim for 30 minutes a day, five times a week, or 45 minutes to an hour, three times a week. See Chapter 6 for more on exercise.

Any amount of exercise is better than none at all.

Socialising

Keep in touch with your friends and family, even though you don't feel like it. The nature of depression tells you to avoid social contact, just when you need it most. Talking with others helps you to see things from a different perspective. If you begin to think, 'Oh, I haven't seen them for ages. They'll think I'm useless,' or other such negative thoughts, remember that is the depression speaking. Joining a support group for depression may be a good idea too. See Depression Alliance at www.depressionalliance.org and MIND at www.mind.org.uk and contact them to find your local support group.

Challenging your thinking

Depression makes you see almost everything negatively. And you think it's true. In truth, your thoughts are just perceptions, and negative ones at that. These perceptions include the way you see yourself, others, your situation, and your past and future. Trying to just 'think positively' doesn't seem to work so easily. You need to question your negative thoughts with more believable, realistic, optimistic thoughts. You'll feel better if the thoughts are actually believable rather than just positive for the sake of it. This isn't easy, but step-by-step you get better at it. It's a life-changing process.

Here are some ways of dealing with negative self-talk:

- ✔ **Ask yourself what a wise and kind friend would say.** Notice any negative thoughts you're having towards yourself. Ask, 'What would a wise and kind friend say to me?' and say the same thing to yourself. For example if you're saying to yourself, 'I'm useless because I'm tired all day,' you may challenge this with the thought 'I'm not well at the moment, that's why I'm tired. A little, gentle walk is probably a good idea now.'

- ✔ **Write down and challenge your thoughts.** When you're feeling particularly low, write down the negative thoughts you're having, and later on, when you feel a little better, have a go at challenging them with more positive, yet believable thoughts. Ask a friend to help you if you can. For example the thought, 'I hate my job. It's boring,' can be challenged with 'I'm lucky to have a job. It may be boring, but I have two great friends there, and it does pay my bills.'

- ✔ **Socialise with positive people.** By spending time with positive friends or family members, you are shown a more positive yet realistic way of seeing things. Also, when you're on your own, imagine what a positive friend would think in your situation and pretend to be thinking like them.

- ✔ **Watch out for thoughts with the words 'should', 'must', 'always' and 'never'.** You may have a tendency to think in extremes. Life isn't black-and-white in that way. 'I'm always late,' is probably untrue. 'I must get better right now!' Why must you? Getting better takes time. 'I'm useless,' and 'I'm worthless,' are painful thoughts that just aren't true. No one is totally useless – as a human being you have intrinsic value, which no one can take away from you.

When you're overwhelmed with negativity, remember it's the depression talking, not you.

Using mindfulness to stay well

Mindfulness, a form of secular meditation and approach to living that's gaining rapid popularity in psychology, has been found to reduce the chance of depressive relapse, especially for those who've had several episodes of depression.

Mindfulness teaches you to become more aware of the present moment rather than just focusing on, or fighting, your negative thoughts. You learn to accept your feelings of depression. This doesn't sound like an effective way of overcoming depression, but is surprisingly powerful. If you fight the feeling of depression, you end up giving the feeling more attention and sink deeper into a negative, downward spiral. By learning to acknowledge and accept your feelings, you ultimately allow them to dissipate more rapidly. You almost befriend your feelings of depression rather than avoiding them. Paradoxically, avoiding your feelings draws you deeper into the feelings themselves.

The next time you have a difficult series of thoughts, feelings, or bodily sensations, try this short 'breathing space' meditation:

1. **Begin by sitting or standing upright.**

   Let your posture have a sense of dignity without making your spine stiff or tense.

2. **Either gently close your eyes or look downwards with a soft gaze.**

3. **Check in with your 'internal weather'.**

   Be aware of your thoughts, feelings, and bodily sensations. No need to change or criticise/judge yourself. Simply become aware of what's going on for you internally for about a minute or so. See if you can accept what's going on for you rather than trying to change things.

4. **Focus your attention on your physical breathing.**

   Feel each in breath and each out breath for about a minute or so.

5. **Shift your attention to your breathing and body as a whole.**

   Get a sense of your whole body breathing if you can for about a minute.

6. **Notice how you're feeling now.**

   You don't need to feel better. This exercise is about becoming aware of what's happening for you in a different perspective, with a sense of acceptance.

Following this mini-meditation, go back to whatever you need to do next, with a mindful awareness – an awareness that is accepting, kind and curious as best you can. Give your full attention to whatever you need to do next, or think about what you can do that would be kind to yourself such as taking a bath, going for a walk or calling on a friend perhaps. Maybe even treating yourself to a little bit of chocolate, and eating it mindfully.

If you like the idea of practising mindfulness, you may like to try the following:

✔ Attend an eight-week group mindfulness-based cognitive therapy course for depression. Visit www.mbct.co.uk/ for help in finding a local teacher.

✔ Learn mindfulness one-to-one with a professional mindfulness teacher. You may need to simply search by using an internet search engine. Check the teacher is experienced and qualified.

✔ Learn mindfulness on your own using a book and CD like *Mindfulness For Dummies* by Shamash Alidina (Wiley) or *The Mindful Way Through Depression* by Mark Williams, John Teasdale, Zindel Segal and Jon Kabat-Zinn (Guilford Press).

Chapter 18

Managing Chronic Disease

• •

In This Chapter

▶ Understanding how relaxation may help your condition

▶ Organising your life to encourage less stress

▶ Finding the right approach to relaxation for you

▶ Exploring sources of support to make things a little more manageable

• •

A chronic disease is a disease that is long lasting or recurrent. Chronic diseases include heart disease, stroke, cancer, chronic respiratory diseases and diabetes. These diseases are the leading causes of mortality in the world. Chronic disease is a huge, global issue, being responsible for over half of all deaths in the world.

When I work with people with chronic conditions, I never cease to be amazed by their courage, resilience and attitude. Suffering day in and day out is unimaginably difficult, and yet often such clients are humble, wise and committed to finding ways to relax more.

Managing chronic disease offers both a challenging and, perhaps controversially, exciting opportunity. If you manage your chronic disease well, you can make significant improvements in what you achieve and how you feel. The hope of some improvement, no matter how small, may be an uplifting thought.

Understanding Long-Term Illness and Stress

Even the thought of relaxation may sound alien to you, especially if you have a serious medical condition. The physical, psychological and social changes that may take place after you are diagnosed with a chronic condition are challenging.

In this section, you'll discover how disease causes stress and some of the benefits of practising relaxation for your health condition and overall wellbeing.

Discovering how your disease causes stress

There is a range of reasons why ill health raises your level of stress. By understanding what's actually causing the stress, you can begin to take a few preventative steps. The clearer you are about the sources of your stress, the more you will begin to feel in control, especially when you take small steps to reduce the stress.

Here are some of the different ways in which a chronic disease may prevent you from relaxing:

- **Lifestyle change:** If you expect to live to 100 years old and suddenly your doctor tells you that you have a chronic disease and five more years to live, that's stressful. You may want to live for longer, to travel the world, to meet your friends more often, to go sailing. . .suddenly your world is turned upside down.

- **Physical impact:** Chronic disease may limit how much you can move physically and prevent you from doing activities that relieve your stress. For example, if you can't move easily, you're less likely to socialise regularly or exercise physically. If you previously enjoyed exercising or playing sport to relieve stress, you may need to find new ways of relieving your stress.

- **Pain:** Chronic pain is a common physical cause for stress in long-term diseases. Pain that lasts for months causes a great deal of stress. Resisting the pain can compound the problem. Accepting the pain is difficult but may be helpful.

- **Lack of acceptance:** If you refuse to accept your condition, there is a constant background sense of anxiety, a sense that something is wrong and needs fixing. Denial of your condition becomes an extra stressor and may even make your condition worse. If you accept your disease, you don't need to fight and struggle.

Mike had been running a music business for 15 years and loved it. He loved being in touch with the general public, sharing his love of music, and discovering new bands and styles. One day, after a particularly difficult period of stress, he had a mild stroke. Mike had to change the amount of time he worked in the business. It was tough. He couldn't move around easily or pick up boxes like he used to, and his legs were stiff, making walking very challenging. He had to find new ways to relax. He discovered breathing exercises, acupuncture and massage helped him. He's now a big fan of integrating relaxation into life. He often tells others of the dangers of chronic stress and the benefits of learning new ways to relax.

To deal with the stress caused by your disease, you need to discover the root of your anxiety. It could be the lack of contact with your friends, your inability to do any work or a negative thinking style. For more on ways to identify your stress, work through Chapter 2. Then you can begin to take small, manageable steps to reduce your stress, which may include relaxation techniques.

Clarifying the benefits of relaxation

Here are some of the benefits of actively taking steps to relax when you have a chronic condition:

- ✔ **Relaxation gives you energy.** You only have so much energy available in a day. If you have a chronic disease, that energy is further limited. By practising something relaxing, you give yourself an energy boost. With a little more energy, your mood may also lift.

- ✔ **Relaxation helps your body repair itself.** The stress response is designed to put all your energy into your muscles to run or fight. The relaxation response is designed to allow your body to heal, repair and grow. See Chapters 1 and 2 for more on this. By relaxing more, you give your body the opportunity to heal, which helps to stabilise or even reduce the symptoms of your chronic illness.

- ✔ **Relaxation can lift your mood.** When you listen to some music, soak in the bath or take part in your favourite hobby, you begin to relax. Relaxation makes you feel more content, satisfied and at peace with yourself. You begin to see the brighter side of things, and small things such as eating a piece of chocolate, seeing the sunshine streaming through the window, or hugging your child make things feel even better.

- ✔ **Relaxation is calming and focusing.** Chronic illness can make you feel disoriented, unfocused and out of control. A little bit of relaxation during the day offers some respite from your worries and concerns. With that relaxation, you may find yourself better able to focus and your mind may feel less 'fuzzy'. Relaxation techniques such as imagery, meditation or even simply stroking your cat attentively are good for making you feel more focused.

- ✔ **Relaxation puts you in more control.** If you find a relaxing technique or routine that works for you, you'll feel more confident and in charge of your life. Little changes make a difference. Rather than having the sense that your disease controls everything you do, you can begin to be in charge. Relaxation offers you a chance to control your incessant worries, changing moods and negative self-talk. Rather than being tossed by the waves of life, you get some rest from time to time.

In Figure 18-1 I show how stress causes disease, which can then feed back to cause greater stress. Relaxation offers a way of breaking this vicious cycle.

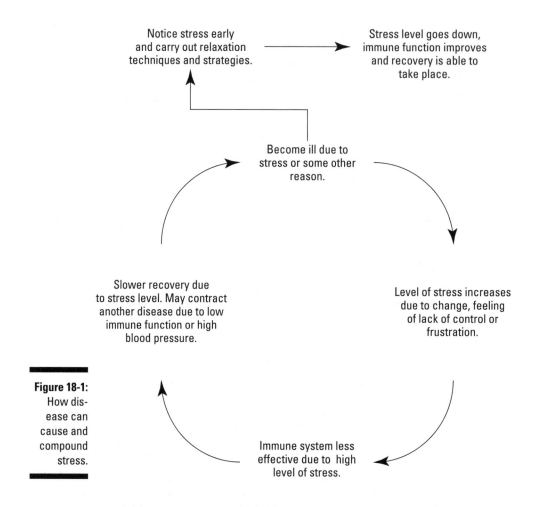

Figure 18-1:
How disease can cause and compound stress.

Managing Your Life to Stay More Relaxed

The choices you make on a daily basis have a huge impact on how you feel, what you think and even your disease. In this section, I help you check if you're taking the right steps for yourself.

Prioritising good nutrition

You are what you eat. If you want to feel better, you need to eat the right foods for your health condition. This may mean cutting out caffeine, excessive sugar, artificially refined foods and unhealthy fats. Instead, try to eat more fruit and veg, wholegrains, seeds, nuts and fresh or frozen foods.

You can still treat yourself from time-to-time with some chocolate or whatever you like to nibble. Just try not to make this a daily habit. On your really difficult days, a little treat may make you feel better.

Maintaining a positive outlook

If you have a chronic disease, you probably find a lot of negative things to think about. If you previously led a very full and active life, your new life with a chronic disease may be very different from how you want it to be. Making some changes to the way you think about your situation may well help you feel better. For more on maintaining optimism, see Chapter 12.

Keeping a diary

Recording a diary of what you eat, what relaxation exercises you do and how you feel is an excellent way of managing your condition. You can then see what seems to help and what doesn't. Keep your diary with you if possible because then it makes it easier for you to enter information as you go through the day. Put as much information down as you have time to do, and be honest with yourself. I show an example diary in Figure 18-2.

Figure 18-2: Recording your day-to-day experiences in a diary can help you manage your condition better.

SITUATION	LEVEL OF PAIN/FATIGUE (/10)	EMOTION	THOUGHTS	RECENT FOOD INTAKE AND EXERCISE	RELAXATION TECHNIQUE — WHICH ONE AND WHAT EFFECT DID IT HAVE?	MORE POSITIVE YET REALISTIC THOUGHTS ABOUT THE SITUATION/EFFECT

Living mindfully

Live your life one breath at a time.

If you have a bad day and think, 'What if this feeling lasts for the rest of my life?' or 'I'm just getting worse,' you're bound to feel stressed and unhappy. Thinking positive in that moment is difficult, but you could have a go at being mindful. Rather than thinking about what's going to happen next week or next year, try to live in the moment. Mindfulness teaches you acceptance and self-kindness and offers ways to deep relaxation. For more on mindfulness, see Chapter 10.

Setting achievable goals to feel better

A journey of a thousand miles must begin with a single step.

Lao Tzu

A chronic illness can take over your life. Maybe you have given up going to the cinema, or walking your dog, or even seeing friends. You may feel fearful to go out of the house or to try a new adult education class.

Setting goals puts you back in control. By setting realistic goals that you want to achieve, and going on to complete those goals, you feel better because you're in control rather than your illness. The secret is to make your goals realistic rather than overly challenging.

Your goals don't have to be huge. By celebrating your small steps, you set up a positive chain reaction and feel motivated to take further steps.

Small steps aren't small, they're giant leaps in disguise. If you have a chronic illness, bear in mind the following principles when you set your goals:

- ✔ Choose a realistic goal that's safe for you to do.

- ✔ Ensure your goal is measurable so that you can be clear when you have achieved your goal.

- ✔ Choose your own goal rather than asking someone else to pick it.

- ✔ Ensure you look beyond your illness and choose what's important in your life.

- ✔ Start with a small step – don't be too ambitious.

Imagine you want to be able to walk outside on your own for 10 minutes, and your doctor agrees this is a good idea. Here are the goals you could set:

1. Exercise your legs for five minutes every day for a week.

2. Walk around your home for five minutes every day for a week.

3. Walk for five minutes indoors and one minute outdoors with a friend every day for a week.

4. Walk outside for four minutes with a friend every day for a week.

5. Walk outside for eight minutes with a friend every day for a week.

6. Walk for ten minutes with a friend every day for a week.

7. Walk for ten minutes outside on your own.

Set goals that are appropriate for your life, your condition and what you want to do.

Pacing yourself

Pacing means spacing your activities so that your energy levels are optimal and you manage your illness effectively. The idea is that if you manage your energy levels in a reasonable and consistent way, your energy will gradually increase. The structure also gives you a greater feeling of control, an important way of feeling more relaxed.

Pacing is particularly good for pain management. Living with pain is stressful, but by using pacing you can keep your pain in check.

At the core of pacing is developing balance. You may currently be either underactive or overactive:

✔ **Underactivity:** This is often the case if you have pain. You avoid more and more activity, but this can lead to greater pain, as you don't use your muscles or joints as much.

✔ **Overactivity:** You may be pushing yourself too much. This can prevent your condition from improving as you experience more fatigue and perhaps pain too.

In order to determine what pace to do your activities, follow the four steps below:

1. **Measure your activity.**

   Choose an activity you want to measure. Let's say gardening. Get a timer and see how long you manage to garden for. Choose an activity that results in significant pain afterwards.

2. **Set your pacing limit.**

   Take the amount of time you did the activity, and reduce it by 20 per cent. So if you managed to do gardening for ten minutes, from now on, aim to do eight minutes.

3. **Stick to your limit.**

   You need to be disciplined and not allow yourself to do more than eight minutes for example. To do this, you'll probably need a timer. The temptation may be to continue after the timer goes, but pacing is about resisting that temptation.

4. **Increase your limit.**

   Once you feel you know your limit and are able to carry out the activity without increasing your pain, you may be ready to increase your limit. Just remember to keep balanced and not to overdo it. You might go from eight minutes to 12 minutes, for example.

Set pacing limits for all your activities, such as doing housework, walking, the number of days you work, the length of time you drive and so on.

Getting some sleep

If you can't sleep, then get up and do something instead of lying there worrying. It's the worry that gets you, not the lack of sleep.

Dale Carnegie

Your chronic illness may be causing you difficulties in falling asleep, making you feel worse the next day. Then, you may try harder to fall asleep, which just keeps you awake, causes stress and may make your illness worse. Try breaking this negative cycle with the following tips:

- **Do relaxation exercises in bed.** Choose deep breathing, visualisation or listening to a guided meditation. And ensure that your bed is comfy. Use pillows under your legs or back if that helps.

- **Be regular.** Wake up at the same time every day, no matter how you slept, using an alarm clock if necessary. Avoid taking naps during the day even if you feel sleepy. But wait till you're tired before going to bed.

- **Cut out or reduce stimulants.** Avoid drinking tea or coffee in the evening, and don't watch television in your bedroom. Create a calm, relaxed environment where you sleep.

Experiment with these suggestions for a few weeks and see what effect they have by noting down how well you slept each night in a diary. Read Chapter 14 for more ideas to help you sleep.

Exercising to relax

If you have chronic pain or a chronic health condition, you may be scared of exercising. But exercising within safe limits helps reduce your stress and may improve your condition, too. Exercise releases endorphins, brain chemicals that block pain signals. Exercise also strengthens your muscles, burns fat and reduces your chance of getting other chronic health conditions.

If your condition involves pain, you may be avoiding certain movements and activities. But although normally pain is a sign that you need to ease off from activity, with chronic conditions, pain may arise even though there is no injury or disease. This lack of activity leads to your joints and muscles weakening and becoming stiff, feeding back to cause more pain and discomfort. This is called the pain cycle, which I show in Figure 18-3.

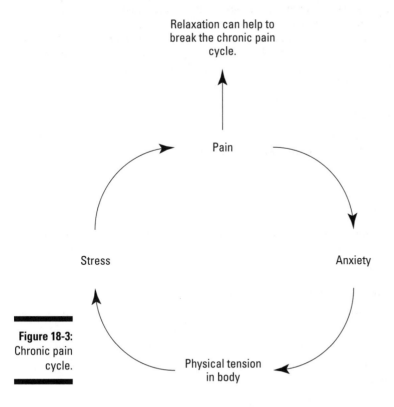

Relaxation can help to break the chronic pain cycle.

Pain

Anxiety

Stress

Figure 18-3: Chronic pain cycle.

Physical tension in body

Work with your health professional to create a realistic, helpful exercise programme for you and begin to challenge your chronic pain cycle.

Using Relaxation to Help You

Being ill is stressful. Having a chronic disease is even more stressful. Stress compounds your feeling of being unwell. Relaxation techniques are an effective way of lowering your stress levels and thereby giving you some control. They can help break the disease–stress cycle that you may be experiencing.

Finding the right relaxation technique for you

The best way to find the right relaxation technique is to try out the various techniques and see what works for you. To help clarify which is best, jot down how you find the various exercises in your relaxation journal (see Chapter 3). I offer a large range of relaxation exercises in Chapters 4 to 13, but in this section, I give you a couple of techniques to get you started. You can do the short relaxation at any time of the day. In addition, try to practise a deep relaxation for 20 minutes or more every day – you could do a mindfulness meditation (see Chapter 10) or the deep relaxation that I describe below.

Short breath relaxation

Get into a comfortable posture. Breathe in deeply, down into your belly if you can, hold it for a few moments, and breathe out slowly. Feel the physical sensation of your breathing in this exercise. Do this for a minute or so, and note what effect it has.

Deep relaxation

Use the steps below to guide yourself into a deep relaxation whenever you feel you need it. It includes some guided imagery and mindfulness of bodily sensations.

1. **Find a quiet, comfortable place to relax.**

   Get your body into a comfortable posture, using pillows and blankets to support you and ensure you're warm. Play some soothing music in the background if that helps. Allow your eyes to close if that feels okay.

2. **Move your attention through your body, perhaps like this: feet, legs, buttocks, belly, hands, arms, shoulders, neck and face.**

   You could either gently tense and relax each part of your body, or simply feel the sensations in each body part. Say to yourself phrases such as 'my feet are feeling relaxed' as you move through your body, if that enhances a feeling of relaxation for you.

Living with a chronic condition

This is some advice from Jane (not real name), a friend online who generously shared her wisdom on my Facebook page.

IMPERMANENCE. . .during a flare, focus on that word during the hard moments and remember it doesn't always feel like that. Even the worst day won't be comprised of all bad moments.

Try to remember this wisely during the good times too, so you pace yourself and try and make them last. Also remember just how wonderful it feels to be alive at those times. I honestly believe that the chronically ill enjoy those times more than those who take their health for granted. In my mind I bottle how I feel when well, and on my worst days I close my eyes, remember the feeling and remember that one day I will feel like that again.

Also, accept yourself. . .accept that you have two lives. . .a well life and an ill life. . .there are still things you can enjoy

during your ill life. For me its music, reading and meditation. . .try not to grieve for the things that you can only do when you're well. . .look forward to them instead and use them as a goal to motivate you to carry on.

If you accept your ill life even with its major challenges and difficult decisions, it is easier to be calm and to pace yourself and when you do this, you get better quicker.

For example, this week I have had to put completing my degree on hold for the third time. . .instead of going back in September this year, I will have to go back in September 2012. I am devastated but it's a decision I have to take because of how ill I am now. However, it is a goal and a motivator to work with my illness and not fight it and give it the time I need to achieve remission I guess. The key is IMPERMANENCE.

3. Calm your mind.

Do this by imagining you are in a relaxing place. This could be a forest, beach, meadow or somewhere indoors. For example, imagine you're walking along a gorgeous beach. Feel the breeze on your face and the sand on your feet. Smell the salty ocean air and see the light of the sun shimmering in the water. Enjoy the feelings of relaxation you experience.

4. Let go of all effort to do anything.

Just allow yourself to 'be'. Say to yourself, 'There's nothing to do, nowhere to go, nothing to achieve right now.' Bring a sense of acceptance to your moment-to-moment experience, including any pain or discomfort you may have. Let things be just as they are.

5. **When you're ready to end your relaxation, slowly count down from five to one.**

   You may feel calm and refreshed once you open your eyes. But if not, don't despair. Relaxation doesn't come instantly, you need to be patient and practise regularly. Be especially kind to yourself if you have a chronic condition. Relaxing whilst having a chronic condition isn't easy.

Avoid immediately rushing around after doing your relaxation technique. Bring a sense of calmness to your activities.

Exploring day-to-day relaxing activities

In addition to practising relaxation techniques, I recommend you do some normal everyday activities that contain an element of relaxation. Here are a few ideas to get you thinking:

- ✔ **Chat with a friend about unimportant, fun stuff.** This will help take your mind off your worries.

- ✔ **Choose a hobby that's easy and repetitive, such as knitting.** Repetitive tasks can be quite soothing.

- ✔ **Do a bit of cooking.** Make something you really like. By taking your time and enjoying the smells and tastes, you'll feel better.

- ✔ **Drink some herbal tea.** It contains ingredients that encourage relaxation.

- ✔ **Have a little cleaning or de-cluttering session.** The sense of satisfaction having done the cleaning is relaxing, and if you do it mindfully the process of cleaning is therapeutic too.

- ✔ **Listen to a favourite radio programme, or download a podcast from the internet.** Podcasts are free online audio shows on almost any topic imaginable.

- ✔ **Read something relaxing.** The act of reading often makes people calm.

- ✔ **Treat yourself to a nap.** If you don't have trouble sleeping, having a nap in the afternoon can be soothing.

- ✔ **Write a letter to someone.** It's much more pleasurable than writing an e-mail for most people, and almost always a joy to receive.

As with all the suggestions in this book, I recommend you try out a few of the ideas in this list at least once and see what works for you. Trying new things is good for your brain too – it likes to learn new things.

Embracing Support to Feel More Relaxed and Healthy

If you have a chronic health condition, you don't need to fight on your own. Help is out there if you know where to look. In this section you'll find ways of getting professional help, guidance in the whole realm of complementary medicine and discover the benefits of support groups.

Getting professional help to manage your condition

If you have high levels of stress due to your chronic health condition, I recommend you get professional help.

The first port of call would be your doctor. Make sure you take your time to explain all the difficulties you're having and ask for information about support in your local area. Your doctor should give you some information and point you in the right direction for the next step. Your doctor may refer you on to other specialists depending on your condition. For more information about your condition, search the NHS website on www.nhs.uk.

Next, try searching for a charity support group in your area. You can do this by either visiting your local library or asking a friend or relative to do that for you. The librarian should be able to identify if there is a charity support group in your area for your condition. There may be a telephone helpline and local support groups you could attend. Alternatively, simply type your health condition and the name of your area into an internet search engine, such Google to see what comes up. Going to a support group, meeting other people and talking through your difficulties can be hugely empowering. Also, the people you talk to may have details of other charity or government support groups, and give you tips on managing your condition effectively.

For example, if you have chronic fatigue syndrome (CFS), you could begin by asking your doctor for a treatment programme, which may include the following:

✓ **Cognitive behavioural therapy (CBT):** CBT is a talking therapy with a professional, helping you change your thoughts, behaviour and actions. These changes can help you to accept your diagnosis and manage it. See Chapter 12 for more on CBT.

✔ **Graded exercise therapy:** This is offered by a trained professional, providing you with a structured exercise programme that helps you to set goals and increase how long you can maintain physical activity.

✔ **Medication:** Your doctor may offer various medications to help you, depending on your symptoms. Your doctor may also refer you to a pain management clinic if pain is a major part of your condition. In a pain management clinic, a specialist assesses your condition and offers an appropriate treatment designed for you. You may also be given medication.

Considering complementary health options

A third of all patients in the Western world use complementary and alternative medicine (CAM) to manage their health and wellbeing. That's millions of people. CAM is an approach to managing health not normally used by medical doctors.

Frequently used types of CAM include the following:

✔ **Alexander technique:** This method teaches you how to remove tension from your body by becoming more aware of your movements in everyday activities.

✔ **Manipulative and body-based practices:** These include spinal manipulation by chiropractors and osteopaths, and massage therapy for relieving pain, injuries, and addressing anxiety and depression.

✔ **Mind–body medicine:** These are practices that integrate the brain, body, mind and behaviour for greater wellbeing. Popular choices include meditation, yoga, acupuncture, deep breathing, guided imagery, hypnotherapy, progressive relaxation, t'ai chi and qi gong.

✔ **Natural products:** These include a range of herbal remedies, vitamins, minerals, probiotics, fish oils/omega 3 and echinacea.

✔ **Reiki:** This is an ancient hands-on healing technique, apparently using life-force energy to heal.

✔ **Whole medical systems such as Ayurvedic medicine and traditional Chinese medicine:** Ayurvedic medicine is an ancient, holistic form of medicine from India based on offering guidance regarding food, exercise, meditation, massage, ethical conduct and medicine. Traditional Chinese medicine is an ancient form of medicine combining the use of herbs, acupuncture, food, massage and therapeutic exercise.

For more on complementary medicine, check out *Complementary Medicine for Dummies* by Jacqueline Young (Wiley). Also, although not UK-based, one of the most comprehensive websites on complementary medicine is at http://nccam.nih.gov/health/whatiscam.

CAM therapies often lack scientific evidence. Minimise your risk by taking the following precautions:

- ✔ Tell your doctor or health care professional which CAM practices you are using to ensure that they are safe.

- ✔ When taking dietary supplements, be particularly careful. They may interact negatively with other medication you're taking, or may even be harmful on their own.

- ✔ Be careful when choosing a CAM practitioner. Check the person's experience, training and qualifications.

Joining a support group

Support groups offer a range of benefits to those that participate. By getting together with others that share the same health condition, you gain the following advantages:

- ✔ You exchange emotional and practical support.

- ✔ You share medical issues and discover that you're not alone with your symptoms or feelings.

- ✔ You receive practical tips and resources.

- ✔ You may discover that you have access to financial assistance or some form of scholarship.

- ✔ You may have the chance to link up with researchers.

Good support groups tend to have strong leadership, up-to-date information, regular meetings targeted to a specific condition and access to professionals. Professionals run some support groups, whereas other groups are run by individuals with the condition. Some groups meet weekly and other, larger groups meet only once a month.

To find a group, begin by asking your doctor. Other ways include asking a reference librarian, relevant association, society or charity organisation. For a list of support groups, visit www.patient.co.uk/selfhelp.asp.

If a group doesn't feel right for you, try another group. You need to feel comfortable with the other members of the group to enjoy the benefits.

Living with a chronic condition

Michelle (not her real name) has long-term chronic conditions – burning mouth syndrome – which she has had for two years, probably caused by extreme stress and brachial plexus – and nerve damage caused by surgery and radiotherapy for breast cancer. She also has a prolapsed disc. She told me about her story on Facebook, having attended a one-day workshop on stress reduction that I did in London. Here's what she said:

I have learned to live with the pain and accept it. I try to sit with the pain and on the very bad days will rest as much as possible. A sleep can make almost any pain seem better. I always say to myself that I 'know this day I am going to feel ill but if I go with it, tomorrow I will feel better.'

I have had CBT and listened to personal development radio phone-ins. What I have picked up from all these is that first you have to learn to love yourself and that happiness comes from within not from things outside of you. Also to not identify yourself by your suffering.

The CBT therapist said that I need to try to not be such a people pleaser and to stop trying to prove myself all the time.

I have been practising yoga for many years and I found this very helpful during the difficult times. I have a good relationship with my yoga teacher.

I often practise mindful breathing, and breathing deeply. I try to be mindful during the day and to accept a thought and then let it drift away – I have learned to let the past go and don't dwell on the future – I feel lucky to be alive after successfully beating cancer. I say to others 'it's all good though' if they ask how I am – try not to be too optimistic or too pessimistic!

Last but not least I bought a young rescue dog, who is full of life and looking after and walking him is a distraction from the pain – I have had to let go of many of the more active activities that I used to like to do because they made the pain worse.

I have found that I needed to master the above ways of looking at myself and life before I was able to tune into any relaxation practice. This has taken some time and required a lot of effort on my part. My therapist said that she couldn't have coped with all that I had had to deal with!

Chapter 19

Anger and Burnout

. . . .

. . . .

Anger is never without a reason, but seldom with a good one.

Benjamin Franklin

*E*veryone has experienced the feeling of anger, whether mild irritation or full rage. Although some anger is normal and useful, excessive anger leads to stress and relationship problems. In this chapter, I offer some insight into anger management and show you how relaxation techniques are ideal for calming your feelings of anger.

Burnout is a physical and emotional exhaustion caused by excessive stress. In this chapter, I uncover ways of preventing and managing burnout.

Mastering Anger Management

Surveys show about 30 per cent of adults worry about how angry they sometimes feel. Anger management shows you ways to deal with anger healthily. You learn to recognise your anger, giving yourself time to cool down and find ways to relax so your anger doesn't fire up unnecessarily. In this section, I help you see what anger actually is and its effects on you, and I show you various ways to cool your temper.

Understanding anger

Anger is a natural emotion, just like happiness or fear. Anger has evolved in human beings and can play a useful function if you keep it within a healthy range. Anger isn't always bad: anger is designed to act as a defence mechanism when you're threatened. However, anger can have negative consequences if it spirals out of control.

Anger works on two levels: your emotions and your physical body. You may feel a huge surge in energy as the stress hormones adrenaline and cortisol are released into your bloodstream. Here are some changes that happen:

- ✔ Your blood pressure increases.
- ✔ Your heart rate and your breathing rate increase.
- ✔ Your muscles become tense.
- ✔ You feel hot and sweaty.
- ✔ You experience churning or butterflies in your stomach.

Over the long term, anger can damage your body. Regular intense episodes of anger may cause the following problems:

- ✔ **Mental health issues:** Increased chance of depression, self-harm and addiction.
- ✔ **Heart and circulation:** Increased risk of heart disease and stroke.
- ✔ **Immune function:** Easier to catch infectious illnesses, such as flu and a longer time to recover from operations and injuries.
- ✔ **Digestion:** Increased risk of irritable bowel syndrome, inflammation of stomach lining and ulcers.

Anger is usually caused by one of the following:

- ✔ An **event**, such as a traffic jam.
- ✔ A **specific person**, such as your colleague or your mother-in-law.
- ✔ A **traumatic memory**, such as your ex-boyfriend's actions.

Most people manage their anger in one way or a combination of the following:

- ✔ **Expressing your anger:** You may do this assertively (healthy) or aggressively (unhealthy).
- ✔ **Suppressing your anger:** You hold your anger in and try to think about something else. The benefit is that you may be more constructive with your energy. The danger is that you turn your anger inwards, causing excessive stress or depression. You could also end up suddenly lashing out or becoming cynical towards others.
- ✔ **Calming your anger:** You use techniques to lower your heart rate and slow your breathing.

Wise use of your anger can lead to effective communication and negotiation. The important thing is to control and release your anger effectively.

Anger can become pleasurable. You may feel as if you're releasing all your pent-up emotions, which, depending on the other person's reaction, may give you a feeling of power. In this way, anger can become an unhelpful addiction, damaging relationships around you.

Discovering whether anger is a problem for you

If you feel angry frequently, intensely or for long periods, or your anger negatively impacts on your relationships, work or leads to physical violence, you may have a problem with anger.

Look at the following statements and see whether you agree with any of them:

- ✔ Waiting in a queue really annoys me.
- ✔ I fly off the handle easily.
- ✔ People really annoy me when they don't act the way I think they should.
- ✔ Sometimes I get so angry I get violent.
- ✔ I find it hard to forgive others when they've done something wrong.
- ✔ When things don't go the way I want, I feel depressed.
- ✔ After an argument with someone, I feel like I hate myself.

Count the number of 'yes' answers you gave and see how well you manage your anger:

- ✔ If you gave 0– 2 'yes' answers you're above average when it comes to managing your anger.
- ✔ If you gave 3– 5 'yes' answers you do have some issues with anger. Learning some anger management skills, perhaps using this book, may be sufficient. You may find professional help of a counsellor and stress management consultant helpful.
- ✔ If you gave 6– 7 'yes' answers you do have a problem with anger management and probably would benefit from professional help.

Remember, this is a very rough guide. There are many excellent, detailed online resources on anger management. Visit www.relaxationfordummies.com/anger-management for some links and in-depth questionnaires.

Trying anger management techniques

Having a set of techniques that you can use to manage your anger when it arises is vital to keeping any unhealthy rage in check. Some of these techniques nip the anger in the bud, before it gets out of control. Others are long-term, preventative approaches.

Try some of these techniques:

Last-minute techniques to prevent anger getting out of control

- ✔ **Count to ten and take deep breaths.** Counting to ten before you express your anger is more powerful than it sounds. In a tense situation, take some deep breaths and count to ten before you react. You may even like to walk away from the situation for a few moments before responding. Think before you speak!

- ✔ **Do some physical activity.** Anger releases powerful, energising chemicals in your body. Use your energy effectively by going for a brisk walk, running, doing physical work around the home or office, or taking some other exercise. The movement releases more helpful brain chemicals, leaving you feeling calmer and better.

- ✔ **Express your anger effectively.** You're better off talking about your issues after you feel calmer. Then you can express your feelings clearly, starting with 'I' statements such as 'I feel upset when you forget to wash the dishes. . .' rather than start with 'you' statements such as 'You really annoy me when you don't wash the dishes.' I statements show that you are taking responsibility for your feelings. You statements sound more threatening and therefore are more likely to create a feeling of anger. See Chapter 15 for more on effective communication.

- ✔ **Find a solution instead of getting angry.** Tell yourself that anger on its own won't improve things – it may just make things worse. Think about finding solutions to your issue. If a pile of clothes left on the floor in your children's room makes you angry, explain to your children what they need to do to help, the reward they get if they tidy up and the consequences they face if they don't keep their room tidy.

- ✔ **Laugh.** Even if you don't feel like laughing, a bit of humour can transform the atmosphere. Just remember not to be sarcastic or your joke will backfire.

Long-term strategies to reduce future outbursts of anger

✔ **Use relaxation techniques.** Try one of the many ways to relax in this book to release tension regularly. Some good examples are deep breathing, imagining a relaxing scene, going for a nature walk, saying the word 'relax' each time you breathe out, meditating, practising yoga or t'ai chi and listening to calming music.

✔ **Forgive and forget.** People don't always do what you expect them to. Holding a grudge is a bit like holding a hot piece of coal – you're the one getting burnt. Rather than being overwhelmed by your own bitterness, consider forgiving the other person.

✔ **Consider getting professional help.** Managing anger can be tremendously challenging. If you find your anger affecting your day-to-day activities, speak to your doctor. You may be offered some ways to manage your anger, or referred to another service for professional help. If you decide to see a therapist or counsellor, ensure they're registered with a professional organisation such as the British Association for Counselling and Psychotherapy (BACP). Their website is www.bacp.co.uk. If you decide to join an anger management class, ensure the trainer is experienced.

Changing your thoughts to simmer down

Your feelings of anger are driven by your thoughts. If you anger easily, you may curse or think in an exaggerated way. Thoughts that evoke anger are called *hot thoughts* or *beliefs*. They can be just internal thoughts or said out loud. They flash into your head, making you feel frustrated or worse. Here are some examples of hot thoughts:

✔ **Name calling:** 'You're an idiot!'

✔ **Making judgements, often with 'should' or 'must' statements:** 'He should definitely give me that refund now.'

✔ **Blaming other people rather than thinking about your own role:** 'This is all your fault!'

✔ **Believing others deserve to be hurt or that you're better than them:** 'It serves you right to have a bad day. You deserve it.'

✔ **Assuming others deliberately harm you:** 'She turned her back on me intentionally.'

Try using the following cognitive behavioural therapy (CBT) approach to make your thoughts more rational and balanced. (For more tips on CBT, see Chapter 12.)

Write down what your hot or angry thoughts could be in certain situations or with certain people who drive your feelings of anger. Here are some examples of thinking styles that tend to create anger. Each is followed by an example 'hot thought,' which caused the anger and a suggested 'balanced thought' that would help to calm you down:

- **Taking things personally:** If you get angry easily, you may take things too personally. For example, if your friend doesn't notice your new hairstyle, you may think 'He doesn't like me,' when actually he has other worries on his mind at the moment and failed to notice.

    Balanced thought: 'Just because he didn't notice my hairstyle doesn't mean he doesn't like me. Maybe he's just stressed about his exams and isn't noticing much around him.'

- **Being a perfectionist:** You may set very high standards for yourself and others, and if they're not met, you feel hurt. And that hurt turns to anger. For example, if you cook a meal for some friends and your partner forgets to get the right type of carrot, you may think, 'Oh no, the guests won't have a perfect meal.'

    Balanced thought: 'Nobody's perfect. I'm a human being and so is my partner. The rest of the meal will be fine. I can offer a nice meal without it having to be absolutely perfect.'

- **Ignoring the positives:** You may focus your attention on all the things others do wrong rather than right, causing you to feel angry more easily. For example, you may lash out at your partner for not calling you when leaving the office, and yet he may have called you on all the other days of the week.

    Balanced thought: 'He didn't call tonight but he almost always does call. I need to remember all the times that he does.'

- **Thinking in black-and-white terms:** This is where you think in all or nothing terms, using words like 'always', 'or never'. You may resort to this kind of thinking style when you get very angry. For example, your friend doesn't turn up to meet you on time. You think 'He's always late. He's totally unreliable.' When he finally turns up you burst out with your anger, when actually he left on time but got stuck in traffic.

    Balanced thought: 'I'm thinking in black-and-white. He has been late a couple of times, but not always. Getting angry won't get him here any quicker. I'll listen to his side of the story when he arrives. Let me try doing some deep breathing whilst I wait for him.'

Now have a go at filling in a table like the one shown in Figure 19-1. Reflect on the last time you were angry and then try to think of a more balanced thought about the situation, like I've given in the examples above. Thinking of a balanced thought is not always easy, but just do your best to begin with – you'll get better at it with practice. Try completing the table every day for a couple of weeks and see if it has a positive effect on your level of anger.

Logic overcomes anger because anger easily becomes irrational. Using more balanced thoughts takes the heat out of the anger. The more you practise balancing your thoughts, the easier and more automatic it gets.

Situation	Thought	Emotion	Behaviour	Balanced thoughts	Bodily sensations
Someone jumped the queue.	He jumped in front of me in the queue. How dare he? What an idiot! I should teach him a lesson!	Anger – 8/10 Sadness – 7/10	Started an argument with the queue jumper.	There's always going to be someone jumping the queue. I can tell him to stop jumping the queue, but there's no need to be angry.	Rapid heart beat Sweating Hot

Figure 19-1: Components of anger – someone jumps the queue.

Remind yourself that anger alone won't fix anything and may just make you feel worse.

Preventing or Coping with Burnout

Imagine this: you've got a mountain of work to do but don't feel you have the energy to carry on. You've been under the stress of a high workload and feel totally exhausted. You only seem to see the negatives of your situation and you can't see a way out. You feel burnt out.

In this section, I help you catch the tell-tale signs of burnout early, so you can take action before things deteriorate. But in case you feel like you've already moved into the more serious side of burnout, I also offer extra help in this section to ensure you make a gradual recovery.

Burnout costs more than just billions

Stress and burnout cost billions of pounds globally. In the UK alone, the Health and Safety Executive reported a cost of half a billion pounds a year. For these reasons, more companies are hiring stress-management experts to reduce the considerable cost of losing staff due to illness. But this is just the financial cost. Think about the emotional cost – the pain and suffering that each employee has to go through both with himself and within his relationship. Consider the social impact – the possible breakdown of the family unit, the impact on children's lives due to the stress suffered by the parents, the shortened lifespan due to stress-related illnesses and the general lower quality of life and wellbeing. I value the opportunity to reduce stress in the workplace because I've met those who've suffered from burnout and want to offer other people the chance to take an active step to reduce their stress before they go over the edge. I personally see stress management and relaxation as essential core training for everyone. After all, as stress is widely accepted as the leading cause of illness in our society, training in ways to relax should be essential for everyone.

Understanding burnout

Burnout is when you feel high levels of physical, emotional and mental exhaustion. This exhaustion is usually due to working excessively under prolonged stress. You feel unmotivated, cynical, and increasingly helpless. Burnout causes high levels of physical, mental, emotional and social damage.

You may have the odd day when you feel low on energy and lack the drive to get on with things – and this of course is normal. But if every day is a bad day, you don't feel emotionally connected with your job, you don't feel appreciated, your daily activities don't seem to line up with your personal values, and the goals you or others set are too ambitious, you may be approaching burnout.

Discovering whether you have burnout

To see whether you may have burnout, ask yourself the following questions:

- ✔ Do you have unexplained aches like headaches and backaches?
- ✔ Do you feel cynical about your work or life?
- ✔ Has your sleep pattern changed recently?
- ✔ Do you have to drag yourself out of bed and fight your way through the chores you need to complete?

✔ Do you depend on drugs, alcohol or food to change how you feel?

✔ Are you irritable and impatient with others?

✔ Do you feel a constant lack of energy?

✔ Do you feel no satisfaction from any achievements you make?

Answering yes to any of the above questions could indicate either burnout or some other medical condition. Therefore it's best to speak to your doctor for a full assessment.

Burnout may be related to your workplace or to your life choices. Here are some of the key factors that cause workplace burnout:

✔ **Conflict:** You are often in conflict with others, whether your manager, a colleague, a customer or at home. Conflict can be highly stressful.

✔ **Lack of control:** You don't feel like you're in control. Someone else dictates what you do and when, and you have no choice. You can't complete the work in your own way. Every aspect of what you do is managed.

✔ **Lack of recognition:** Your work goes unrecognised. You don't feel as if you're valued for the hard work you put in. You may get negative feedback but rarely any positive feedback.

✔ **Poor management:** You have no clear idea of where things are going. Leadership seems confused.

✔ **Too much work:** You feel you have too much work and can't cope with the workload. This lasts for longer than you like. You have a feeling of being too busy to do anything else and feel totally snowed under.

✔ **Unclear role:** You don't understand what your role is supposed to be. Expectations seem to keep changing.

✔ **Wrong job:** If the work you're doing just isn't right for your personality, you're likely to find the job stressful.

Here are some of the key factors that cause burnout due to your life choices:

✔ **Lack of close social relationships:** Having someone close to talk to is a powerful way of reducing stress.

✔ **Not getting enough sleep:** If you're not finding enough time to sleep, you are putting an extra stressor on yourself.

✔ **Taking on too many jobs and responsibilities:** Afraid to say no to any opportunities. Not asking others for help.

✔ **Working too much:** Not spending enough time in leisure – socialising, exercising, relaxing.

Figure 19-2 shows how a range of factors can build up to cause burnout.

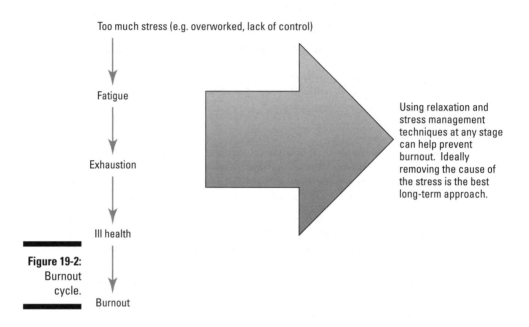

Too much stress (e.g. overworked, lack of control)

Fatigue

Exhaustion

Ill health

Burnout

Using relaxation and stress management techniques at any stage can help prevent burnout. Ideally removing the cause of the stress is the best long-term approach.

Figure 19-2:
Burnout
cycle.

Using strategies to prevent burnout

> *It is a very good plan every now and then to go away and have a little relaxation. . .When you come back to the work your judgement will be surer, since to remain constantly at work will cause you to lose the power of judgement.*
>
> Leonardo Da Vinci

You can prevent or handle burnout through several self-help strategies. The important thing is to take some action. When you are faced with high levels of stress, it's difficult to decide what to do. This is because you're locked into a panicky state of mind. Looking through the list of options below may help you to decide on the best option for you and help you think more clearly:

✔ **Determine the cause of your stress.** Find out what is causing the burnout for you. Is it too much to deal with at work? Is it because you're not finding time to relax and socialise?

✔ **Manage your stressors.** Make a plan to reduce your stress. See if there is any way you can directly reduce the areas that are causing you stress. Discuss with a trusted friend or colleague – they may have some useful suggestions.

✔ **Get support.** Maybe you need to seek out the support from a professional counsellor or medical professional. Alternatively, a regular meet-up with friends or family may be just what you need.

✔ **Consider changing your job.** Some people spend years in a job that's just not right for them. Have an honest look at your current skills set and job. Consider other professions that may suit your personality better. Take time to reflect and speak to a careers advisor for guidance.

✔ **Discuss your options.** If you have an issue at work, talk to your manager. Could you take some time out to rest? What about job share, flexitime, working part-time or doing some work from home? Would some further training help? Could someone coach or mentor you?

✔ **Consider an attitude shift.** If you're being cynical and negative, you're probably compounding any underlying stress. Take a brief time out and see things differently. Plan breaks at work, even if for a few minutes every hour or so. Write down areas of your work that you do enjoy – the pay, the benefits, some colleagues or clients, the commute? Seek ways to improve your outlook. Spend time with more positive people and their positive outlook may rub off on you.

Your health is extremely important – you can't live without it. See your doctor or other health professional as soon as you suspect burnout is looming.

Recovering from burnout

If you feel totally exhausted, you need some time to recover. You're not being selfish. Rather, by taking care of yourself, you'll get better sooner rather than later.

To deal with burnout, try using the three Rs:

✔ **Recognise:** Notice signs of burnout for you.

✔ **Reverse:** Take action by using relaxation techniques (see Chapters 4–13) and seeking support from family, friends or a professional such as a therapist or doctor.

✔ **Resilience:** Take action to build your resistance to stress in the future. Practise relaxation techniques regularly. Make your goals realistic rather than too challenging, accepting what you can't change. See the positive aspects of your life and build relationships with helpful people.

Catherine's experience of burnout

This is Catherine's (not real name) story. She contacted me through the *Relaxation For Dummies'* Facebook page, an online social network:

Not every burnout is caused by just too much work. I found out for me that my burnout two years ago did not result from work, but from dealing with a difficult relationship and work. I see more and more that in the times when I am really exhausted about work, it's not about work. Work is not exhausting, but the attitude of avoidance, the thought 'I don't want to be here now, I want something else' – this is what really makes me tired. The solution is

acceptance. I am experimenting with this at the moment – sometimes engaging myself MORE at work makes it less exhausting.

When I first realised I probably have burnout, I started with mindfulness by reading a book on the subject. I learned that I have special spots on my body which hurt or felt tense when something was wrong – when I'm stressed or angry without showing it. By observing the feelings in these spots on my body (for example, in my upper back) I learned to realise quickly when it's too much for me, and, even more, I learned exactly what caused my feelings of stress and exhaustion.

Here are some ideas to help you get back up again:

- ✔ **Find out why you are burned out.** Reflect on the various factors that have led your stress levels to be so high and try to reduce at least some of them.

- ✔ **Ensure you get enough sleep.** Don't spend time watching TV or on the internet when you should be in bed.

- ✔ **Take things easy for the next few days or weeks.** Give yourself more than sufficient time to recover.

- ✔ **Eat healthily.** Have plenty of fruit and vegetables and aim for a balanced diet.

- ✔ **Exercise gradually.** Go at the right pace for you. This may be just a short walk or less to begin with.

- ✔ **Use relaxation techniques.** Try progressive relaxation, for example, detailed in Chapter 4.

Part VI
The Part of Tens

The 5th Wave   By Rich Tennant

"Okay, you've got the breathing down, but wouldn't you be more comfortable in a different workout suit?"

In this part . . .

In this part you'll find a lovely summary of the main ideas in this book. Uncover the ten golden rules for relaxation, ten quick and easy ways to relax, ten deep relaxation techniques to help you get really chilled out and ten resources for further help, including websites, organisations and recommended books and CDs.

Chapter 20

Ten Golden Rules of Relaxation

*T*he idea that you need to follow a set of rules to relax sounds like a contradiction in terms. But trust me, rules do help. Children feel insecure without some guiding rules. A society without rules would collapse into mayhem. If you want to relax effectively, following a few rules, principles or guidelines lets you gain maximum benefit.

The rules I outline in this chapter combine what scientists have found to be effective approaches to relaxation together with what my clients tell me helps them relax.

Accepting What You Can't Change

Acceptance is vital when change isn't possible. If you're in a situation and there really is no way out, refusing to accept implies a constant struggle for nothing. You're chasing your tail. Only after you accept can you find rest. Lack of acceptance just causes stress.

For example, if your company increases everyone's workload, you may not be in a position to stop the change. You just have to accept, and focus on what you can control. Perhaps you can apply for a job in a different company, or work out a way of working smarter rather than just harder.

Don't try to control the uncontrollable.

In the realm of intense emotions, acceptance is particularly powerful. If you feel sad, there's no point in denying the fact. To pretend you're okay and sweep the feelings under the carpet doesn't give your feelings the recognition and respect they deserve. You begin to fight with your emotions, and the emotion of sadness just grows stronger. Research into depression shows that denying and fighting the feeling of depression is one of the ways that the illness is sustained. Through acceptance and mindfulness, you stop trying to avoid your feelings, and they naturally subside much quicker and have less intensity.

Being Kind to Yourself

When things don't go according to plan, it's easy to fall into self-criticism. You say to yourself things like, 'I should've told him to come early,' or 'I'm an idiot,' or 'I can't do anything right,' or 'I'm so emotional all the time.' These self-judgemental thoughts from your inner critic, which we all have in varying degrees, are self-destructive. Your inner critic drains your energy and makes you feel stressed from the inside out.

Here are some ways to be kind to yourself:

- **Forgive yourself when things go wrong.** You're a human being and can't do everything perfectly. To help you forgive yourself, ask yourself:

   - Was it completely your fault?

   - Will it matter in a few weeks or months?

   - Did anything go well?

- **Listen to your body.** Notice when you're too tired or stressed and need a break. Give your body what it needs.

- **Say nice things to yourself and notice how you feel.** Reflect on things that have gone well recently rather than only on what's gone wrong.

- **Practise a self-compassion meditation.** See Chapter 13 for an example.

- **Treat yourself without feeling guilty.** You may choose a night off to watch a movie, a nice novel, a good haircut, a quick chat with your best friend, a little bit of shopping or an early night for a change.

- **Motivate yourself through self-praise** when things go well, rather than getting angry with yourself when things go badly.

Each time you do a relaxation technique, or choose to do something you find enjoyable or pleasurable, is an act of kindness in itself and a positive sign of progress towards self-kindness. Even reading this book shows you have some capacity for self-kindness, so give yourself a pat on the back!

Choosing Relaxation Techniques that Work for You

Everyone is different. Some people like chocolate and others hate it. Each person has a different set of genes, experiences and temperament. For these reasons, everybody relaxes in a different way. There is no right or wrong way to relax. Variety is the spice of life. Try different approaches and see what you like or what appeals to you. If you've tried meditation many times and it just drives you crazy, maybe you need to try something different, like yoga or self-hypnosis.

To relax effectively, try to find a technique or range of techniques that work for you. You can choose from progressive relaxation, guided imagery, meditation, physical approaches like t'ai chi or yoga, autogenics, deep breathing, massage, hypnosis, exercise and more.

Everyone has the ability to relax. But not everyone relaxes in the same way. Find what you enjoy and would like to practise almost daily.

Expressing Yourself

If you're stressed, you probably have the same thoughts or feelings circling round. Try getting the thoughts out in the open in some of the following ways:

- ✔ **Talk:** Chat about your situation with friends, family, colleagues or a professional counsellor. Talking is a hugely powerful way of getting from stressed to relaxed. Humans are social animals and have a fundamental need to connect with others.

- ✔ **Write:** Note your thoughts and feelings in a journal. Using a journal is tremendously cathartic. You release pent-up emotions without worrying about what the other person thinks. Some research has found writing in a journal to be more powerful than talking to someone.

- ✔ **Draw or paint:** Try expressing your feelings artistically if you enjoy this sort of expression.

- ✔ **Play an instrument:** If you think you can't play, have a go anyway but try not to stress your neighbours with the noise.

By expressing your emotions, you acknowledge them. Acknowledging stress is the first step on the road towards relaxation and wellbeing.

Making Time for Daily Relaxation

Discipline is remembering what you want.

David Campbell

Everybody on the planet has 24 hours in each day available to them. The difference between people lies in how they use that time. The only way you can have time to relax is to prioritise relaxation. If you frequently think, 'I don't have time to relax,' you probably don't value relaxation as much as all the other errands that you need to do. Don't underestimate the danger of stress. Put relaxation at the top of your 'to do' list.

If you can manage to make relaxation a daily habit, like brushing your teeth or having a shower, your life feels better. Daily relaxation takes discipline. Doing something for 21 days usually helps to create a habit. You may need to force yourself on some days, but it's worth it in the long run.

If you're short of time, here are some ways you can combine relaxation techniques with other activities:

- ✔ **Try deep breathing on the train or bus.** See Chapter 5 for tips on breathing exercises.

- ✔ **Practise a peaceful place imagery exercise in bed.** Try this just before you go to sleep. Have a look at Chapter 9 for some ideas.

- ✔ **Do mindful walking or exercise.** By being aware of the physical sensations in your body and aware of your thoughts and emotions you are, in effect, practising a mindfulness meditation. Check out Chapter 6 for mindful walking and Chapter10 for more on mindfulness in general.

- ✔ **Give your daily chores and errands your full attention.** By connecting with your senses as you act, you train your mind to be both focused and calm. Repetitive activities done mindfully engage the relaxation response.

- ✔ **Exercise with friends.** By doing this you combine two highly powerful ways to relax: physical activity and socialising. See Chapter 6 for ideas to get you moving.

Noticing When You Need to Relax

Imagine walking to your car and discover you have a flat tyre. After changing the tyre, you arrive late at work. You miss an important meeting. You start to feel a headache coming on. You grab a coffee to give yourself a boost and accidentally spill half of it on your shirt and computer. The day just gets worse. Your headache begins to throb; you have a stomach ache and start looking for a packet of biscuits. You feel stressed and your body's warning signs are on high alert.

Some pressure is necessary in life, otherwise you feel unmotivated and bored. But, like many people nowadays, you may be under too much pressure, which turns into stress. Because of your busy, distracted lifestyle, you may not even recognise how stressed you are, which can be dangerous. Your stress levels may have been too high for hours, days or even years without you noticing. That's like driving your car at full speed and ignoring all the warning lights that tell you to stop and get a service. The first step is to notice those warning lights.

You may have been tense for so long that you're used to the feeling of tension and feel that it's 'normal'. Take a fresh look at the sensations in your body, mind, health and behaviour to determine whether you're under too much unhealthy stress.

Here are some of the possible signs of stress to look out for, but remember, each person reacts differently to stress and sends out different warning signs:

- ✔ **Physical signs:** Racing heart, sweating, easily unwell, nausea, chest pain, loss of libido, headaches, neck/back pain, upset stomach, dry mouth.

- ✔ **Mental signs:** Worrying, lack of concentration, rapid thinking, unable to switch off, seeing negatives too often, memory problems.

- ✔ **Emotional signs:** Short-tempered, frustrated, angry, feeling lonely, depressed, irritability, anxiety.

- ✔ **Behavioural signs:** Don't want to socialise, poor sleep patterns, eating too much or too little, procrastination, using drugs or alcohol to relax.

Without finding a way to relax and ease your stress, you have a higher chance of developing a chronic disease such as high blood pressure, heart disease, diabetes and depression. Using relaxation techniques, or simply doing more things you enjoy, may protect you from unnecessary future suffering.

Recognising that you're under too much pressure and need to find a way to relax is key. Use a journal or notepad to help you recognise when you feel most stressed and when you're most relaxed. See Chapter 3 for how to do that.

Don't suppress your discomfort of the feeling of stress. Your body is warning you to relax.

Preparing Your Mental Attitude for Relaxation

After you spot the stress signals, you need to prepare yourself to relax with the right mental attitude. I suspect you lead a busy life and so finding time to relax on top of everything else may be stressful! Try to remember that relaxation helps you get more, rather than less, out of your day.

Here are some ways to prepare you for relaxation:

- ✔ **Accept that acquiring relaxation skills takes time.** Acquiring a new skill is about trial and error. You probably need to try a few different ways, methods and techniques to see what works for you. Some relaxation techniques may make you feel more stressed at first. Don't give up. You can do it with the right combination of activities. Where there's a will, there is a way.

- ✔ **Overcome feelings of guilt.** You're not being selfish by relaxing! By finding ways to relax you're looking after yourself and those around you. If you work yourself to the ground, you're not helping anyone. In fact, that leads to more work for others. Let go of feelings of guilt when relaxing. Excessive work is an ingrained attitude of our society and is the reason why almost everyone is stressed.

- ✔ **Put relaxation in your diary.** It's easy to forget to make space for relaxation, so block out some 'me time' in your diary or add a reminder on your phone. Book an appointment with yourself!

- ✔ **Plan to start gradually and build up.** If you've never practised relaxation techniques before, start small. Begin with a five-minute exercise in deep breathing or lying down and listening to a short meditation. After you feel comfortable with relaxing for five minutes, you can gradually increase the time to 10 or 15 minutes.

There is no ideal length of time to relax, but try to do 10–20 minutes daily to notice some benefit. If you want to achieve deep relaxation and undo chronic stress, go for about 45-minute sessions daily. Start with ten minutes a day and increase each session by five minutes every week or so.

If you decide to do a relaxation technique for ten minutes, stick to your plan. Don't give up after two minutes because you feel bored or tense.

Doing a short relaxation technique twice a day may be more effective than doing one long session because you take time from your normal, everyday activities twice a day to relax. Each time you make a conscious effort to relax rather than do your normal activities, you shift from your normal habitual patterns to being more relaxed. Experiment to see what works for you.

When you first learn to relax with a new technique, ensure you're in a warm, comfortable, safe and quiet environment. As you become more skilled in relaxation, you can get into a relaxed state of body and mind in the midst of noise but this is difficult to start with.

Seeing Relaxation as a Skill

I have not failed. I've just found 10,000 ways that won't work.

Thomas Edison

Just as activities such as driving, walking and speaking are all processes that take time and effort to learn, so is relaxation. Relaxation is a skill. As you practise relaxation, you get better at achieving a relaxed state. Eventually, you can relax almost instantly, at will, just like you can scratch your head or make a cup of tea. And your ability to relax deeply is enhanced too.

Finding out how to ride a bicycle takes time and effort. The first time you tried to ride, you probably failed. You probably fell off and hurt yourself a bit. That's okay and totally normal. You need to get back on the bike and try again. Success comes from seeing failure or mistakes as part of the discovering process.

Relaxation is a discovering process and you're bound to make mistakes at first. If you expect instant and deep relaxation and don't get it, don't give up! Be as persistent as you can.

You don't actually ever fail at relaxation. You try a technique and notice what happens. If you feel more relaxed, great. If not, try again, a few more times. If the technique still doesn't work, try another technique. If none of the techniques work, you may want to seek the professional help of a counsellor or therapist if stress is a problem for you.

In my experience, you're likely to go through the following steps if you're determined to become skilled at relaxation:

1. Decide to study a relaxation technique and try it.

2. Feel a bit relaxed but not great.

3. Try several other techniques. Some work better than others.

4. Continue to practise the technique that works for you.

5. Begin to feel less stressed generally and more at ease with yourself.

6. Start exploring deeper relaxation techniques, perhaps working with a teacher or reading around the subject.

Let go of all your expectations from the relaxation exercise if you can. Just try the technique and see what happens. Think of it like an experiment or a game.

Taking Control of Your Life

Feeling out of control is one of the main causes of stress. Your stress arises due to problems. Problems have solutions if you work through each problem step-by-step. Remaining passive and giving up often makes the stress worse. You need to take some action.

Deciding to take control of your situation is empowering and uplifting in itself. Working towards a solution makes you feel more in control. Finding a solution you're happy with is the key.

To help gain some control over your life, bear the following points in mind:

✔ Confront whatever is the cause of your stress and work out a solution. Take a step back and look at the issue objectively. Then break the problem into bite-sized chunks that you can deal with. If you can't work out an answer, call a friend or family member to help you.

✔ Practise saying no. You need to set some boundaries. If you say yes every time someone asks you to do something, you attract people who like asking for favours. Begin by saying no to small things that you can manage, and build yourself up for the bigger requests. Having too much work to do and not enough time to do it will make you feel out of control.

✔ If you have a disagreement or argument with someone, avoiding the issue doesn't help. Often, avoidance can make things worse. Use a relaxation technique to calm yourself, and then go ahead and speak to the other person. See Chapter 15 and 16 for tips on communication.

Understanding the Amazing Power of Relaxation

It has been estimated that 75 to 90 per cent of all visits to primary care physicians are for stress-related problems.

American Institute of Stress

You're much more likely to practise relaxation if you understand what relaxation is and give relaxation a high priority in your life. Stress is a physical, mental and emotional automatic reaction that takes place in your body and mind. When you're stressed, your heart beats rapidly, your blood pressure rises and your muscles tense up. If you used the stress response as it was designed, every time something stressed you, you would have a fight, run away or just freeze. As none of these actions is socially acceptable, stress builds up within you.

Fortunately, you have an innate capacity that's the opposite of the stress response. This is called the relaxation response. You can use relaxation techniques to turn on the relaxation response.

Relaxation undoes what stress causes. The relaxation response lowers your blood pressure, encourages deeper, smoother breathing, calms your mind, lifts your mood and increases creativity, intelligence, and decision-making skills. You can reverse the harmful effects of chronic stress by practising regular relaxation.

> *The relaxation response is a physical state of deep rest that changes the physical and emotional responses to stress . . . and the opposite of the fight-or-flight response.*
>
> Herbert Benson

By regularly evoking the relaxation response, you reverse the damaging effects of pent-up stress. You create positive changes in your brain and body that stop you getting stressed so easily, building your resilience to future stressors.

While doing a relaxation technique, you may not feel any positive changes taking place. However, physical and psychologically beneficial changes take place even though you can't feel them.

Here are a few of the many benefits of relaxation:

- **Appearance:** Want to look more attractive? Then relax more. By regularly relaxing, your skin looks clearer and you're less likely to put on extra weight by avoiding emotional or stress eating. If you encourage relaxation into your life by sleeping well, eating healthily and exercising, you look beautiful on the inside and on the outside.

- **Productivity:** If you're relaxed, you can focus more effectively than when you're excessively stressed. Taking a break to relax pays back many times over. You just need to access your inner discipline and wisdom to find time to relax.

✔ **Health:** Regular relaxation can help boost your immune function. So you don't get the flu so easily at one end of the scale. Relaxation can even reduce your chances of heart disease, stroke and high blood pressure.

✔ **Wellbeing:** Regular relaxation makes you happier. Stroking your cat, dancing, enjoying music, making love, and laughing with friends are great ways to relax and enjoy yourself.

Relaxation isn't just about falling asleep or being so chilled out that you can't do any work. Relaxation strategies are a set of tools available to you when you're stressed to enable you to ease off the gas pedal and let go a bit. In my experience, most healthy, successful, focused and kind people have a range of ways they use to relax regularly.

Many people don't consider using relaxation techniques until they're at the point of a breakdown. By valuing the benefits of relaxation, you can start prioritising relaxation now, using techniques that work for you.

Chapter 21

Ten Quick Ways to Relax

*O*ne of the secrets of staying relaxed is being able to spot your stress rising during the course of the day, and then using quick stress relievers to calm you down to a more focused and less frantic state.

When people ask me what I do for a job, and I answer 'stress management', they almost always ask for a tip. The little exercises I offer in this chapter are simple to teach and learn. Try them for yourself and, if your friends and colleagues ask why you look so relaxed, try teaching them the exercises too.

I recommend you try one of the techniques in this chapter several times a day for a couple of weeks. Then do the same with another exercise in this chapter. After you've tried them all for a couple of weeks, decide which techniques work for your temperament and lifestyle. Begin by using the exercises when you're not stressed so that you get the hang of how to use them. As you become more proficient and skilled at relaxing, you can use the techniques during your stressful episodes.

Breathing Deeply

If I had to choose just one technique to teach you to relax, I would pick deep belly breathing.

In deep belly breathing, also known as diaphragmatic breathing and abdominal breathing, you use the full extent of your lungs rather than just your chest to breathe. To do this, your diaphragm moves down, pushing your belly out and creating more room for oxygen to enter your body. In comparison, shallow breathing uses just the chest area to breathe, with the rib cage moving and not your belly. I describe deep breathing in detail, and show the process with a diagram, in Chapter 5.

Stress causes you to breathe shallowly and rapidly. This type of breathing reduces the amount of oxygen in your body. By breathing deeply when you feel stressed, your body assumes that you're in a safe place and starts to relax automatically.

1. **Sit, lie or stand in a comfortable posture.**

   Loosen any tight clothing if you can. Choose to have your eyes open or closed.

2. **Place one hand gently on your chest and one hand on your belly.**

   If you're in a public place and don't want to do this, just be aware of the sensations in your belly.

3. **Breathe in slowly through your nose.**

   As you breathe in, let your belly expand. You may be able to feel this with your hand.

4. **Breathe out slowly through your nose or pursed lips.**

   Let your belly naturally contract as you breathe out. Try to breathe out for longer than you breathe in.

You can do this exercise from anything between just one breath to a few minutes, depending on how much time you have.

To enhance the relaxation effect of this exercise, try some or all of the following:

- In this technique your most important breath is your exhalation. When you're stressed, you tend to inhale and exhale rapidly. By breathing out slowly your brain increases the sense of relaxation within your system.

- As you breathe in and out during the exercise, connect your attention with the physical sensation of breathing. This is called mindful breathing and helps you shift your attention away from your worries and concerns for a while, offering a different perspective.

- Repeat a relaxing word or phrase to yourself as you breathe out. Try the phrases 'relax', 'this too will pass', or 'calm'. You can even choose a neutral word like 'one', or a spiritually meaningful phrase for you. Experiment!

✔ Count how long you breathe in and out. For example, try breathing in for four seconds, holding your breath for two seconds and breathing out for six seconds. As you breathe in, count 1. . .2 . .3. . .4 and hold 1. . .2. . .and breathe out 1. . .2. . .3. . .4. . .5. . .6. Use the second hand of a clock or watch to start with if you can't count seconds.

Building Your Optimism Muscle

Picture this: you're having a tough day at home. The baby just won't stop crying and the phone won't stop ringing. You feel anxious, annoyed and tense. All you can think about is all the things you've got to get done and how bad a parent you are.

As soon as you notice this pattern occurring, stop for a moment and follow the STOP exercise for positive thinking:

S – Stop! Say the word 'stop' to yourself, and stop what you're doing for a few moments.

T – Take three deep, mindful breaths. This means feel each breath in and out.

O – Observe your thoughts, especially any negative, unhelpful thoughts. Become aware of the thoughts popping into your head. Notice your feelings and bodily sensations. Do you feel anxious? Is your heart racing? Noticing and observing what's happening helps you to decide how to best look after yourself.

P – think Positive but believable thoughts. This is about thinking in a more optimistic light, but not so much that you don't believe it to be true. Thinking in this way is a powerful antidote to your negative self-talk.

For example, imagine you feel stressed and think, 'I can't control the kids at all. I'm a terrible parent. I'm useless. I'm having such a bad day.' Then you remember the STOP exercise. You stop what you're doing, take the phone off the hook for a few minutes and sit down. You take three deep, mindful breaths and begin to feel a tiny bit more relaxed. You listen to your own thoughts and notice that you're criticising yourself with sentences like 'I'm useless at coping.' You begin to replace the unhelpful sentences with more positive but believable thoughts such as 'I'm having a difficult day today but I'm not useless. I've worked so hard for my children. I'm not perfect, but I'm doing my best in the circumstances. Things will settle down in a couple of hours and I'll feel better.'

As with all the other exercises in this chapter, try this STOP exercise with low-level predictable stress to start with, such as after checking your e-mails or when you're cooking dinner.

Coming to Your Senses

The secret of health for both mind and body is not to mourn for the past, worry about the future or anticipate troubles, but to live in the present moment wisely and earnestly.

Buddha

One of the quickest ways to relieve stress is to connect with your senses. This brings you into the present moment. In the world of the senses you briefly let go of the huge traffic jam or demanding boss. Your body and mind then begin to relax.

 To achieve relaxation in this way, you need to know which particular senses and stimuli are most effective for your brain and body. For you, it may be hearing the music of Bach, squeezing a soft ball or inhaling the scent of lavender.

Explore all your senses and find out which sense, or combination of senses, is most relaxing for you. Here are a few ideas to get you started:

✔ **Sight:**

- Look at a photo of a loved one.

- Gaze at the view out of your window.

- Place some flowers or a plant on your desk.

✔ **Sound:**

- Listen to a relaxing piece of music or nature sounds.

- Pop outside and listen to the sounds around you.

- Sing a song or whistle a tune.

✔ **Smell:**

- Carry a small bottle of your favourite scented oil.

- Smell some of the flowers in your room.

- Light an incense stick or scented candle.

✔ **Taste:**

- Chew some gum.

- Eat some dark chocolate.

- Enjoy a piece of fruit.

✔ **Touch:**

- Gently rub your thumb and fingers together and notice the subtle sensations.

- Stroke your cat or dog.

- Notice the sense of touch between your feet and the floor as you walk.

✔ **Movement:**

- Squeeze something squashy, such as a rubber ball.

- Stand up and stretch, or do a couple of yoga postures.

- Dance or jump around – maybe not in front of your moody boss though.

Begin by using this technique when you're under low-level stress. For example, try one of these stimuli every day for a week during your commute to work. Note what effect it has. Then try a different stimulus the next week. With experience, try this technique for a different stressor, like after the morning school run or before public speaking. And remember to have some fun with experimenting!

Your imagination is as powerful as using your senses. If, for example, you feel stressed at work, but you don't have your cat with you to stroke, imagine petting her. You may feel better.

Doing Something Pleasurable

If you think you don't have time for any fun, you probably really need a bit of pleasure time. Pleasure and fun are, of course, subjective. What is pleasurable for one person may be unpleasant for another person. So although I suggest a few things in this section, make sure you choose something pleasurable for you.

If you repeat the same pleasure too often, it stops being so pleasurable. This is called habituation. A piece of chocolate once a week tastes better than a piece of chocolate every hour or day.

Here are a few quick and simple pleasures you may like to try:

- ✔ Colour a picture in a colouring book using some crayons.
- ✔ Do some knitting.
- ✔ Drink a cup of your favourite tea.
- ✔ Eat some chocolate slowly and mindfully.
- ✔ Light a candle.
- ✔ Listen to some of your favourite music.
- ✔ Play a computer game.
- ✔ Practise a short piece of music on a musical instrument.
- ✔ Try a sudoku or crossword puzzle.
- ✔ Watch a short, funny video online.

Thinking what to do in the heat of the moment is hard. Try making a list of things you like doing. Then next time you feel stressed, pull out your list and do one of the things on it.

Getting Physical

Exercising when you feel stressed is an efficient way to relieve anxiety and relax. The stress response is designed to get your body moving, so moving your body fast helps to relieve the stress. Physical activity boosts your body with feel-good endorphins and distracts you from your worries. After a brisk walk, you may find a solution to your problem, or see the situation in a more balanced way. In this section I suggest a range of different exercises you can do. Have fun trying them out. You can even rate how relaxed you feel before and after the activity. See Chapter 6 for more suggestions on integrating physical activities into your day.

- ✔ **Clean the house.** Try focusing on your senses so that you're more mindful and attentive to what you're doing.
- ✔ **Go for a brisk walk.** Listen to some of your favourite music at the same time if you feel like it.
- ✔ **Do a few push-ups, sit-ups or star jumps.** These will get your heart pumping.
- ✔ **Go running for ten minutes around the block.** Doing this two or three times a day is enough exercise to keep your heart healthy too.

✔ **Work through a series of stretches.** Be sensitive to your body and see what sort of stretches you would enjoy, without overly pushing yourself. I give lots of stretching ideas in Chapter 7.

Aim to do at least 30 minutes of physical activity a day, five days a week.

Practising Peaceful Place Imagery

Peaceful place imagery is a form of guided imagery and a popular way to relax. The idea is to use your imagination to take you to wherever you find relaxing. Amazingly, your body will respond as if it really is at that calming place. Doing this sort of exercise makes you feel more in control of your thoughts and emotions, improving your sense of wellbeing.

Many of my clients enjoy this exercise and find the process relaxing.

1. **Find a place you won't be disturbed for a few minutes.**

   Close your eyes if you can.

2. **Become aware of the feeling of your own breathing.**

   Take a few deep, slow, smooth breaths.

3. **Think of a place you find relaxing or peaceful.**

   Choose a place where you feel secure and at ease. It can be a familiar place or something you've invented.

4. **Create as vivid a picture as you can.**

   Don't worry if the image is not clear. Just doing your best is absolutely fine. Consider what the sounds, smells, tastes and feelings are like too.

5. **Imagine yourself in this peaceful place.**

   Imagine how calm, relaxed and at ease you are. Notice how relaxed your muscles are, and how safe and happy you feel. Enjoy this peaceful place for as long as you have time for.

6. **When you're ready, imagine stepping slowly back out of the peaceful place into the present moment, knowing that the peaceful place is always there when you want it.**

You need to practise this guided imagery a few times and then you'll be able to use it in the heat of a stressful moment.

If you find your mind wandering around too much, try using a guided audio recording to help you focus. Use the CD accompanying this book or see Chapter 3 if you want to make your own audio.

Smiling or Laughing

When you feel stressed, you probably feel like doing exactly the kind of things that sustain or deepen the stress, such as avoiding talking to other people, not going out, stopping exercising, eating unhealthily, drinking lots of caffeine, overdoing the alcohol or using drugs. You probably don't feel like smiling or laughing.

Smiling and laughing are highly effective ways to cut the tension and release your stress. Smiling reduces stress hormones such as cortisol, adrenaline and dopamine, and increases mood-lifting hormones such as endorphins. Smiling even reduces your blood pressure. Even forcing a smile on your face has been shown to promote greater levels of positivity.

Laughter, including fake laughter, releases healthy hormones into your bloodstream. And fake laughter often turns into real laugher anyway. Try it and see.

See Chapter 13 for some tips on finding a smile or laugh. These tips may seem like common sense, but when you're stressed your brain doesn't always think straight and you need all the help you can get.

Trying the RELAX Technique

The RELAX technique offers quick stress relief by combining several popular relaxation exercises. I recommend you write down this technique or download it from www.relaxationfordummies.com/relax-card and put the paper somewhere easy to access, such as in your wallet or on your computer.

R – **Remove yourself from the situation**. Just pop to the bathroom or get a glass of water if you need a reason to go somewhere. Changing your environment even for only a few minutes can make a huge difference.

E – **Exhale and inhale slowly and deeply.** Let your exhalations be slightly longer than your inhalations. A few slow, deep breaths can change your body's physiology within seconds.

Also do a little **Exercise**. Go for a walk, jump up and down or do ten star jumps. Exercising uses up your stress hormones rather than letting them swim around your body.

L – Lightly massage yourself. You can use your fingertips to massage around your eyebrows and temples. You can also rub your shoulders or any other part that needs some loving. Try smiling at the same time and allow your posture to be upright and open rather than closing down.

A – Accept what you can't change. If you haven't done as much work as you'd have liked, accept the fact now. You don't have to accept injustice, just accept what is unchangeable at the moment. Let go of controlling the uncontrollable. If your boss will not reduce your workload, you can't keep fighting the fact. You're going to have to find a new way of managing the work, perhaps through delegation.

X – eXpect things to turn out well. Notice any harsh, critical, negative thoughts and turn them to more positive, yet still believable thoughts. You may not pass this interview, but it will improve your interview skills.

Using a Three-Stage Mini-Meditation

This meditation is sometimes called a 'breathing space meditation' or a 'mindful check-in'. The aim of meditation is not to blank your mind. The idea of meditation is simply to focus your mind on something and to bring your attention back to your chosen object, without self-criticism, each time you notice your mind has drifted off.

1. **Sit, stand or lie down in a comfortable posture.**

   Assuming an upright, dignified physical posture enhances the effect of this meditation.

2. **Stage 1: Become aware of your thoughts, feelings and bodily sensations for about a minute.**

   Ask yourself, 'What thoughts are arising? What feelings can I notice? What bodily sensations can I notice?'

3. **Stage 2: Feel the physical sensation of your breathing for about a minute, around your belly.**

   Feel each in breath and each out breath. If your mind wanders, gently bring it back.

4. **Stage 3: Open your attention to your body as a whole, including your breathing.**

   See if you can get a sense of your whole body expanding and contracting as you breathe in and out.

This meditation takes about three minutes. You can shorten or extend it for any length of time you choose.

Visualising a Successful Outcome

Imagine you have a presentation coming up and you're stressed up to the max. If you do nothing, you get more nervous and anxious, and you turn up sweating and shaky. Fortunately you have an alternative – visualisation. This exercise can take just one minute, but ideally give it a few minutes if you have time. Visualisation is powerful stuff. When you go to your local coffee shop and the waiter says, 'Would you like a cup of hot coffee with steamed milk and topped with a touch of whipped cream and a sprinkling of chocolate?' you form an image in your mind, as if the coffee is already there. It's more effective than saying 'Want a coffee?' The vivid image creates an emotional reaction.

You can create a similar feeling of relaxation by using the power of images in your mind too.

Many people think they're not good at visualising, but you probably visualise all the time already, without knowing. Most people think in a combination of thoughts and images. Your anxious feelings before something like a presentation are probably due to an image of yourself making a fool of yourself, or losing your job, together with some scary thoughts. Give visualisation a few tries to see if it works for you.

The same neural pathways are stimulated in your brain when you imagine a situation as when you're actually there. So you can trick your brain into thinking you're on a million-pound holiday when you're sitting at home – nice!

Here's how to visualise success to relax:

1. **If you can, close your eyes and get into a comfortable posture.**

2. **Take a few deep, smooth, slow breaths to help you towards relaxation.**

   Let go of any tension in your muscles as far as possible.

3. **Imagine a successful outcome to your situation, project or goal that is currently causing stress.**

   Visualise what it would look like for you to succeed. Where are you? What are people saying? What is it like to feel the success? What are you wearing? What can you smell, taste or touch. Go through all the senses and be as vivid as you can. Do this for as long as you have time. It could be just for a few minutes.

4. **Give yourself a few moments to open your eyes and tune back into the present moment.**

Visualising a successful outcome also helps you to reflect on exactly what you want to achieve and makes you more likely to take active steps to move towards that positive outcome. So not only do you feel a bit more confident, but you also achieve greater success.

Chapter 22

Ten Ways to Deep Relaxation

Take rest; a field that has rested gives a bountiful crop.

Ovid

Experiencing deep relaxation from time-to-time is essential for you to be able to function at your peak performance.

Imagine a toy car run by a rechargeable battery. Every night the battery is recharged, but not quite enough. The car runs slower and less efficiently over time. In the same way, you recharge your energy every time you go to sleep, but sleep doesn't always fully recharge you. Deep relaxation offers you a boost in energy by recharging you. Without charging, you can't expect to function well. If you see relaxation in this way, hopefully you won't feel so guilty about taking time out – you're just boosting your energy levels.

You can't rush relaxation, because relaxation is the opposite of rushing. Rushing implies being under pressure; relaxation is about easing off the pressure and having a break. Deep relaxation takes an investment of time but is well worth it. Your health is your wealth.

Deep Self-Hypnosis

Self-hypnosis can lead to a deep state of relaxation. Let go of any mystical or magical ideas of hypnosis, and think of it as a useful tool to achieve deep relaxation. For full details on using self-hypnosis for relaxation, see Chapter 9.

To achieve a deep sense of relaxation in self-hypnosis, bear in mind the following tips:

- ✔ Find a quiet, comfortable place where you won't be disturbed.

- ✔ Prepare your affirmations before you start so that you aren't thinking about them during the hypnosis.

- ✔ Before you start the session of hypnosis, do some relaxation through deep breathing or by any other favourite method of yours.

- ✔ Allow yourself 15–30 minutes to enter a deep relaxed state.

Guided Imagery

You use your imagination all the time. Tap into this inner power through the use of guided imagery. In the exercise below, you imagine yourself in a place you find peaceful and secure. With experience, your body will react as if you're actually in that peaceful place, and become relaxed. You can then use this technique anytime during the day, when you feel too stressed.

1. **Find a relaxing, quiet, place and turn off any potential distraction.**

   This is time for you. If you want, play some relaxing music in the background, or perhaps a nature sounds CD. Or just lie down outside if you can, and listen to the real sounds of nature.

2. **Close your eyes.**

3. **Imagine your most relaxing place.**

   It could be outdoors or indoors. You can be with others or on your own. You can imagine a place you've visited before, somewhere you've never been, or a combination of the two. Some people like to be on a beach, in a hammock, in a warm log cabin, in a forest or walking through a field. Choose a place that works for you. The key is to use all your senses to imagine what it's like there.

   Here's an example I like: you walk along the beach with bare feet and enjoy the warm sand. You look out at the beautiful clear, blue water. As you walk along the shore the warm water caresses your feet. The warm sun gently heats your glowing skin, which sparkles and glows as you stroll. You see a hammock tied between two large palm trees. You climb effortlessly into the hammock and gently rock as you listen to the birds and smell the flowers nearby. You feel so relaxed and notice a smile on your face. You are given a glass of cool, refreshing lemon juice, which you enjoy sipping.

4. **Enjoy your feeling of relaxation in your imagined place.**

   Let the feeling of deep rest sink into your muscles and bones. Let go into relaxation. You only need to relax as much as you feel comfortable doing so.

5. **When you're ready to end the exercise, slowly open your eyes and have a nice stretch.**

   Don't be concerned if you find yourself zoning out. Sometimes you may find your body moving in a strange way or feel a little dazed afterwards. Having these kinds of experiences is normal. If you keep falling asleep during this exercise, try sitting more upright, or even standing up. Alternatively, try doing it at a time of day when you're more awake.

When you're in a deeply relaxed state, press your thumb and index finger together. Now associate relaxation with that sensation – you're programming your body to relax with your finger and thumb touching. Whenever you want to get into a state of relaxation, simply press your thumb and index finger together and you can begin to access the feeling of relaxation immediately.

Hot Bath

Having a hot bath is a deeply relaxing experience for many people. See Chapter 15 for more tips on making your bath extra relaxing.

Think about how you can relax in the bath by offering some pleasure to each of your senses – the heat of the water for your sense of touch, the scent that you add for your sense of smell, some music in the background for your sense of hearing, dim lighting and a few candles for your sense of sight and a herbal tea for your sense of taste.

Massage

Human touch has an automatic effect on relaxing the body. Massage helps to tease out the tension in your muscles and offers you some 'me time'. Swedish massage and shiatsu are the most popular types of massage for relaxation.

Self-massage is an alternative and free option, which many people forget about. You can do self-massage anywhere. Try the little sequence below to see if self-massage can work for you. Chapter 8 has lots more massage tips.

1. **Work on your shoulders.**

   Press the muscle on your left shoulder using your right palm or fingers. Close your eyes and breathe smoothly and start to either gently squeeze or make circular movements. Repeat on your right shoulder with your left hand.

2. **Knead your neck.**

   Reach around and gently squeeze the back of your neck, beginning at the base. Gradually make your way up the back of the neck. Repeat as many times as you wish.

3. **Feel your face.**

   Place your fingers in the centre of your forehead. Draw lines from the centre of your forehead to your temples. Smooth out your forehead. Move your way down to your eyebrows. Then use your fingers to make small circular motions around your temples. Continue with this circular motion down to your cheeks and further down, massaging your jaw muscles.

4. **Finish with your feet.**

   Sit on a chair and rest one foot on your knee. Slide your thumbs up and down the sole of your foot. Then push your thumb or knuckles into any tense areas of your foot. Squeeze each toe with your thumb and finger. Finish by squeezing and releasing your whole foot with both hands. Repeat on the other foot.

Don't massage to the point of pain.

Mindful Body Scan Meditation

I have taught this technique to many of my clients and most people find it deeply restful after they practise it a few times. The meditation takes about 30–45 minutes. Ideally you lie down on your back, on a bed, mat or soft carpet. If you're a beginner, you may prefer to be guided in this exercise using an audio CD. You could use the CD that accompanies the book *Mindfulness For Dummies* (Wiley), or you could buy the 'Guided Mindfulness Meditation' CD by Dr Jon Kabat-Zinn from an online audio store.

1. **Lie down and make yourself comfortable.**

   Feel the natural sensation of your breathing for a few minutes.

2. **Shift your attention to your toes.**

3. **Very slowly, move your attention up your body.**

   The idea is not to try to relax but to be aware of the sensations that you notice. You may find your mind wandering off from time-to-time, but that's fine. Don't judge or criticise yourself.

4. **After scanning your whole body, just lie there and rest for a few minutes.**

   Enjoy any feeling of relaxation that has arisen. If you don't feel relaxed at all, just accept how you feel at the moment. Mindfulness is about being in the moment and accepting the sensations just as they are.

I describe the full body scan in more detail in Chapter 10.

When you do a body scan meditation, don't try to relax. Think of the meditation as an awareness exercise. Your awareness will naturally lead to relaxation in the long term.

Progressive Muscular Relaxation

This is a popular method of relaxation, especially for people who find it difficult to feel sensations in the body and like a slightly more physically active way to relax.

1. **Get comfortable, either sitting or lying down.**

   Loosen any tight clothing.

2. **Begin relaxing by taking a few deep, slow, smooth breaths.**

3. **Move your attention to your right foot.**

   Notice the sensations in that foot.

4. **Tense your right foot to a count of about ten.**

   Notice how the sensations in the foot change.

5. **Relax your right foot.**

   Take a deep breath as you notice the more relaxed sensation in your right foot.

6. **Repeat Steps 3–5 for your left foot.**

7. **Gradually move up your body in this way, tensing and relaxing each part of your body.**

   Here's a sample sequence you can follow: right foot, left foot, right calf, left calf, right thigh, left thigh, buttocks, stomach, chest, back, right arm and hand, left arm and hand, shoulders, neck, face.

8. **Finish by enjoying any feeling of relaxation that has arisen.**

   Take a few slower, deep breaths to deepen your experience.

Relaxation Response Meditation

Relaxation response meditation is a really simple meditation exercise to create a state of deep relaxation very rapidly. Benefits of the relaxation response meditation include improved focus and concentration, a deeper state of natural relaxation every day, greater awareness of when stress arises in your body, and an improved ability to relax after a stressful event.

The basis of the technique exists in almost every religious tradition. The technique that I describe here is secular, so anyone can practise it.

The meditation simply involves repeating a word or phrase to yourself and focusing your attention on it, without straining or trying too hard. See Chapter 10 for help in choosing a phrase and more details on developing this technique.

1. **Sit in a comfortable posture.**

   Close your eyes.

2. **Feel the natural sensation of your breathing.**

   Each time you breathe out, repeat your chosen word, phrase or prayer to yourself.

3. **When you notice that your mind wanders off to other thoughts, gently guide your attention back to your chosen word or phrase.**

4. **Bring the exercise to a close after about 20 minutes.**

   Keep an eye on a clock rather than setting an alarm. That's a more gentle, relaxing way of ending the meditation.

Have a laid-back passive attitude in this meditation, rather than putting in too much effort and trying too hard. This is your time to relax.

Stretching for Relaxation

When you're stressed, your muscles tense up. Stretching your muscles is a great way to relax. Take your mind off your worries and anxieties by noticing the physical sensations in your body as you stretch and being aware of your movements. If you don't like the idea of doing proper yoga, just do some natural stretching, a bit like a cat does.

Enjoy stretching after a long day at work. The more you focus on the sensations of your body and your breathing as you stretch, the more you'll enjoy it.

Combine your stretching with some relaxing music if that helps you to be in the moment.

When you stretch, try to follow these tips to make your stretching effective:

- **Breathe slowly, smoothly and consciously.** Feel your breathing as you stretch. Avoid holding your breath. Tune into the sensations in your muscles and joints as you stretch.
- **Don't stretch too far.** Remember, you're not in a competition. You shouldn't find the stretch painful. And remember to avoid bouncing in the stretch.
- **Take your time.** You're better off sustaining a gentle, relaxing stretch rather than forcing a deep stretch, which can lead to injury.

T'ai Chi

T'ai chi is essentially meditation in movement. The philosophy of t'ai chi is based on the idea that relaxation requires a balance of energy, or *qi*, to flow around the body.

T'ai chi emphasises awareness of the sensations of your breathing, together with the sensations of movement of your body. In this way, you let go of your worries and concerns and train your brain to live in the present moment. You are taught to maintain a healthy physical posture, helping you to release tension from your body. Through moving your arms and legs in a smooth, controlled way, you help to improve your flexibility and send nutrients into your joints. You also gradually strengthen your muscles, ligaments and tendons.

Find a local t'ai chi teacher, or read Chapter 7 to get started.

Yoga Nidra

Yoga nidra is a yoga exercise that helps to create total, deep relaxation. It is said to bring supreme stillness of mind and profound insight. Regular, persistent practice helps you enjoy the relaxing benefits of yoga nidra.

Yoga nidra means 'yogic sleep'. The idea is to enter a state similar to deep sleep while actually remaining awake. The technique has been used for thousands of years. According to yoga, the three main states of consciousness are waking, dreaming and deep sleep. Yoga nidra offers a way to enjoy conscious deep sleep.

1. **Lie down on your back in a quiet place.**

   Cover yourself with a blanket if necessary. Let your arms be by your sides, with palms facing up, and let your feet naturally fall away from each other. Use a pillow for comfort.

2. **Move your attention through your body, starting from the top of your head.**

   Feel the sensation in each body part from the top of your head, through to the tips of your toes.

3. **Move your attention back up through your body again, from your toes all the way up to the top of your head.**

   As you do this, imagine breathing in a sense of relaxation or calm, and breathing out any tension or stress.

4. **Become aware of your body as a whole.**

   Play with the idea that your whole body gently expands as you breathe in, and contracts as you breathe out.

5. **Do some spinal breathing.**

   Imagine your breath can move up and down your spine. As you inhale, imagine or feel your breath moving up from the base of your spine and out of the top of your head. As you breathe out, imagine or feel your breath going down from the top of your head to the base of your spine. Play with the idea without trying too hard or taking it too seriously. Enjoy the feeling if you can.

6. **Go through some of the *chakras*, or energy centres.**

   Chakras are important centres of energy according to yoga philosophy. Try these three chakras in sequence: the space between your eyebrows; your throat area; and the centre of your chest. For each energy centre, rest your attention there together with an awareness of your breathing for a couple of minutes. Notice if there is an associated colour in each chakra if you are a visual person and find it restful. Enjoy any sense of relaxation, stillness or silence that arises there.

7. **Now simply rest as deeply as you can.**

   If you feel calm and relaxed, stay in that state. If you feel agitated, notice the various thoughts and feelings that are coming up and allow them to drift away. Watch them come and go. Do this for about 10 minutes or so.

8. **To bring the exercise to a close, become aware of your breathing.**

   Become aware of your body as a whole and start to gently wiggle your fingers and toes. Allow your eyes to gently open when you're ready.

Chapter 23

Ten Resources for Further Help

*I*f you've read this book and are seeking further help in specific areas, look through this chapter to see if anything catches your eye. I've included a range of websites, resources for children, some relaxing music, guided relaxation, movie recommendations and more.

Getting in Touch

I specialise in teaching mindfulness and other relaxation techniques to organisations, clinicians and the general public. I help to manage stress, anxiety, depression and other stress-related illnesses.

On my website at www.shamashalidina.com you can:

✔ Begin a free e-course in mindfulness or relaxation.

✔ Download mindfulness and relaxation audios.

✔ Read my blog and other information on relaxation.

✔ Attend a workshop or group course in mindfulness or relaxation.

✔ Book a workshop with me in your organisation.

✔ Begin training to be a mindfulness trainer or coach.

✔ Book one-to-one mindfulness consultations in London, and distance learning courses over the telephone worldwide.

I'd love to hear from you. Feel free to get in touch and let me know how the journey of relaxation is going for you! I read every email. Or stay in touch on facebook.com/shamashalidina or twitter.com/shamashalidina.

Trying Physical Relaxation DVDs

DVDs are useful for learning the physical mind–body approaches to relaxation, such as yoga, t'ai chi and qigong. Here are some of the more popular DVDs available on the market at the moment:

- ✔ *Yoga for Stress Relief* by Barbara Benagh
- ✔ *Beginner T'ai Chi* by Stephen Luff
- ✔ *Qi Gong Fire & Water* by Matthew Cohen

Grab these and find more recommendations on www.relaxationfor dummies.com/relaxationdvds.

Watching Comedy Films for Light Relief

I enjoy comedies and uplifting movies. If you don't know where to start, try these, rated top ten in a recent survey:

1. *Forrest Gump* (1994)
2. *Dr Strangelove or: How I Learned to Stop Worrying and Love the Bomb* (1964)
3. *City Lights* (1931)
4. *Toy Story 3* (2010)
5. *Modern Times* (1936)
6. *Amelie* (2001)
7. *Life Is Beautiful* (1997)
8. *The Great Dictator* (1940)
9. *The Apartment* (1960)
10. *Singin' in the Rain* (1952)

If you don't like any of these, ask your friends for recommendations as they may have a better idea of your taste. If you can watch the movie together with your friends, you'll enhance your relaxation as you share the experience together. But sometimes, it's nice to watch a movie on your own too. Don't forget the popcorn!

Relaxing to Music

Like movies, music is very much down to personal taste. Try the following classical pieces to relax with:

- *Canon in D Major* – Pachelbel
- *Eine Kleine Nachtmusik* – Andante – Mozart
- *Air on a G String* – Bach
- *Fantasia on 'Greensleeves'* – Vaughan Williams
- *Etude in E Major* – Chopin
- *Nuvole Bianche* – Ludovico Einaudi
- *La Mer* – Debussy
- *Somewhere over the rainbow* – Keith Jarrett
- *The Heart Asks Pleasure First* – Michael Nyman

You can often purchase compilation CDs with relaxing classical music on it.

If you don't find classical music relaxing, try chilling out to well-known pop tracks:

- *Let it be* – The Beatles
- *Return to Innocence* – Enigma
- *Only Time* – Enya
- *Adiemus* – Karl Jenkins
- *Imagine* – John Lennon

Reading Books

If you want a book to help you relax, works of fiction are helpful as they take your mind off your worries and concerns.

If you want to read more about relaxation and how to achieve relaxation, you might like to check out the ones listed below. Try not to get too bogged down in theory. After some reading, dive in and practise some daily relaxation techniques and see how you find it.

- ✔ *Mindfulness For Dummies* by Shamash Alidina (Wiley). I couldn't help it!
- ✔ *Stress Management* by Edward Charlesworth and Ronals Nathan (Souvenir Press). A nice style of writing with a wide range of techniques for you to try.
- ✔ *Relaxation and Stress Reduction Workbook* by Martha Davis and Elizabeth Robbins Eshelman (New Harbinger Publications, US). Informative and evidence-based approaches to relaxation in a workbook format.
- ✔ *Total Relaxation* by John Harvey (Kodansha America, Inc). Clearly written and relaxing to read through. Nice way of explaining different levels of relaxation.
- ✔ *Stress Management For Dummies* by Allen Elkin (Wiley) A classic book and great companion to this book.
- ✔ *Wherever You Go, There You Are* by Jon Kabat-Zinn (Piatkus Books). An easy bedtime read, expounding the gentle art of mindful living by one of the leading teachers.

Find links to these books on www.relaxationfordummies.com/relaxation-books.

Using Guided Relaxation Audios

Most people find guided relaxation audios helpful. If you search for a CD or audio download, you may become a little overwhelmed by the choice. You can find meditations, hypnosis, progressive relaxation, visualisation and guided imagery, autogenics, and more. Try these CDs if you're looking for more:

- ✔ *Ultimate Relaxation* by Dr Hilary Jones – a popular guided relaxation CD.
- ✔ *Total Relaxation* by Richard Latham and Jane Warren – a relaxation involving lots of visual experiences.
- ✔ *Stress Relief* by Martin Rossman – a combination of deep breathing and guided imagery exercises, beautifully produced.

I've put together links to those CDs and more at www.relaxationfordummies.com/guidedrelaxationaudios.

Looking at General Relaxation and Stress Reduction Websites

Here are some websites that have high-quality information on relaxation and stress management that I would recommend. You can find links to all these websites on www.relaxationfordummies.com/links too:

- www.apa.org/topics/stress This is the American Psychological Association, which represents psychology in the US, with the largest association of psychologists worldwide. The website outlines what stress is, offers a range of tips for dealing with chronic stress, and advice on when and how to get help. Updated regularly.

- http://helpguide.org/mental/stress_relief_meditation_ yoga_relaxation.htm. This non-profit resource offers a wealth of high-quality information on relaxation and stress management in a well-presented and accessible way. Also offers lots of sound advice on mental and emotional health.

- http://www.mentalhealth.org.uk/help-information/ podcasts/ http://www.mentalhealth.org.uk/help- information/podcasts. A free set of audio tracks produced by a Mental Health Charity in the UK, including progressive relaxation for better sleep and a quick-fix relaxation exercise, as well as many more.

- http://www.mind.org.uk/help/medical_and_alternative_ care/mind_guide_to_managing_stress.A detailed guide to managing stress from one of Britain's leading mental health charities.

- http://www.nhs.uk/Conditions/Stress/Pages?Introduction. aspx.This is the website for the National Health Service in the UK. It offers lots of high-quality information on stress, as well as all the stress-related illnesses. Worth browsing, especially if stress is affecting your health.

- http://www.patient.co.uk/showdoc/577. My doctor recommended this website to me once. Here you can find links to many different resources for managing stress, from charity organisations to self-help guides.

- http://www.radiosrichinmoy.org/free-online-music-radio/ free_relaxation_music/. This website offers a range of free relaxation music. You could play your favourite music from the website in the background as you use a relaxation technique.

- www.relaxationfordummies.com.This website goes along with the book, offering a free 30-day e-mail course in relaxation, relaxation downloads, tips, links and ways of interacting with others reading the book.

Helping Your Children Relax

Children lead stressful lives. With the unrelenting peer pressure to be 'cool', the constant information overload of the internet, texting and online social networks, exams, bullying and perhaps having to cope with their parents separating, today's children have a lot to deal with.

Here are some resources you might like to use with your children:

- *Enchanted Meditations* for Kids [Audiobook] [Audio CD] by Christiane Kerr. A lovely set of relaxation exercises and visualisations that are an ideal way to unwind at the end of the day

- *YogaKids: Silly to Calm* (DVD) by Marsha Wenig (Gaiam Limited) – a DVD with engaging yoga exercises for children.

- *Relax Kids: The Wishing Star* by Marneta Viegas (O Books) – a friend of mine who was a teacher used this with her class, with great success. The children used to ask for the stories as they enjoyed the feeling of relaxation they experienced.

- *Teaching Meditation to Children: The Practical Guide to the Use and Benefits of Meditation Techniques* by David Fontana & Ingrid Slack – an excellent guide offering ways for you to coach your children into the art of meditation at a pace and in a way that is engaging and interesting for them.

- `http://kidshealth.org/kid/centers/relax_center.html` – a website for children, with lots of colour and written in a way that makes relaxation [WORD MISSING HERE]

- `http://www.relaxkids.com/` A set of resources you can buy to help your children relax. Also has a list of classes for children, and resources for schools.

- `http://www.calmforkids.com/` CDs, training, resources for schools and ways of finding a local teacher.

Reducing Stress in the Workplace

If you find it hard to relax because of the pressures at work, use some of these websites, together with Chapter 16 on reducing stress at work. Some of the organisations are suited for managers to help them reduce the stress of their employees.

- International Stress Management Association (UK) – `www.isma.org.uk`.

- Health and Safety Executive (UK) – `www.hse.gov.uk/stress`

✔ American Institute of Stress (USA) – `www.stress.org`.

✔ Business Balls (General Information) – `www.businessballs.com/stressmanagement.htm`.

✔ Mindtools (General Information) – `www.mindtools.com/pages/main/newMN_TCS.htm`

Finding Relaxation Classes in your Area

If you'd like to do relaxation exercises in a group with others, there's probably a range of different options available to you. The benefits of learning relaxation in a group include learning new tips from a teacher, getting to interact with other people socially, and it helps you to realise that you're not the only one suffering from stress – that's a stress-relieving realisation in itself.

Try these methods of finding a suitable relaxation class:

✔ `http://www.hotcourses.com/` This is the UK's largest course finder. Search for relaxation, stress management, yoga or whatever style of relaxation you wish to learn more about.

Contact the adult education college in your area. You could ask them about suitable courses in relaxation. If you don't know the name of the college, try calling your local authority – it should know.

✔ `http://www.bwy.org.uk/instructor/find.htm` Find a local yoga teacher that has been accredited by the British Wheel of Yoga on this website.

✔ `http://www.taichifinder.co.uk/` Use this website to find a local tai chi or qigong teacher.

Local gyms often have classes such as 'Body Balance' or Yoga which many people find relaxing.

✔ `www.google.co.uk` Use the world's most popular search engine. Type in the name of your area followed by 'relaxation class' or 'stress management class' and see if you find anything suitable.

✔ `http://www.bemindful.co.uk/learn/find_a_course` Find a mindfulness-based stress reduction course near you, using this website produced by the Mental Health Foundation, a major mental health charity in the UK

Remember to check the qualifications and experience of your teacher before doing a course to ensure you're getting the best possible learning experience.

Appendix

Audio Tracks

● ●

*O*ne of the best ways to learn relaxation techniques is to listen to a guided relaxation audio regularly. You'll have received a CD with this book, including five different guided relaxation techniques for you to try. I'd recommend listening through the whole CD once so you know what to expect. Then, practise the first relaxation technique twice a day for a couple of weeks or so and see what effect it has. Then move on to the next relaxation technique on the CD, and so on. In this way, you give each relaxation technique adequate time to see if it works for you.

Relaxation is a skill that requires regular practice – it's not always an instant quick-fix. After you've been listening to the CD for some time, you may like to practise on your own, without the CD – you don't have to listen to the CD every time you practise your technique, if you don't want to.

Here is a list of the tracks on the accompanying audio CD to guide you through the different relaxation techniques:

Track 1: Introduction   (4 minutes)

Track 2: Belly Breathing   (7 minutes)

Track 3: Progressive Muscular Relaxation   (16 minutes)

Track 4: Mindfulness of Senses Meditation   (7 minutes)

Track 5: Loving Kindness Meditation   (18 minutes)

Track 6: Guided Imagery   (20 minutes)

Play your favourite music in the background as you listen to the relaxation techniques if you like – this can enhance the relaxation effect for some people.

Index

• S •

FOR DUMMIES®

Making Everything Easier!™

UK editions

BUSINESS

Bookkeeping For Dummies
978-0-470-97626-5

Leadership For Dummies
978-0-470-97211-3

Starting & Running a Business All-in-One For Dummies
978-1-119-97527-4

REFERENCE

British Politics For Dummies
978-0-470-68637-9

DIY For Dummies
978-0-470-97450-6

Researching Your Family History Online For Dummies
978-0-470-74535-9

HOBBIES

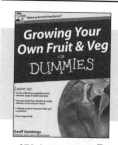

Growing Your Own Fruit & Veg For Dummies
978-0-470-69960-7

Allotment Gardening For Dummies
978-0-470-68641-6

Electronics For Dummies
978-0-470-68178-7

Asperger's Syndrome For Dummies
978-0-470-66087-4

Basic Maths For Dummies
978-1-119-97452-9

Boosting Self-Esteem For Dummies
978-0-470-74193-1

British Sign Language For Dummies
978-0-470-69477-0

Cricket For Dummies
978-0-470-03454-5

Diabetes For Dummies, 3rd Edition
978-0-470-97711-8

English Grammar For Dummies
978-0-470-05752-0

Flirting For Dummies
978-0-470-74259-4

IBS For Dummies
978-0-470-51737-6

Improving Your Relationship For Dummies
978-0-470-68472-6

Keeping Chickens For Dummies
978-1-119-99417-6

Lean Six Sigma For Dummies
978-0-470-75626-3

Management For Dummies, 2nd Edition
978-0-470-97769-9

Neuro-linguistic Programming For Dummies, 2nd Edition
978-0-470-66543-5

Nutrition For Dummies, 2nd Edition
978-0-470-97276-2

FOR DUMMIES®

A world of resources to help you grow

UK editions

SELF–HELP

Cognitive Behavioural Therapy For Dummies
978-0-470-66541-1

Creative Visualization For Dummies
978-1-119-99264-6

Mindfulness For Dummies
978-0-470-66086-7

STUDENTS

Philosophy For Dummies
978-0-470-68820-5

Student Cookbook For Dummies
978-0-470-74711-7

Sociology For Dummies
978-1-119-99134-2

HISTORY

The Tudors For Dummies
978-0-470-68792-5

Medieval History For Dummies
978-0-470-74783-4

British History For Dummies
978-0-470-97819-1

Origami Kit For Dummies
978-0-470-75857-1

Overcoming Depression For Dummies
978-0-470-69430-5

Positive Psychology For Dummies
978-0-470-72136-0

PRINCE2 For Dummies, 2009 Edition
978-0-470-71025-8

Project Management For Dummies
978-0-470-71119-4

Psychometric Tests For Dummies
978-0-470-75366-8

Reading the Financial Pages
For Dummies
978-0-470-71432-4

Rugby Union For Dummies, 3rd Edition
978-1-119-99092-5

Sage 50 Accounts For Dummies
978-0-470-71558-1

Self-Hypnosis For Dummies
978-0-470-66073-7

Study Skills For Dummies
978-0-470-74047-7

Teaching English as a Foreign Language
For Dummies
978-0-470-74576-2

Time Management For Dummies
978-0-470-77765-7

Training Your Brain For Dummies
978-0-470-97449-0

Work-Life Balance For Dummies
978-0-470-71380-8

Writing a Dissertation For Dummies
978-0-470-74270-9